Roger Planchon:
director and playwright

Roger Planchon

Roger Planchon:
director and playwright

YVETTE DAOUST

CAMBRIDGE UNIVERSITY PRESS

Cambridge
London   New York   New Rochelle
Melbourne   Sydney

Published by the Press Syndicate of the University of Cambridge
The Pitt Building, Trumpington Street, Cambridge CB2 1RP
32 East 57th Street, New York, NY 10022, USA
296 Beaconsfield Parade, Middle Park, Melbourne 3206, Australia

First published 1981

Phototypeset in V.I.P. Melior by
Western Printing Services Ltd, Bristol
Printed in Great Britain at the University Press, Cambridge

British Library Cataloguing in Publication Data
Daoust, Yvette
Roger Planchon.
1. Planchon, Roger
2. Theatrical producers and directors – France –
Biography
842'.9'14   PN2638.P6   80–49806

ISBN 0 521 23414 X

*This book is dedicated to Paul Davies,
and to Cécile and Ninian Mellamphy,
for much support and encouragement.*

Contents

Illustrations

ix

Acknowledgements

I would like to thank Roger Planchon and members of the Théâtre National Populaire, Villeurbanne, for welcoming me to their theatre, inviting me to attend play readings and rehearsals, and letting me use their archives. Above all I would like to thank Dorothy Knowles who suggested this topic for my PhD thesis, and who has been a constant source of inspiration and practical help.

Note on dates and translations

I have chosen to treat Planchon's work thematically rather than chronologically: however, to help readers keep track of time, the date of each play's première appears in the contents list and at the head of each page, as well as in the text.

Translations from French articles and books, from Planchon's unpublished plays, and of his unpublished comments, are my own. They are neither official nor definitive. Quotations from the unpublished plays are given in the original French in the endnotes.

1

The birth and life of the Théâtre de la Cité de Villeurbanne

IN March 1972, the French government announced that it was taking the unprecedented step of moving its first subsidised popular theatre, the Théâtre National Populaire (TNP), from the Palais de Chaillot in Paris to a municipal theatre in the working-class suburb of Villeurbanne, near Lyons. Roger Planchon, its new director, was already a leading figure in the popular theatre movement. After taking over the Théâtre de la Cité de Villeurbanne in 1957, he had painstakingly built up a local public around a nucleus of cultural activity there. He refused to leave Villeurbanne for Paris. Because they wished to have Planchon and his recently-appointed co-director, Patrice Chéreau, at the head of the Théâtre National Populaire, the government gave the Théâtre de la Cité de Villeurbanne the status, subsidy, and responsibilities of the Théâtre National Populaire. What was, and is, the TNP? And why, since 1972, has it been firmly established in the provinces?

The TNP was originally founded by Firmin Gérnier in 1920, but it was only under Jean Vilar, who was appointed its director in 1951, that it became a stable and creative theatre. Its official purpose had always been to attract a working-class public to the theatre; Vilar was the first to make practical changes in order to fulfil that purpose. The TNP had previously given reduced-price showings of other theatres' productions; Vilar created a permanent company at the TNP, and put on original productions there of a high artistic standard. He made the theatre more accessible to working people in general: he abolished tipping, started performances earlier, and provided a reasonably-priced restaurant in the theatre. He started *Festivals de banlieue*, yearly tours of the Parisian suburbs. Following the example of Jean Dasté, who directed theatres in Grenoble and St-Étienne in the 1940s, Vilar built up a network of contacts in trade union and other organisations. Using these contacts, Vilar was able to offer reduced-price bookings for groups, and to establish weekend theatre seminars at the TNP, inviting groups of working-class people to take part in two days of playgoing, discussions, and talks by actors and technicians, all at a moderate price.

Jean Vilar's work at the TNP was contemporaneous with that of many provincial companies, but it became better known, partly because of Vilar's status as a director, and partly, also, because of the pre-eminence of Parisian theatres in France. Jean Dasté's Comédie de St-Étienne, Maurice Sarrazin's Grenier de Toulouse, Roland Piétri's Comédie Dramatique de l'Est (Strasbourg), Gaston Baty's Comédie de Provence (Aix-en-Provence) – all these had been set up in the 1940s, and many more provincial theatres with a purportedly 'popular' aim were founded in the 1950s and the 1960s. Roger Planchon's theatre was one of these.

Born in the Ardèche in 1931, Planchon grew up in Lyons and was educated at a Catholic school there. He left school very young, working first in his father's café and then as a bank clerk. Still in his teens, he began giving readings of Michaux and Apollinaire in a Lyons cabaret in the evenings. He decided to spend a year in Paris, where he organised his own crash course of museum and art-gallery visiting, reading, and theatre-going. On his return to Lyons, Planchon enrolled in some drama courses, which included periods of work/study in the centres dramatiques (drama centres) of the time. He worked with Hubert Gignoux, later to become director of the Centre Dramatique de l'Ouest.

Eventually, Planchon formed a drama group of his own with a few friends, some of whom are still with him (Robert Gilbert, Jean Bouise, Claude Lochy, Isabelle Sadoyan). The group began by working in the daytime at ordinary jobs and rehearsing plays in the evenings. They put them on in whatever parish hall was available. They produced a farce set in 1900, Bottines et collets montés (Ankle-boots and Starched Collars), they put on Twelfth Night, and they rehearsed a great number of other plays which they couldn't afford to put on. In 1949, after winning first prize in an amateur theatre competition with their Bottines et collets montés (financed from Planchon's savings), they decided to turn professional.

The group produced their farce again in the only venue they could find, a church youth club on the banks of the Saône. The parish priest objected, however, to Planchon's atheism and leftist sympathies, and the company had to find a new home. In 1952, they found an old disused printer's shop in the rue des Maronniers, and at their own expense, hiring themselves out as labourers to the contractor, they converted it into a hundred-seat theatre which they named Théâtre de la Comédie. The actors had to begin by building up a permanent audience. They started, astutely, with a number of farces, which were good draws and which, because they demanded versatility, were also good training.

One of these farces was based on the life of the eighteenth-century French bandit, Cartouche. It was put on a hundred times, the first time a play had had such a long run in Lyons. With its slapstick fun, its self-mockery, and its satirical allusions to local figures and to contemporary events, *Cartouche* was clearly a precursor of the musical comedies of Planchon's later career. At one point, the frail heroine, dragged

Cartouche, at the Théâtre de la Comédie, 1954

into the bandits' lair, cries piteously, 'You aren't going to kill me, are you?' This is a comedy, isn't it?' 'No, my lovely,' roars Cartouche's fearsome female lieutenant, 'this isn't a comedy, it's a melodrama!'[1] The dialogue lampooned, in passing, well-known people and institutions in Lyons: Cartouche's enemy plans to torture him by making him read Le Progrès, a leading daily in the city (whose drama critic, Jean-Jacques Lerrant, was one of the first to appreciate and publicise Planchon's work).

The company of the Théâtre de la Comédie was already seeking to draw a non-élitist public. Criticised for never producing the French classics, Planchon retorted that like seventeenth-century directors, he preferred to put on plays written by contemporary dramatists. Gradually the troupe built up a following of students and young people with productions of Kleist, Synge, Lenz, Büchner, Brecht, Vitrac, Calderón, Ionesco, Vinaver, Adamov, and Shakespeare.

In 1956, the company instituted 'mardis', Tuesday evening debates; the production on these evenings was preceded by an introduction to the play, its author, and its context, and was followed by a discussion between audience and actors. In one of these early interchanges, some spectators suggested a way in which the blocking (the characters' positioning on stage) might be improved at a specific point, a suggestion which was tried out in later productions. The actors of the Théâtre de la Comédie set themselves high standards. By their encouragement of, and openness to, direct criticism, they were deliberately turning their followers into increasingly demanding theatre-goers.

Many of the ideas which were to influence Planchon's later work were already apparent in these first years at the Théâtre de la Comédie, including his admiration for Brecht, and his belief that the techniques of the cinema could be used on stage to attract a new public. He was convinced even then that the most effective way of bringing people in a provincial city to the theatre was by creating a permanent resident theatre company on the spot. He was to look back later on this first stage in his career:

The story of the Théâtre de la Comédie is that we laid a wager that we would play every evening . . . It is something to which I believe I was one of the first in France to devote myself: to create a permanent theatre, so that things went on in a simple, regular way.

What the centres dramatiques were doing at that time [1952]

consisted of playing in a city for two days . . . We said, at the time, very loudly, 'Decentralisation which consists in going from town to town is not good because you reach only, in fact, a superficial clientele. They are the two thousand people who would, in any case, go to the theatre . . . And what we were trying to do, what I personally was trying to do, was to impose the idea that the public must be extended, but starting in depth.'[2]

In 1957, the municipality of Villeurbanne (a working-class sister city to Lyons) offered Planchon and his company the use of their large local theatre, the Théâtre de la Cité de Villeurbanne. Here Planchon established his company and began the task of attracting a genuinely 'popular' audience, an audience in which there would be a representative number of working-class people. 'Theatre', claimed an editorial in the theatre's magazine, 'is a privilege to be shared in order that there be no more privileges.'[3] As Jean Vilar had done at the old TNP in Paris, Planchon started by making his theatre more attractive, putting up displays on playwrights or on various aspects of theatre in the foyer. He reduced prices, arranged group bookings, invited groups to 'journées', day-long theatre seminars modelled on the TNP weekends. He set out to find his audience, not by organising tours, since he was in the heart of a working-class area, but by sending out members of the troupe to give lunch-hour talks on theatre in factory canteens, by putting up posters in the factories, and by addressing people through loudhailers as they left work. Planchon collaborated closely with trade unions, youth groups and schools, and kept in touch with the views of his public through discussions and surveys. 'We are not working for the public,' he said, 'we are working with it.'[4] Like Vilar, like many young directors, he was committed to making working-class people aware that culture was not someone else's privilege, but their own right. In his theatre, settled in the midst of a solidly working-class area, he was one of the first to have a genuine opportunity to put this ideal into practice.

In 1959, the newly-formed Ministry of Cultural Affairs under André Malraux began to attack the long-standing problem of over-centralisation in France. One of its policies was to lend support to provincial drama groups, and it created a hierarchy of subsidised provincial theatres: the *troupe permanente* (permanent company) had the lowest status and received the smallest subsidy; the next grade was that of

centre dramatique; and the final distinction was to become a
maison de la culture (cultural centre), a centre offering a
varied artistic programme around the nucleus of a theatre
troupe. In December 1959, the Théâtre de la Cité became the
first *troupe permanente* and the first permanent subsidised
provincial theatre in France. In 1963 it became a *centre
dramatique*, and furthermore, Roger Planchon was offered
the directorship of a new *maison de la culture* which was to
be built in Villeurbanne. The Ministry of Culture agreed to
pay half the cost of the *maison de la culture* if the local
authority paid the other half; it also wanted Planchon to be
appointed director.

Planchon was delighted, especially as his old municipal
theatre had been proving inadequate. There were 1300 seats,
but only 600 spectators could see and hear reasonably well.
The acoustics were, by everyone's account, terrible. Furthermore, the 1930s building was inflexible and ill-adapted
to the variety of activities which Roger Planchon and his
troupe had initiated over the years. The Théâtre de la Cité felt
that a new *maison de la culture* could be organised in collaboration with the many organisations and groups with whom
they were already working. However, the authorities in Villeurbanne saw things differently, and hoped to saddle the
new *maison de la culture* with an administrative council
made up of prominent citizens. Planchon wanted artistic
control, and he wanted his public represented on the
decision-making bodies. When Villeurbanne eventually
decided to spend its money on an incineration plant for
domestic refuse instead of a new theatre, Lyons considered
taking on the *maison de la culture* project. The mayor, M.
Pradel, hoped, however, to appoint a theatre administrator
separate from the company, whereas Planchon felt that this
role should be played by the artistic director, so that artistic
priorities determined administrative policy and not the
other way round. In the end, Lyons, like Villeurbanne, abandoned the idea.

Planchon believed that 'theatre is not an isolated artistic
manifestation, but rather belongs in a social context', and
that it should be, 'not a solemn and reserved place to which
the middle class go on Sundays, but a real centre of culture
where anyone, as he or she pleases, is free to come in at will'.[5]
Accordingly, he always welcomed within the walls of the
Théâtre de la Cité de Villeurbanne artists from other theatres

and from other fields of endeavour. Orchestras from abroad, singers, jazz musicians, and ballet companies performed at Villeurbanne, and the theatre therefore attracted not only theatre-goers but a wider audience. Following the example of Toulouse and Bordeaux, the theatre also opened a Cinéma National Populaire (CNP) in Lyons in 1968. Its aim was to present good cinema on a normal competitive basis, but to make it accessible to the lower-paid by a system of group bookings and season tickets. The new cinema abolished tipping and the selling of sweets, and provided comfortable seating, the best projection standards, and short films related to the main feature instead of advertisements and outdated news. It was well received, and two more CNPs were subsequently opened in Lyons.

Following on the tradition of the *mardis* at the Théâtre de la Comédie, at the Villeurbanne theatre the troupe organised *semaines culturelles*, week-long programmes consisting of talks and exhibitions in factories and visits to the theatre by the workers for plays and discussions. Early in its career, the Théâtre de la Cité also organised school programmes, with the cooperation of educational authorities. Members of the company were always ready to go out, on request, and talk to various groups, institutions, and organisations about the theatre, its current preoccupations, its forthcoming productions, etc. These talks, the tours of the theatre building, the preparatory lectures, the debates and discussions which the Théâtre de la Cité organised, were meant to lessen any feeling of strangeness which a new spectator might have when coming into the theatre for the first time. The theatre's system of group bookings for clubs, associations and trade unions also contributed to making a spectator feel at home, on an outing and sharing an experience with people he knew.

Roger Planchon's opinion of his public, his estimation of their tastes and of their capacity for enjoyment and appreciation, evolved from the beginning through continuous contact with them. The first, obvious problem, their lack of sophistication, was turned to advantage, as Planchon pointed out: 'The popular public, the new public, is what interests us most, because by working for them, we are led to carry our research always a little further, and because our research can only be appreciated at its full value, at first, by new eyes, unclouded by any routine or familiarity.'[6] Because

Planchon's new audience was generally a cinema-going audience, Planchon attempted to integrate the language of the cinema into his productions on the stage. These 'borrowings' from the cinema were readily accepted by the Villeurbanne public. In his first visit to Paris in 1959, however, Planchon was surprised to discover that people more accustomed to stage conventions did not understand cinematic sets or scenes. He reflected that 'What is taken for granted by a cinema public, perhaps theatre-goers take longer to get used to . . . one must realise that audiences are different and that one is addressing people who have a different way of thinking, a different way of laughing, and one must take this into account.'[7] It was perhaps then that Planchon began to realise how much his work had already been affected by his audience. Indeed, the public's opinion, which Planchon was always at pains to discover, helped to determine the entire orientation of his theatre's work. The grass-roots contacts which the members of the troupe established with the public were an education for both. People speaking in factory canteens had to express themselves clearly, quickly, and confidently enough to maintain interest. They had to reflect on their work and the direction which it was taking. The actor Jean Bouise said of these visits that

It's not always so simple: presenting theatre, the nature of our work, our repertoire, all the practical propositions designed to attract the spectator to the theatre, and then saying that you are ready to come back to answer the criticisms heaped up on you, speaking about all this when the fellow is at table and has only twenty minutes, is sometimes quite curious.[8]

As the years passed, the discussions and debates and the reactions of his audiences gradually shaped Planchon's vision of what theatre should and can be. He repeatedly pointed out the value of this kind of interaction: '. . . only theatre, today, involves the constant presence, in flesh and blood, of a creative group in the midst of the public, and the bond which is established between a permanent troupe and its public is irreplaceable'.[9]

The first productions put on at Villeurbanne were of *Henry IV* and *Les Trois Mousquetaires* (*The Three Musketeers*), because a questionnaire had revealed that local people were interested in Shakespeare and Dumas. This was, in a sense, bowing to popular demand. Yet there was never any question of sacrificing artistic integrity to a facile or 'populistic' form. *Henry IV* was presented in all its complexity and richness. The production of *Les Trois Mousquetaires* lampooned the novel's misogynous heroism and romantic patriotism. Every production had to be intellectually accessible, at least on one level, to a relatively uneducated audience; yet no production was to be oversimplified or patronising. Planchon's approach to any play is that of an extremely intelligent individual, who is intimately aware of the preoccupations and attitudes of his audience even as these may change:

Of course one explains and comments in a production; but I've never believed in making a theatre to attract 'the masses' with comprehensible plays or acceptable stories. What you have to do is put into the performance something of the way people outside culture see things. There's no intermediate step, no easy way in – you have to turn the whole thing round at once.[10]

In 1966, nine years after Planchon had moved into Villeurbanne, the young man who was to become his co-director, Patrice Chéreau, was beginning his career in the Parisian *banlieue* (suburbs). It was only in the 1960s that the French government recognised the need for permanent theatres on the periphery of Paris, the dormitory cities which were just as cut off from the cultural life of the centre as the remotest provincial town.

On the periphery as in the provinces, there were theatrical groups which had been in operation since the early fifties, without government recognition or subsidy. Many more grew up in the sixties.[11] Chéreau was director of the theatre in Sartrouville, a dormitory city in north-west Paris, for three years. Like Planchon, he worked with schools and with trades unions; he even presented rehearsals at union meetings for criticism and debate. Like Planchon also, he tried hard to elaborate a kind of cultural policy with his public.

In 1968, all the subsidised theatres – those in the provinces, those in Paris – were brought up short by the May 'events'. Many never recovered. Drama was in occupied factories and universities and in street demonstrations. Even those theatres working for 'the people' began to feel irrelevant. Many drama groups went on strike in sympathy with the workers; some went out to entertain people who were occupying their place of work. Planchon's company cancelled a planned tour of Canada, out of solidarity with the

workers of France. On 30 May, President De Gaulle made a
speech in which he blamed the events on organised dissi-
dent groups and on the Communist Party in particular, and
called on his followers to resist the threat of totalitarian
Communism. He postponed a promised referendum, and
dissolved the National Assembly, promising elections if the
revolutionary pressure abated, but hinting at tough measures
if it did not. After this speech, Jean Vilar resigned from
Avignon in protest and said that he was unwilling to take any
government-subsidised post. Jean-Louis Barrault's Odéon
was occupied; when Barrault refused to turn off the electricity in the theatre, as ordered, he was dismissed from his post
as its director. Many drama festivals were postponed, shortened, or cancelled. Theatrical events were created everywhere, but by students and other young people, not by professionals.

It was time to take stock. On 25 May 1968, directors of
popular theatres from right across France met at Villeurbanne, and, after days of discussion, issued a joint statement.[12] The statement admitted that theatres had failed to
reach what they called the 'non-public', defined as 'an
immense body of human beings made up of all those who
still have no access and no possibility of access to cultural
reality in the forms which it persists in taking . . .' The traditional culture to which theatres had been trying to introduce
their audiences remained foreign and useless. Culture must
be, for the working-class person, 'a way of breaking out of his
present isolation, of escaping the ghetto, by seeing himself
more and more consciously in a social and historical context,
by freeing himself more and more from the deceptions of all
kinds which make him, in himself, a party to the situations
inflicted upon him'. The directors thought that theatre
would have to politicise people, to make them aware of their
own socially-imposed cultural deprivation. What was
needed was '. . . an entirely different conception [of culture]
which does not refer to a given pre-existing content, but
which expects, from the mere coming together of people, a
progressive definition of a content which they can recognise'. The Villeurbanne statement, unfortunately, ended
with a whimper, requesting a reorganisation of subsidies and
of the administration of cultural affairs.

The most useful concept to come out of the rhetoric of the
Villeurbanne conference was that of a 'progressive defi-

nition' of culture. Indeed, the difficulty which faced all directors in reaching a working-class audience was that they – even Planchon – were trying to attract them to plays consecrated by the middle class. 'Culture' is less a sum of knowledge than an attitude to new knowledge, and the working class, in France as in Britain, has its own culture. Ariane Mnouchkine, director of the Théâtre du Soleil, was keenly aware of the paternalistic dilemma of those who wish to 'take culture to the masses'; before the events of May 1968, she said . . .

creating popular theatre consists in speaking to the pro-letariat . . . Which is very like paternalism, and ends up being as dangerous as stubbornly doing good to people in spite of them. Because, this proletariat who have been dispossessed of theatre do very well without it thank you and do not demand it, and they are quite right! Their need for spectacle is largely filled by the cinema, television, music hall, spectator sports . . .[13]

What was the effect of this reappraisal on Planchon? The pause in his theatrical productions in the summer of 1968 was followed by a complete, if temporary, break with Vil-leurbanne; the troupe left on a prolonged tour during nearly two years' renovation of the theatre buildings. The Villeur-banne conference seems to have increased Planchon's soli-darity with other theatre people in France and abroad. He joined with other directors and actors to oppose the dismis-sal of Barrault, to protest against a banning of Armand Gatti's play on Franco at the TNP, to support Paolo Grassi when he was threatened with dismissal from the Piccolo Teatro in Milan. More importantly, however, Planchon seemed to come to a pragmatic realisation that his original aim had been unrealistic. After ten years of work at Villeurbanne, only eight per cent of his public was working class. 'One cannot hope', said Planchon in 1969, 'to attract a whole working-class public to the theatre. The important thing is to make them understand that culture exists, but that it remains a privilege. The rest is demagogy.'[14]

Patrice Chéreau, too, gave up the idea of attracting a working-class audience through established theatrical form and content. 'Agit-prop theatre in France in 1969', he declared, 'awaits neither a talent nor a vocation, but rather the situation which will make it necessary to those it will address . . . and who will create it themselves.'[15] In

November 1968, Chéreau put on a play called *Le Prix de la révolte au marché noir* (*The Price of Revolt on the Black Market*), a *création collective* which parodied, as Planchon's *La Mise en pièces du 'Cid'* was to do, contemporary styles of, and ideas about, the theatre. Like Planchon, Chéreau left his theatre; he went to work at the Piccolo Teatro in Milan. His ideas on the role and power of theatre altered fundamentally after 1968. For Chéreau, for Planchon, for many other dedicated theatre people, May 1968 was a watershed.

In 1972, when I was working in the archives of the new TNP in Villeurbanne, workmen were renovationg the building, and I asked a painter with whom I had struck up a conversation whether he had ever been to this theatre. The answer came immediately, an astonished '*Moi?*' The theatre was a building to work on, but as a place of entertainment it remained totally foreign. It is the realisation that workers come into theatres only to build them which has made Planchon turn more of his attention, on the one hand, to the ongoing work of attracting and maintaining a *provincial* audience, working class or not, and, on the other hand, to his personal work as a playwright.

The government, in its decision to turn the Théâtre de la Cité de Villeurbanne into the Théâtre National Populaire, showed that it, too, was aware of a certain failure in its previous programme. M. Jacques Duhamel, then Minister of Cultural Affairs, said that traditional methods of reaching the public seemed to have gone as far as possible, and that it was time for a change.[16] The new TNPs organisation was from the start quite different from that of the old TNP and of the Théâtre de la Cité de Villeurbanne. With Roger Planchon and Patrice Chéreau as artistic directors and Robert Gilbert as administrative director, it has the specific mission of bringing theatre to all French cities, including but not favouring Paris. In order to ensure that each of its visits is properly prepared and has as widespread and long-term an effect as possible, the TNP relies on the structures for audience contact which have been built up by the host theatre in each city. Planchon and his actors make themselves available for talks and meetings with groups of interested people whenever possible. The company also divides into two sections, one under Chéreau and the other under Planchon, each presenting a different play. As the artistic approaches of the two men are also completely different, a visit by the TNP can be very enlivening: two weeks of Planchon's *Le Tartuffe* followed by two weeks of Chéreau's *La Dispute*, for example, would provide a great stimulus to discussion. Planchon was quite right to exclaim about the new TNP in 1972: 'We will celebrate theatre for a month in every city!'[17]

2

Planchon's approach to the theatre

LIKE most directors of the *théâtre populaire* movement, Planchon was strongly influenced by Brecht. When he began his career at Villeurbanne, this influence was almost overpowering. At this point, as he admitted later, he was copying Brecht outright: 'We should respect his [Brecht's] stage productions to such a point that we not only use them as inspiration, but modestly set about copying them . . . Epic theatre is a new dramatic form, and we should learn to dismantle and reassemble models of it. After that, we will be able to see how to make it more effective.'[1]

Of course, Brecht was not Planchon's only source of inspiration. Another major influence on his directing style has been that of the cinema. Planchon's early productions, and notably his 1957 production of Shakespeare's *Henry IV*, also benefited from the ideas of Jean Vilar and from those of Antonin Artaud; they combined the neatness and polish of Vilar's style with the kind of violence which Artaud recommended. Furthermore, Planchon's rewriting of Marlowe's *Edward II* in 1960 was in a lyrical style quite different from the emotionally austere Brechtian model. Nevertheless, Brecht's ideas on direction have influenced the entire course of Planchon's work.

First, Planchon believes in approaching a play by studying the *fable*, the events or actions, rather than the psychology of the characters. As early as 1958, he was saying: '. . . a *mise en scène* in itself means nothing. What counts is the development of the scenes, their relation to one another, the relation between a character and his language, that which he uses now, that which he will use later . . . It is the situation which counts, its relation to the other situations of the same character.'[2] It was to be an oft-repeated principle. Let us look first at what the characters *do*, he said again and again, and not at what they *say*: 'A play progresses only through its events . . . Actions can be in flagrant contradiction with the words spoken.'³ This idea of sticking to the events was not invented by Brecht; it comes from Aristotle's *Poetics*. Planchon read Aristotle, and in 1964 he surprised everyone by declaring that he had become a 'classical' director, one who asks, for instance, not, 'Who is Tartuffe?', but rather, 'What does Tartuffe do?'

Secondly, Planchon adopted from Brecht the important concept of a *langage scénique*, a stage language: the idea that the presentation of a play on the stage, its translation by an acting company into a visual and auditory medium, is as meaningful in its own right as the written text. A play is thus only fully realised as a work of art when it is presented on the stage. By incorporating this idea into his work, Planchon distinguished himself from the influential Jean Vilar, who believed that the director should be a tool of the playwright. Planchon is well aware of his debt to Brecht in coming to understand that the stage interpretation and the text are two equally important halves of a dramatic production:

The lesson which we can learn from Brecht the theoretician is that . . . stage language . . . has a *responsibility* equal to that of the written text and, finally, a movement onstage, the choice of a colour, of a set, of a costume, etc., this involves a complete responsibility. The stage language is totally responsible, in the same way as the text itself is responsible.⁴

These two major theories, that of the importance of the *fable*, that of the significance of the stage language, were to affect all the aspects of Planchon's work as a director.

If the stage language is as important as the text, then each element in this language assumes a great significance. Planchon believes that there is no such thing as a 'neutral' or 'innocent' presentation of a play. The director's interpretation manifests itself in every detail of the staging, the lighting, the music, the backdrop, and in each individual prop; even the physical appearance of the actor is a choice and therefore an interpretation. Playing with a simple set or with no set at all is also a choice, according to Planchon: 'One does not act without a set, one acts with the intention of acting without a set, which is quite different. There is no neutral set . . . every object placed on the stage or every absence of an object . . . has some kind of significance.'⁵ Because the set will 'speak' in any case, it is clearly best, in artistic terms, if the director decides consciously what it is going to say.

René Allio was Planchon's set designer at the Théâtre de la
Cité de Villeurbanne for many years, and their entente was
exceptionally good. He and Planchon saw the work of the
director and the work of the set designer as complementary.
An assistant director at the theatre once defined the director
as '. . . un monsieur qui écrit le spectacle dans l'espace' (a
man who 'writes' the play in space).[6] One might add that it is
the set designer who provides the means with which the
director can 'write' the play onstage. Allio saw a set as an
outil à jouer une pièce (a tool for performing a play).[7] It must
be functional in the most basic terms: it must provide all that
is necessary for the actors and/or the stagehands to change a
scene rapidly and, in Planchon's productions, often in full
view of the audience. A set must also give the audience some
indication of the setting, in time as well as place. In planning
this aspect of a set, René Allio tried to find forms typical of
the period portrayed in the play, but which, at the same time,
were reminiscent of forms recognisable to the audience.
Finding analogies between our century and others in dress
and architecture often required considerable research, and
Allio more than other set designers of his day insisted on the
importance of careful documentation.

As well as creating a tool for the acting of a play the set
designer, in collaboration with the director, creates a visual
language which underlines the themes of the play. Allio
tried to do this, '. . . sometimes in a precise and almost critical way, sometimes in a more diffuse and subtle fashion'.[8]
Like Planchon, Allio believed that each object acquires a
special significance when it is placed in the stage area,
which is a space defined by convention. As soon as the actor
appears on the stage, his body gives a scale to the set as a
whole. The audience perceives the familiar human form, and
judges everything else in relation to it. The objects which
surround the actor, therefore, must have the same degree of
realism and of verisimilitude as the actor. Since each element, including even the actor's appearance, has a meaning,
all objects must be chosen and juxtaposed with some thought
for their interrelated meanings. Allio once gave an example
of this interrelationship: he said that a costume, although it
has an obvious relation to the actor who wears it, is chosen
primarily for its appropriateness to the character. If it is
necessary to change the costume, thus defined, in order to
adapt it to the actor, then the actor is wrong for the part.[9] The

set designer's role is to predict what significance an object will acquire on the stage, among other specific objects.

Two particularly modern facets of staging have extended the scope for experimentation in stage design: electric lighting and modern sound effects. Erwin Piscator, the German director, had already experimented with the use of film and with cinematographic lighting effects in the 1920s. Since then the stage has remained three-dimensional and, in any design, the structural and atmospheric possibilities opened up by lighting must be taken into consideration. In any case, as the Théâtre de la Cité was trying to attract a public nurtured on television and film, it was especially necessary for it to borrow, as much as possible, the techniques used by these media. Lighting was only one of these techniques.

Music, in the same way as lighting, and because of the increasing sophistication of acoustical equipment, can open up the stage imaginatively; it can suggest a far greater and more flexible space than that actually available. The Théâtre de la Cité was a rarity among contemporary French theatres in that it had a resident composer, Claude Lochy, who is still with the Théâtre National Populaire. According to Lochy, the musical accompaniment of live plays is an art sadly neglected in France. He said in 1959 that the Théâtre de la Cité was attempting to discover the function of music written directly for the stage. Brecht believed in using music as an independent and yet integral part of the stage language. Its role has been explored by Claudel, for whom it was an extension of the spoken text beyond its literal meaning to attain a cosmic significance. Lochy's own ideal was a musical score which would serve the text, not by playing the role of a psychological or of a naturalistic illustration, nor as background 'musak', but as an autonomous comment: 'Thus music is no longer merely the emotional catalyst for the spectator, but, on the contrary, it is what keeps him alert, what disconcerts him.'[10]

Planchon and his actors share an enthusiasm for the cinema, which has long been a source of inspiration as well as a point of contact with a public used to film conventions. Planchon has always integrated cinematic techniques into his *mises en scène* because he regards theatre and film as closely related. In his productions, projectors are used with an instinct for their appropriateness at any given moment. He has used them to light a scene from various angles, to pick out one small section of a set, to alternate between close-ups and long-distance 'shots', like a camera. In his production of Brecht's *Schweyk im Zweiten Weltkrieg* in 1960, he used a revolving stage in a similar way, not only to facilitate scene-changing, but to show a tableau from a new vantage point or to dwell on certain scenes and speed up the movement of others. Plays were sometimes chopped into short cinematic sequences. Planchon made the audience aware of the existence of a foreground and a background on the stage. He used slide projections as Erwin Piscator had done, and, as Brecht did, he used bands of material with comments and slogans for the public to read. He made an important use of offstage sounds in many of his productions; a 'collective' voice in *Edward II*, for example, or receding footsteps in *Bérénice*, or the cries and laughter of an imagined television audience in *La Langue au Chat*. Subjecting plays, whether classical or modern, to this rejuvenating treatment earned Planchon his reputation as a radical artist very early in his career.

Even as he uses these ideas for staging, Planchon remains, in one respect at least, a faithful disciple of Brecht. Sets, music, and techniques of lighting or of stage design are never used without being revealed for what they are. When René Allio was at the Théâtre de la Cité, he made a fine distinction, in his theory of staging, between *représentation* (performance) and *présentation* (presentation). The *représentation* was made up of those things which serve the performance of the actor and make the episodes of the play clear. The props in this category should be realistic in a traditional way – that is, unrealistic seen close up in order to seem more realistic from afar. The *présentation*, on the other hand, was made up of those things which contribute to the show as a whole. This *présentation* must, in Allio's opinion, *avouer le théâtre* (acknowledge that this is theatre).[11] The details of the set should support the illusion,whereas the set as a whole should be a commentary on the play.

Obviously, the two categories overlap, and the distinction would be of little practical use to a budding set designer. The Théâtre de la Cité were working for a new class of theatre-goers, but at the same time they were committed to Brecht. Allio's distinction between *présentation* and *représentation* was an attempt to reconcile the Brechtian distancing effect, which appeals to the intellect, with the need to create a dramatic illusion for a public that wanted full-blooded, if intelligent, drama. This striving for a balance between illusion and commentary creates an underlying tension in all Planchon's work. With great intelligence and sensitivity he is usually able to make the stage illusion just perceptible without destroying its essence. In Planchon's production of *George Dandin*, for example, a critic noticed that the straw was real, but that the set did not quite hide the backstage machinery. Planchon struck the balance with most ease in his musical comedies, *Les Trois Mousquetaires*, *O M'man Chicago*, *La Mise en pièces du 'Cid'*, perhaps because laughter is both an act of alienation and an act of involvement on the part of the spectator. Whether it is through humour, caricature, or self-revealing stage sets, Planchon never fails to remind his audience that they are in a theatre.

This principle is fundamentally opposed to naturalism. To make the spectator constantly aware of being in a theatre is to treat him as an intelligent adult. By making his public conscious of the theatrical illusion, Planchon is demanding the right, as the critic Dominique Nores points out,[12] to tell it a false story, a story which can be real only within the mind of each spectator. Thus it is another way of extending the play's resonance beyond the stage and beyond even the medium of the theatre, into the realm of the public's imagination.

Planchon's preoccupation with concrete day-to-day reality, as well as his fidelity to the concept of studying a play through its events, has helped to shape his method of directing actors. What he demands of them is that they appreciate their role rationally, step by step; just as each scene must be analysed in depth, so must each character be considered carefully in his own right. It is necessary to regard each role as a composition, a structural entity, and to make each character at once typical and unique. Just as the play must be shown to take place in a specific historical context, so the characters in it must be shown to be people of their time and of their situation. Characters are looked upon as primarily social beings.

Repeatedly, Planchon has stood firm against over-playing, or 'pathetic' acting. In his first experience with Parisian actors in 1958, his main problem was to get them to rid themselves of a tendency to play emotionally, *de jouer lyrique*. The best actors sometimes overplay their roles in the belief that they are enriching them. Planchon thinks that actors must subordinate their acting to the events of the plot:

'In the theatre, everything which reinforces the story (the *fable*) comes out right.'[13] In 1972, Planchon affirmed categorically: '... my style is absolutely stripped bare of pathos. When I see an actor plunging into pathos, I feel he's lying.'[14]

In the same way as Planchon's productions show respect for the audience's intelligence, his way of entering into a play shows considerable confidence in the actors. Claude Lochy gave an account of the way in which roles were assigned in Villeurbanne in 1962:

The casting is never made definite at the start, except for one or two roles. We read the play out loud. We discuss it . . . Each actor creates a *mise en scène* for the role which he has chosen. Roger sees each actor alone to see if the role which he had the day before suits him. Little by little, after fifteen days, the casting has crystallised. Roger, of course, demands an effort and a style of acting, but discussion is always possible.[15]

The Théâtre de la Cité worked as a community, and so does the new Théâtre National Populaire. The emphasis is on team work, on discussion, on the contribution of the group to the production. Actors can make suggestions, improvise, and disagree during a rehearsal. When I attended the rehearsals for Planchon's own play *La Langue au Chat*, for example, the actor playing the Pope, Pierre Asso, requested that one of his lines which had been cut be reinstated; he felt that it ended his speech with a delightful pun ('Revelation has been replaced by Revolution', scene 11, p. 4). Planchon agreed. This emphasis on an exchange between director and actor, and the belief in collective endeavour, are ways of discouraging 'star' performances and of increasing the coherence of the troupe.

In a sense, actors in Villeurbanne are in a privileged position and were so even at the start of the theatre's career, in comparison with their Parisian counterparts. Employed full-time for a year, they enjoy a degree of financial security which allows them to take time and to reflect on their work. Planchon saw the importance of this advantage when the troupe went to Paris. Actors in the capital have to rush from one audition to the other, and take on any available work, simply in order to make a living; they are seldom able to concentrate fully on one role at a time. Planchon concluded after the theatre's first visit to Paris that 'Any artistic adventure, of whatever order, demands a continuity which does

not exist in Paris . . . All the artists involved in a show must
have the time, once their work is finished, to meditate upon
it, to rethink it. This is the indispensable condition for making one further step forward.'[16]

It is necessary to give the actors freedom of thought and
expression, but it is also necessary to shape their work into a
unified and coherent whole. Even for the *créations collec-
tives* in the theatre's repertoire, a director's hand is necessary. Planchon has a way of leading an actor, through conversation, in time, to make the same discoveries that he
himself made in his preliminary work. Gérard Guillaumat,
one of the Villeurbanne actors, described Planchon's control
over the acting team and his way of inciting the actor to think
about his role and about the play as a whole:

With Roger, at the start, you have a feeling of freedom. You have the
impression that you could do anything. In the end it is not so.
Gradually you feel caught in a rigorous *mise en scène*. For each
play, it's different . . . Planchon places the actor in such a position
that he must automatically feel lost. Being lost, the actor asks
himself questions. He becomes curious. He is no longer interested
only in his own role but in the whole play. Roger Planchon pro-
vokes the actors. A good director must be a *provocateur*.[17]

This carefully planned 'provocation' stimulates actors to
take that one step further, to play their role more intelligently. Planchon gives his actors a definite framework
within which to work, but rather than imposing it arbitrarily
from without, he manoeuvres them into a recognition of it
and an acceptance of its necessity.

Planchon's sense of humour is of great assistance in making rehearsals run more smoothly and in giving actors a
perspective on their roles. During rehearsals for *Dans le vent*,
for instance, he once gave Jean Bouise, one of his actors, a
very picturesque indication of his character's emotional
situation in a conversational scene: 'You are sitting on a
brazier. Someone comes to ask you how you are. You answer,
"Fine", and try to smile.'[18] Planchon has even refused to direct
actors in another language than French, because they would
not understand his jokes. He feels that humour has an essential and delicate role to play: 'I am trying to define a certain
style but it's very fine, very French if you like, very . . .
humorous. To play the kind of theatre I want, I need . . . *very
intelligent actors*. The more intelligent they are, the more

they can play what I want them to play.'[19] Planchon's style
has been described as being between parody and realism.
This may well describe the tension of a performance in
which the actor's perspective on his role is essentially witty.

The plays which Planchon directs, whether classical or
modern, other people's or his own, are rooted in a specific
milieu. He believes that all plays have a social significance.
This is one constant line of approach in all his interpretations. No work of art can be understood if it is detached from
the historical context in which it was born. Whatever a play
has to say, its setting and the stage language through which it
is translated must show that what happens does not happen
in a vacuum.

At the beginning of his career, Planchon made definite
statements about history in his *mises en scène*. Later, he
came to prefer a more understated, 'dry' presentation.
According to Planchon, there is in this respect an essential
theoretical opposition between Brecht and Aristotle: Brecht
believed in giving all plays which he directed a demonstrative structure and a clear conclusion, like the lesson at the
end of an Aesop fable. Aristotle, on the other hand, was
interested only in the conflict, without giving it a demonstrative value. The progression from a demonstrative theatre in
the Brechtian mode to a less tendentious style of production
was a major development in Planchon's work. Planchon
claims that his work is critical, in that it shows up those
aspects of society which he considers objectionable, but that
he does not now put forward any formula or political ideology as a solution. A director who makes a point of revealing
social ills cannot escape the charge of didacticism completely. Nevertheless, Planchon's later productions have
moralised politically far less than his earlier ones. In this
movement away from Brecht, it is interesting to note that
Roger Planchon's main preoccupation was a very Brechtian
respect for the spectator's intelligence; he believes that it is
up to the public, and not the director, to find the answers.

When Planchon attempted to define himself and to
explain his aims and methods as a writer, many of the con-
cepts which had always guided his work as a director
became clearer. He wrote his first play in 1962. He had been
asked to make a film based on his early Théâtre de la Comédie production, *Cartouche*, and when he set about writing
the film script, he found that he really preferred to write a

play. He began to write for two major reasons. First, he felt
that he had been trying to say too much through other
people's plays; he put on a version of Marlowe's *Edward II* in
1961 which was virtually a new play. He decided, as he later
admitted, that 'As long as I was mistreating other people's
plays . . . it might be honest to write and to mistreat
myself.'[20] Secondly, he wanted to get away from the influence of Brecht, and avoid repeating himself in his *mises en
scène*. In this he was successful: 'Although the experience of
directing was of no benefit to me for writing, on the other
hand, writing freed and renewed me for directing. For twelve
years I had not got away from the influence of Brecht. I was
only copying, as best I could, but copying.'[21]

Unlike other directors, such as Baty, who wrote with the
staging in mind, Planchon wished to write like someone who
had never set foot on a stage. He felt that to fit his writing to
his staging would be unwise, and in a sense unethical: 'I said
to myself "you must never write something just because you
know you'll be able to direct it" . . . the temptation would
have been to write . . . with a set in mind, so that the text
would fit the set.'[22] Having taken this decision, Planchon
discovered that his past experience of the theatre was of no
use to him as a writer; a seasoned director, he was nevertheless an absolute beginner at writing.

Although as a director he moved away from Brecht after
becoming a writer, Planchon found that Brecht remained a
strong influence on his writing: 'You could say that all the
plays I've written have been a long meditation on Brecht's
work. I think the two writers who are the closest to Brecht are
Peter Weiss and myself. He's taken one side of Brecht, I've
taken the other.'[23] Even Brecht's method of writing was, to a
certain extent, imitated at the Théâtre de la Cité. Brecht used
to write among friends, asking for advice, reading out parts,
and getting as many opinions as possible. Planchon, too,
makes each of his plays as collective a creation as possible by
giving readings of freshly-written plays to groups of actors,
technicians, guests, etc. Their comments and criticisms are
taken into account and the play is gradually modified. It can
go through many transformations before it is presented onstage. Even quite late in the rehearsals for *La Langue au Chat*
parts of the text and the *mise en scène* were altered more than
once. At one point in these rehearsals, a harried sound technician asked Planchon about a recent alteration: 'That

change for the "love crusade" – is it definitive now, for the moment?' In an art so open to change and so sensitive to people's reactions, the 'definitive' version might well not remain definitive for longer than a moment.

Although Brecht's influence is still perceptible in Planchon's work, he was for Planchon a point of departure and not a horizon. Brecht's plays like his *mises en scène*, are demonstrative. Furthermore, they belong to a specific historical context. Arthur Adamov, and Brecht's followers in France today, such playwrights as Armand Gatti, Michel Vinaver, and Planchon, have taken a different direction. In the early 1960s, and especially after the *événements* of 1968, Planchon saw the limitations of Brecht for a contemporary French audience: 'Brecht . . . formulates the problems and puts them in question form. The play gives the answer. The clearer the answer, the less interesting it is. On the other hand, the more ambiguous it is, the more the answer becomes interesting aesthetically and morally.'[24] Planchon has said that he loves the play which asks questions but gives no answers because, 'It is not polite to give any in the spectators' stead.'[25]

Planchon's plays, like his own *mises en scène*, have a clear historical background. He believes that we are all caught within a given historical situation which we help to create and to perpetuate, but by which, at the same time, we are determined. Planchon does not wish to bring about the revolution through the theatre, however; even the events of 1968 did not transform him into a political agitator. When the general trend in France was toward agit-prop (as in André Benedetto's street performances in Avignon), Planchon was taking a different direction:

The young seem to want to go towards theatre which is immediately effective, theatre of raw, 'mobilising' documents, but, for my part, I am tending towards a meditative theatre, which allows the spectator to sit back in front of a story which is told to him slowly . . .

Although, like everyone, I am haunted by the difficulty of History, which is something really tragic, I belong to a generation which is asking itself questions on what 'Revolution' means, as opposed to what is happening in certain left-wing theatres in which people wish to bring about Revolution.[26]

The public, in Planchon's theatre, is meant to come to its own conclusions. His plays are intended primarily to make people look again at what they have taken for granted and question it.

Planchon's plays show an Adamovian concern for the here-and-now. Indeed, he chose to work in the theatre because it is an immediate art which lives from day to day, and which in a sense has no past. When he puts on a play for the second or the third time (as he did with Le Tartuffe, to give only one example), he is not content to do it as it was done before. Each production is thought out afresh. It is not only perfectionism, but a love of the immediate and the perishable which prevents Planchon from using the same interpretation of a play twice. If this trait was already evident in his work as a director, it has become manifest in his own plays. His unpublished plays are rewritten each time he recreates them on the stage.

Planchon's entire artistic perception has been shaped by approaching reality from its most humble and apparently trivial side:

I have a passion for what is concrete. Everything that is really palpable, concrete, pleases me. I like life in its most elementary state, without heightening.

It's the whole feeling of life passing, something very fragile which doesn't last, which is miraculous in the true sense of the word.

You see, you are never large enough for the things you live through. A woman giving birth, a man and a woman making love – these are things which are absolutely prodigious! And people never manage to measure up to this wonder, they don't reach its dimensions, and it's only by approaching the humblest side of things that you can measure up to this everyday miracle. That's what I'm trying to capture in my writing and my productions.[27]

Planchon's production of George Dandin was a spectacular example of his use of the day-to-day to create an ambience and uncover new facets of an old play: the set showed a farmyard with all its mud, its hay, and the activity of the peasants working from dawn to dusk, and thus gave a dense background to the quarrels and monologues of the principal characters. Each ordinary object, every humble person, has a part to play in the 'everyday miracle' which Planchon attempts to portray through the theatre.

Working for an audience which is 'outside culture' has made Planchon extremely wary of over-abstraction or artificiality. As a self-taught man brought up in a working-class home he knows, in a personal way, what will provoke boredom or mockery in an uneducated person. This pragmatic quality of Planchon's inspiration is, however, tempered by two things. The first is a fascination with dreams and with their importance in the lives of most people; he admits that he uses the framework of his own dreams in writing. The second is his love of poetry.

Planchon came to the theatre, like many of his contemporaries, through surrealism. He has always enjoyed poetry. It may be his own enthusiasm for poetic texts which influenced him to emphasise the text in his own plays. He has often spoken of a crisis in the theatre in the early sixties, which led many directors to abandon spoken language on the stage. Since then,

> ... the tendency to abandon the text has never ceased to affirm itself. For my part I have turned my efforts in the opposite direction. Indeed, I have taken care to give a definite importance to the text in what I wrote, being careful, however, to impose a certain discipline on the writing. For me, this is continuing in the direction of such works as those of Brecht and Vitrac.[28]

Certainly a poetic bent was evident in Planchon's very first play, *La Remise*, and it has become increasingly apparent in his later writing.

Like Adamov, and like Gatti, Planchon attempts in his own plays to portray history through its effects on believable human beings. He admits that he has always written for a specific public: 'I have written ... for my Villeurbanne public, with external events, the news items read in *France-Soir*, but with their personal reactions to these events. I have always written for the French, never for foreigners. Villeurbanne is a small town made up of workers, somewhat *embourgeoisés*.'[29] From being thus centred upon a specific milieu, Planchon's artistic vision has been formed by it. He realised the extent of his own 'provincialism' late in his career; he said in 1972: 'I am totally provincial. I have a profound feeling for the French provinces of which I am a part. Formerly, it was on the level of general ideas. But now that I write plays, I sense that my plays are, more and more, the French provinces.'[30] Indeed, his plays in both their settings and their themes are basically provincial. In a highly centralised nation such as France, where great historical events are usually initiated in Paris, the provincial view of history is always marginal and oblique. The citizen in the provinces, especially in the rural areas, is usually eventually caught up in historical events, but often in spite of himself and without understanding how. The effects of social or economic upheavals, new attitudes and progressive ideas, come from the Parisian centre to a province unready and often unable to assimilate them into its own mentality. The characters in Planchon's plays are constant outsiders.

When he wrote his play on the French Revolution, *Bleus, blancs, rouges*, Planchon was surprised to find that, although he had been careful to speak of '. . . the French Revolution in its specific Frenchness . . . yet the play also works as a description of people caught up in a time of great historical change anywhere'.[31] It is often in a work of art which, like Planchon's, is most rooted in a specific time and place that one finds a universal quality. The difficulty of writing with a historical context consciously in mind is that the characters may become reduced to the level of examples or puppets. It is a problem which many politically-aware writers have encountered, from Brecht to Adamov to Gatti. Planchon and Gatti are two contemporary playwrights who have succeeded in combining a historical awareness with a truth of individual characterisation, who have achieved, in their characters, Lukács' ideal of an '. . . organic unity of profound individuality and profound typicality'.[32]

According to Roger Planchon, two important trends in contemporary theatre are that which he calls the 'Mystico-Sacré', by which he no doubt means the Artaud-inspired ritualistic theatre of such people as Jerzy Grotowski, Fernando Arrabal and the Latin American school, and that of political agitation, best demonstrated perhaps by such directors as André Benedetto. Planchon follows neither of these directions; the former is one to which he is temperamentally unsuited, and the latter amounts, in his view, to preaching to the converted. He is a thinker about politics, rather than an agent for immediate political change: 'I create political theatre, but I'm interested essentially in the problematical aspect of politics . . . For me, a situation in the theatre is true insofar as it has its roots buried deep in everyday life.'[33]

A recurrent theme in Planchon's latest statements is his aim to arouse a new sensibility. Perhaps he would agree with a statement made by Claude Roy, the journalist and writer, about the purpose of good theatre. In 1964, Gatti's play *La Vie imaginaire de l'éboueur Auguste Geai*, and Planchon's play *La Remise* were shown in Paris in the same programme. A left-wing critic, Marc Pierret, accused both Gatti and Planchon of using their own working-class forebears as dramatic characters, not with any political purpose, but merely to give a middle-class audience an evening's entertainment. Claude Roy wrote a very sensitive reply to Pierret's criticism:

> Good theatre . . . has no immediate use . . . a beautiful play only makes people conscious . . . Conscious of fragility, of time passing, of tenderness, of violence, of fury, of pity, conscious of what it takes to make and unmake a man . . . it is certain that, in any case, before understanding and transforming, one must feel . . . Roger Planchon and Armand Gatti . . . are people who stir up the heart. The human spirit is a thing which it is wise to stir up before putting it to use.[34]

PART I

The director

3

Contemporary drama: the social context

> ... a work of art, and especially a play, becomes real only if it
> is placed in a definite social context.
>
> Arthur Adamov

BRECHT

Der gute Mensch von Sezuan (The Good Woman of Setzuan)
IN January 1954, Planchon and his troupe were asked by
Édouard Herriot, then mayor of Lyons, to put on a play as
Lyons's contribution to the drama section of the art festival of
Lyons–Charbonnières. They decided to produce *Der gute
Mensch von Sezuan*, known in France as *La Bonne Ame de
Sé-Tchouan*.

Performances took place in a large gambling casino in
Charbonnières. Short of money as usual, the company used
everything in the casino, including the tables. As in the
Chinese theatre, foot-bridges crossed the room through the
audience, who were surrounded by the sets and indeed
became a part of them (a situation which looked forward to
Michel Parent's productions of Arrabal in the 1970s). The
actors wore costumes which were beautiful, but faded and
worn, to convey the blend of poetry and realism in the play.
Introducing Brecht to a provincial audience of the fifties, and
with inadequate means, was an ambitious project. It wasn't a
great success.

The next year, the Théâtre de la Comédie produced the
play once again, in a different style. Sets were austere with
natural substances – wood, earth – predominating. Planchon
was trying to move away from the fairy-tale and toward the
fable. The production, however, still aroused sympathy for
Shen Te, the suffering heroine.

The third time the play was put on, in 1958, Planchon and
company had moved to the Théâtre de la Cité de Villeurbanne. By then Planchon had met Bertolt Brecht in Paris and

31

discussed the play with him. The 1958 production, directed with the assistance of Claude Lochy, was a genuine recreation: Planchon's basic approach was to emphasise the philosophical dilemma in *La Bonne Ame*; the problem of being 'good' in a 'bad' society.

The experience gained at the Théâtre de la Comédie was useful. It had showed that the play was effective if it took place on a small stage. In the large Villeurbanne stage area, Planchon and Allio, his set designer, found a way of creating a small space within a bigger one: the sets and the *mise en scène* as a whole suggested an unlimited space, that of the park or of the city of Sé-Tchouan, for example; each scene, however, took place in a definite, limited part of the stage. René Allio used an enormous backdrop covered with wash-drawings and vertical calligraphic designs based on Chinese script. The props were modelled on objects depicted in documents of the day – that is, of China in the 1930s. The paintings widened the stage space and gave the play a legendary quality appropriate to a *fable*; the props added a touch of realism, and unified the action by giving it a fixed point around which to revolve. Props and different backdrops were lowered from the flies, or changed in the half-darkness; the stage was also filled, in Planchon style, with numerous extras, moving to the sound of a whistle as though they were being refereed through an organised game. (Planchon may have been borrowing from his productions of *Les Trois Mousquetaires* in which whistles and organised, dance-like movements were used extensively.) The costumes, even those of beggars and wretches, were designed after careful study of Chinese dress and of previous Berliner Ensemble productions. Because the actors were not sufficiently trained to act with masks in true Brechtian style, they played without, except of course for Shen Te when disguised as Shui Ta (played by Isabelle Sadoyan). The music was that which Paul Dessau had composed for the Berliner Ensemble.

Brecht in the fifties was still relatively unkown in France; furthermore, the members of Planchon's troupe were young, and their left-wing views seemed subversive to the Lyons authorities. Now that they were an officially subsidised company they therefore had to overcome considerable official opposition in order to stage *La Bonne Ame de Sé-Tchouan* at all. After rehearsals for the play had started, Planchon had to make an abrupt change in the season's programme. As he himself said later: 'I was rehearsing

Brecht's *La Bonne Ame de Sé-Tchouan* when I was made to understand that it would be best to give up this project for the moment, otherwise all my subsidies would be cut off. We had to put on *Les Trois Mousquetaires*. Helter-skelter!'[1] The play was finally put on, but there was little press coverage. One understands why when one reads the critic Pierre Marcabru's account of his meeting with Planchon after the show: 'I congratulate him; he looks abashed and says: "Please don't talk about it, I have given a written promise to do all in my power so that nothing at all is said about my work. I got the right to put it on on this condition only."'[2]

Pierre Marcabru and Gérard Guillot both saw the production and wrote about it, nevertheless. Both were particularly impressed with Planchon's control of the acting team and with the unity of the troupe. They were and are an exceptionally well-coordinated group, used to Planchon's direction. Marcabru praised in Planchon's work '. . . a very special way of letting go and of holding back the actors, of blocking them in full swing; a kind of brutality in his manner of attacking the public headlong, incontestably great gifts when it comes to measuring, organising, directing violence', and also commended '. . . this meticulous firmness which gives *La Bonne Ame de Sé-Tchouan* a power of provocation whose regular and tenacious pressure recalls the Berliner Ensemble'.[3]

Schweyk im Zweiten Weltkrieg (*Schweik in the Second World War*)

Planchon presented Brecht's *Schweyk im Zweiten Weltkrieg* under the title *Schweyk dans la deuxième guerre mondiale* in October 1961 at Villeurbanne. Jacques Rosner was assistant director.

Brecht's play is based on Jaroslav Hašek's unfinished novel *The Good Soldier Schweyk*. Erwin Piscator had put on a version of Hašek's story at the Theatre am Nollendorfplatz in 1929, an adaptation by a writers' collective that included Gasbarra, Mehring, Jung, Lania, and Brecht. In it marionnettes on a moving platform represented troops departing for the front. There were no fixed sets: Schweyk played amongst moving props and walked on moving footways. He was surrounded by Grosz's political and satirical cartoon films. Genuine documentary films were used for the war scenes. Planchon's production was to keep up this tradition of openness to technical innovation.

Brecht wrote *Schweyk im Zweiten Weltkrieg* in 1943. He altered the character of Hašek's anti-hero in important ways. Brecht saw Hašek's hero, not as a crafty saboteur, but as a worldly-wise opportunist, and indestructible man of the people. He changed Hašek's anarchistic and solitary bachelor into a man who longs for at least enough order to eat one's fill and enjoy being with one's friends. Still, Brecht's Schweyk is anything but a hero. Although his ineptitude makes everyone laugh, as one laughs one feels a nagging doubt about his actions. They bring on reprisals, and they include fighting on the Russian front. It is only his survival and the eventual downfall of his oppressors that 'justify' his behaviour. Hašek's Schweyk is opposed only to a brutal and stupid army discipline; Brecht's Schweyk confronts one of the most sinister regimes in history. In Brecht's play, therefore, the opposition between the 'Higher Regions', where Hitler and his acolytes live, and the 'Lower Regions', where the common people live, is crucial.

René Allio's sets were designed to underline this basic opposition, to comment on the character of Schweyk, and to make the play, its sources, and its setting, clear to the public. Just as, in his post-war productions, Brecht had used colourless sets and costumes to produce a 'sobering' and anti-heroic effect, Allio decided to use a very limited range of colours. For most people the mental images associated with the Nazi era are without colour. It is not just that they are distant in time, nor that they are horrifying, but that most of us have seen the events of the Nazi period only through the black and white newsreels and newspaper pictures of the time. Allio therefore designed the costumes in shades of white, black, and grey, so that they would 'speak' to the audience. In order to remind spectators of the original Schweyk, however, Josef Lada's illustrations for Hašek's novel were reproduced in bright colours on panels framing the stage. Bright colours were also used for the scenes of Schweyk's dreams during his long march through the snow in search of Stalingrad; they sharpened the contrast between his grey reality and his irrepressibly optimistic aspirations. The nightmarish scenes set in the 'Higher Regions' were staged in a uniform blood-red, '. . . an expressionistic proceeding if ever there was one', explained Allio, 'but from which one must not shrink, to illustrate these scenes in which caricature, and a parody of opera, particularly

Wagnerian opera, prompt one to use extremely powerful forms'.[4]

In general, Planchon, following Brecht's textual portrayal of them, made the Nazis into caricature figures through the stage language. There is a violent and unrealistic scene in the play, for example, in which Schweyk is taken to Gestapo headquarters in the offices of a bank and interrogated. For this scene, the set was entirely false, and quite absurd. It was uniformly black, there were coffin handles instead of door knobs, there were revolving doors between offices, and the secretary was played by a man in a grey skirt.

The music is another important element of caricature in the play. The company used Hans Eisler's score for the Berliner Ensemble, and indeed Eisler visited the theatre himself. There were three different sorts of music. For the mimed sequences, the style was that of large male-voice choirs, with a good brass and cello accompaniment, following a polka or marching rhythm. There were also numerous songs, accompanied by a honky-tonk piano, recalling both the folk music of central Europe, and the Nazi airs of the thirties and forties. For the dream-like sequences which take place in the 'Higher Regions', the actors became opera-singers performing to a mock-Wagnerian accompaniment, again appropriately Hitlerian. Because half the play was sung, the Théâtre de la Cité had to ask for the help of singers and of a 45-piece orchestra from the Opéra de Lyon.

Planchon, as the programme for the Villeurbanne production shows, saw Hašek's hero as the descendant of a long line of popular heroes, from the Guignol of Lyons to Falstaff, Till Eulenspiegel, and Charlie Chaplin. Schweyk as played by Jean Bouise at Villeurbanne was neither Hašek's nor Brecht's hero, but a more linear, more provocative character. Schweyk is an ordinary, slightly cowardly, slightly stupid man, resisting brutality with apparent inertia, but quite ingenious in his fight for survival. Jean Bouise is a brilliant comedian, and it may be that his performance so impressed critics that they forgot the ambiguities of the character in their delight with the interpretation. Peter Lennon, for example, felt that even the physical appearance of this 'jewel of an actor' designated him for the role of Schweyk:

I could imagine no more cozy and confident take-over of the Schweyk personality than that accomplished by Bouise: he has a crafty eye, a mouth made for imbecility, a hoarse and offensively contented laugh, and the swaggering assurance of a Candide who knows that the world is even more of a cretin than he is; add to this his exceptional mimetic gifts and an insouciant control of timing . . .[5]

Bouise's interpretation, like much of the *mise en scène*, was inspired in part by folklore, in part by marionettes, and in part by animated films. He invented, in fact, a style to suit the role, a style which suggested, as most of the critics noted, all popular heroes rolled into one. Much of the praise for the performance, however, suggests that Bouise's Schweyk was a popular hero whose acquiescence in the war is overlooked because of his wit, his likeability, and his capacity for survival. Had the character been over-simplified and made too likeable?

There is an ambiguity inherent in the character of many folk heroes. Passive resistance or, at least, resistance by assumed stupidity often involves an acceptance of evils which cannot be avoided except by giving one's own life. In order to put Schweyk into perspective, Planchon put him in the context of a meaningful stage language. The widow Kopeka is the real resistance fighter in the play, and her unambiguous heroism shows up Schweyk's instincts for self-preservation. Schweyk, in a sense, collaborates. Told to march, he marches. But there is an ironic twist to his docility. He marches on a revolving platform. March as he will, he remains in the same spot. The scene of this long and pointless march on a revolving platform is an image of the essential question of the play: is Schweyk's kind of resistance only *accidentally* harmful to the Reich? Bouise did indeed make Schweyk likeable, and possibly therefore more accessible and familiar to a Villeurbanne audience. But the ambiguity of his morality was maintained throughout the production.

One aspect of Planchon's production which aroused much comment was his use of the revolving stage, not because it was a new prop (it had been used by the Berliner Ensemble as a way of speeding up the action), but because he used it in a cinematographic way. He said in the programme that '. . . we have tried to find, especially, a technique which is more like a language. Just as a camera in a film, by its mobility, by the way in which it divides space, by what it shows or conceals, is really in itself an actor.' In the Villeurbanne set for Schweyk, the props were set in a circle around the stage, and when a given prop was needed, the actors simply picked it up and put it on the revolving stage, where it became a part of the action. The revolving platform was also used to emphasise certain scenes, to show them from different angles and from varying distances, and to speed up or slow down the pace of the action. As in a circus spectacular, the show was continuous. The technique radically affected the structure of the play; by concentrating attention on one group of actors, for instance, then abruptly breaking it away. The public had the impression of being behind all four walls at once. In general, critics were extremely impressed with this stage innovation, and many considered it an inestimable advance in the technique of staging and the art of theatre direction. Pierre Marcabru called it '. . . a milestone in the history of theatre . . .'[6] Perhaps one should add 'French theatre', in view of Piscator's work. Only the critic Bernard Dort took exception to the use of the revolving platform. Many scenes in the play take place at an inn (l'auberge du Calice), and Dort thought that Brecht had meant the inn to give an impression of fixity and intimacy in a turbulent, strife-torn world; he

Schweyk dans la deuxième guerre mondiale at the Théâtre de la Cité de Villeurbanne, 1961, Jean Bouise (right) as Schweyk

SCHWEYK DANS LA DEUXIEME GUERRE MONDIALE

compared it to a Noah's Ark. By placing the inn on the revolving stage, and opening it up on all sides, Planchon had disregarded the contrast between its permanence and the chaos of the war raging outside its walls. Planchon wrote a lengthy reply to Dort, arguing that the inn had been staged as 'open' purposefully, in order to make a point about war. He used Dort's own metaphor of the Ark:

The Ark is *primarily* open, how could it not be open? And the people in it experience the raids, the arrests, the brutality; the era is an unsettled one; then comes the war, with its battles, its bombings, etc.; *'tournoyante'* [whirling, in both a concrete and a figurative sense] is a daring modifier, but an expressive one. The revolving stage, you can be sure, was more than a technical expedient.[7]

The quality of Planchon's direction and of the staging in general for this production was too outstanding to escape notice. After the use of the revolving platform and the brilliance of Jean Bouise's performance as Schweyk, the critics noticed especially, once again, the remarkable coherence of Planchon's troupe. Even the amazing Bouise, far from stealing the limelight, seemed always to inspire the other actors with his infectious vitality. The company gave an impression, wrote Bertrand Poirot-Delpech, '. . . exceptional these days, of solidarity, of a team knowing where it wants to go and lucidly obedient to its directors, beyond any bids for money or prestige'. He went on to conclude: '. . . it will escape no living theatre buff that their show, as it is, represents one of the best chances of associating a new public with an art which is in danger of dying'.[8] Once again, Planchon had fulfilled his aim.

VINAVER

Aujourd'hui ou Les Coréens (Today or The Koreans)
When it began to be known that the Théâtre de la Comédie was producing contemporary plays, one of many young playwrights who sent scripts to Planchon was Michel Vinaver. His play *Aujourd'hui ou Les Coréens* was outstanding for its simplicity and realism. The Théâtre de la Comédie put it on in 1956.

The play is set in Korea during the war. A group of soldiers is lost in the jungle. One of them is left for dead by the others, but struggles on alone and reaches an enemy village, where he is taken in and cared for. Gradually he begins to understand the villagers and the purpose of their struggle, and eventually he decides to stay. Vinaver deliberately sets off one type of existence against the other: the soldiers' makeshift, day-to-day camaraderie, their unceasing and pointless motion, against the stability of the village, not unscathed by the war, but surviving as a human community.

The play alternates between soldier scenes and village scenes. The sets were made up of reversible panels representing on the one side the dense vegetation of the jungle surrounding the soldiers' successive encampments, and on the other the slats of the village huts. Black-outs were used to change the sets, punctuated by the crackle of distant gunfire and the eerie sounds of jungle wildlife.

The play's 'political' message created some controversy. The Korean war had ended in 1953, and the French had withdrawn from Indo-China in 1954. The play is far from being apolitical, but its political theme is imbedded in, indeed one might say subsumed by, its 'human' themes. Vinaver himself regarded the play as a kind of paradigm of the theatrical experience which seeks to remove a spectator from his past, place him outside himself, and reintegrate him into a new present. The hero of the play goes through this sort of initiation, but Vinaver thought that the play as a whole should show a movement into a new time and a new world view:

History is irreversible. But it is also a creation, from moment to moment. Every action can be taken as an original action. It is not escapist theatre which abolishes all memories, which wipes the slate clean of images and significance, which presents a world in which relations between beings and with things are emptied of all depth, given without connotations, literally observed.[9]

Planchon was no doubt attracted by this matter-of-fact approach to reality. The hero of *Les Coréens* does not expound the philosophy behind his decision to stay on in the village, or even rationalise it. It is freely made and yet it seems the only right decision. It was Planchon who was to ask, not 'Who is Tartuffe?' but 'What does Tartuffe do?'. It was Planchon, also, who was to be constantly fascinated by the integration of our personal motives with our political acts – a key theme in this play.

The play ends very positively, with life having the last word, as in *Le Cochon noir*. It was a tremendous success, attracting Parisian critics, and thus brought the Théâtre de la Comédie recognition in Lyons.

Par-dessus bord (Overboard)
The next play by Vinaver which Planchon put on was of a very different stamp. Although again it pits tradition against change, this time it is the brassy 'brave new world' which emerges triumphant.

Par-dessus bord was produced in March 1973 and in June 1974 at the Théâtre National Populaire. The play depicts the rivalry between a long-established French firm of toilet-paper manufacturers, Ravoire et Dehaze, and a powerful

Vinaver's *Les Coréens*, Théâtre de la Comédie, 1956 – Korean captured by American soldiers in the jungle

American company, United Paper, which is trying to capture the French market. In France, we learn at the beginning of the play, toilet paper is still considered a rather embarrassing product, and Ravoire et Dehaze hold the market with a tough, yellowish, old-fashioned paper which they have made for years. When United Paper begin to make an impact on the market with their softer product, Ravoire et Dehaze retaliate by packaging theirs in red, white, and blue wrappers, in an appeal to their customers' patriotism. The attempt, which in the light of later events appears pathetically unimaginative, fails. When the president of the French firm has a heart attack, his son decides to call in American advertising consultants. Their approach to selling is ruthless; they make the directors of the company recognise (albeit reluctantly) that for everyone there is a certain degree of pleasure in the act of defecating, and that it is on this unavowed pleasure that their advertising must capitalise. A new, soft, modern product is developed, an attractive name found (after a series of hilariously delicate suggestions), and Ravoire et Dehaze successfully launch 'Mousse et Bruyère' (Moss and Heather) on the market. Eventually they are bought out by the American company, and in the process it is not only old ideas and old products which are thrown 'overboard', but unproductive employees as well.

The play is written from the point of view of a middle-management executive, who is eventually thrown overboard. Vinaver himself works in a firm, and has first-hand knowledge of business, contemporary trends in production, marketing, office politics, and management attitudes. His text presents special problems: there are many characters in it and in its entirety it would take perhaps ten hours to perform. Furthermore, the dialogue is deliberately conceived to create a sense of discontinuity in time; Vinaver explained that he wished to present events so that 'business time', 'personal time', and 'social time', were juxtaposed, and thus to provoke a certain 'friction' between them.[10] He spoke of 'exploding' scenes so that one scene could be shown up as a stereotype when it is interrupted by another, contemporaneous scene taking place elsewhere. Planchon, of course, saw that this could not be done on the stage; while a film can jump from one scene to the next at every four lines, a stage production cannot. Vinaver's play has too many settings to be presented all at once onstage, as in the *décor*

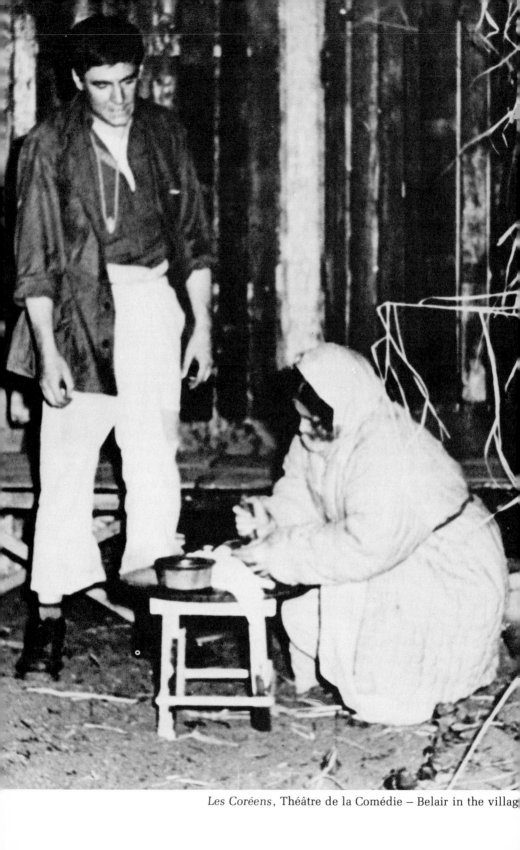

Les Coréens, Théâtre de la Comédie – Belair in the villag

explosé (exploded set) of Planchon's *La Remise* or of Gatti's
La Vie imaginaire de l'éboueur Auguste Geai. For one scene,
the office party, 60 or 70 people would have been needed (the
firm is supposed to have 350 employees!), and Planchon
could not see a stage filled with so many people unless they
were all involved in the action. He did consider staging all
the different interwoven stories simultaneously in a large
hall, so that one could go to the play one evening and see the
story of the sales representative, another night to see that of
the management, etc. Finally, however, he followed Vinaver's own suggestion that 'each carve his own play from it
[the text], improvise within it'.[11] Planchon's production
lasted four hours in Villeurbanne, and he cut it down to three
and a half hours before taking it to Paris.

Planchon called Vinaver's play a 'texte éclaté provoquant
des frottements entre un monde et un autre' (an exploded
text creating friction between one world and another).[12]
Dialogue which was split up in the text was regrouped in the
production, but Planchon found a way of translating into
stage language the friction between different time levels and
different stories. The company tried to establish '. . . a permanent counterpoint between the sung, danced, and mimed
sequences, and the memorable story of the battle, of the
reconciliation, and of the union of the société Ravoire et
Dehaze and the United Paper Company'.[13] Thus in the text
the banality of a scene is shown up by its juxtaposition with
another scene on a different level, whereas on stage it was
shown up by the intrusion of musical comedy. Because it is
written by someone on the inside, the text is absolutely
realistic. For the advertising sequences in particular, Vinaver made a collage of actual business documents. This
authenticity in the writing made it possible to present the
play in a less realistic way on the stage – the text was translated into an exuberant stage language, itself a parody of the
advertising world, the world of the image and of mass-
marketing. Planchon considers, and rightly, that no other
playwright has Vinaver's sense of modern dialogue, of the
form and flavour of contemporary 'thought' put out by the
media and absorbed half-consciously into the minds of individuals. Years earlier, Planchon had presented *Paolo Paoli*
in as straightforward a manner as possible because it was
written by a poet with little notion of day-to-day office life.
Because Vinaver, on the other hand, is involved in business,

because he is able to recreate speech of the kind which fills people's minds today, his extremely realistic play could be presented in a fantastical way on stage.

Planchon's *mise en scène* emphasised that the struggle was between American marketing techniques and French traditionalism. He filled the stage with the national symbols of both countries: on the one hand the French cockerel, *poilus* (First World War veterans) and their *Madelon* (their song); on the other hand, the bald eagle, tommy-guns, Mickey Mouse, majorettes, and chewing-gum. Sales representatives did little dance steps; the American buyers wore Stetsons. These symbols correspond to images which people hold at the back of their minds, and to which they respond even though, consciously, they know they are not realistic or rational. Much of the wit of the staging lay in this deliberate hyperbolic reference to people's preconceived association of ideas. It is a technique used to some extent in all Planchon's own musical comedies, which is not only essentially theatrical, but also essentially 'popular'.

Karel Trow who had composed the music for *La Langue au Chat*, created for *Par-dessus bord* another stylish and rhythmical accompaniment, with music-hall overtones. Planchon chose the form of the American musical partly because Vinaver's own text requires some dancers, partly also because the era of American industrial expansion was also that of the musical's greatest popularity. It also seemed appropriate to denounce a society's mentality through its own forms of entertainment. Planchon himself had done just that in *La Langue au Chat*, using television, and again in *Folies bourgeoises*, using French boulevard plays.

As Planchon had done in *Dans le vent* in 1968, Vinaver here deplores American ideological and economic imperialism in Europe. Here, again, 'made-in-America' ideas are adopted uncritically in France. In its spoof of advertising and in its rapid television commercial rhythm, Planchon's production of *Par-dessus bord* strongly recalled *La Langue au Chat*. The show was like Planchon's own musical comedies, not only because of the colour, the music, and the dances, but because of its quality of critical description. Vinaver describes a reality (the business of a firm) so utterly accurately that the description itself, while it is thoroughly entertaining, prompts us to reflect on contemporary business, on its use of people, on its manipulative marketing techniques, on its domination by America, etc. The balance which he achieves in his text was recreated on stage by a director whose own musical comedies aimed at the same sort of equilibrium between fun and realism. No one can deny that the play and the production brought up serious and even worrying issues, but they did so in a manner both wry and colourful. The play was the greatest success of the 1974 Villeurbanne season, probably by reason of its authenticity, as much as its fun.

ADAMOV

Paolo Paoli
The Théâtre de la Comédie in its early years put on two of Arthur Adamov's plays, *Le Sens de la marche* and *Le Profes-seur Taranne*. Their 1953–4 season included his adaptation of Marlowe's *Edward II*, and in 1957–8 the theatre put on *Paolo Paoli*, not only in Lyons, but also in Paris. It was important as the first play which the Théâtre de la Comédie presented in Paris before moving into their Villeurbanne theatre.

Planchon's cooperation with Adamov was so close that on one occasion, when the latter gave a talk at the Théâtre de la Cité, he was introduced as *l'auteur maison* (the writer in residence). Adamov found an unusual understanding of his aims and his principles in Roger Planchon's company. Lyons was one of the few places in France where he could see his works staged. He was originally Russian. He was born in the Caucasus in 1908, in a wealthy family who brought him up to speak French. They were forced to leave Russia in 1912, and moved to Germany. Adamov came to Paris in 1924, and there became involved with political and literary revolutionary groups. Although they are, at the very least, remarkable, his plays met with little understanding or interest during his lifetime. After years of artistic frustration, poverty, and phys-ical illness, Adamov died in 1970.

Paolo Paoli, one of Adamov's early plays, is an attack on a society in which everything – including human life – is used only for its exchange value. Set in the early twentieth cen-tury, it focuses on a dealer in rare butterflies, and shows how his trade, esoteric and far removed though it may seem from the contemporary political scene, is in fact an integral part of it. The dealer Paoli's business conduct is not only a symptom, but also a shaper of the values and even of the events of his day. The play is structured like a 'chronicle play': the scenes are connected with excerpts from contemporary newspapers, chosen by Adamov for their ironic relevance to the action of the play. In production these quotations and pictures were projected on a screen.

When Roger Planchon decided to stage the play, Adamov found that he agreed totally with the ideas of this young director. They had the same opinion of the characters and of the differing levels of caricature in the play. The affinity between Planchon and Adamov extended even to their ideas on stage language. In a posthumous tribute, Planchon was to write of his collaborator and friend:

He liked to see, on stage, simple, elementary objects: a typewriter, a 'bistro' clothes rail. *He was allergic to all aestheticism . . .* The bike, the clothes rail, were to come onto the stage without any transposition, like totems. It was up to the director to charge them with 'energies'. For Adamov, there was space, and these scattered, absurd, ridiculous totems, which were to remain in the empty space when all the characters had disappeared.[14]

This 'allergy' to aestheticism corresponded to Planchon's intense distaste for over-pathetic acting. If the objects on the stage were over-stylised, could they not, like actors, be accused of 'over-signifying'?

On his tiny stage at the Théâtre de la Comédie, Planchon had found that ordinary objects loomed larger than life. He had turned this to advantage by making the drama revolve around the objects rather than the actors. It was a technique well-suited to such a play as *Paolo Paoli*. The set designer, René Allio, introduced to Planchon by Adamov, worked with Planchon for the first time on this production, and it was a promising beginning. The play has two levels, that of the mundane, day-to-day dealings of Paoli, and that of the national and international context in which his activities are set. To convey the first level, Allio designed a small room, at once an entomologist's cabinet and an industrialist's office, stuffed with butterfly collections and bric-à-brac. The black, brown, and burnt-sienna tones of the era predominated.

While the local level of the play was illustrated in the small stuffy office in which wheelings and dealings take place, the sense of a world scale of events was created in the intervals between scenes. Planchon was to use this idea in his own plays, notably *La Remise, Bleus, blancs, rouges,* and *Le Cochon noir,* relating the immediate and local action to its political, national, or international context by means of slide projections, textual references, or mimed sequences between the scenes. In *Paolo Paoli,* Adamov's carefully-chosen extracts from the media of the day were projected on a white background, and Planchon and Allio added a sound accompaniment of crowd noises, commercial jingles, martial airs, etc. Adamov was pleased with this contrast between frivolous music and the projections of terrifying photos or cynical press statements.

The political message of the play was, by today's standards, restrained: Adamov simply showed that capitalistic trade can reduce people to the level of objects. Nevertheless, it was considered too daring by the Commission des Arts et Spectacles, a government body which was a source of financial help to Planchon, at the time heavily in debt. The Commission des Arts et Spectacles threatened to stop subsidising Planchon if performances of *Paolo Paoli* were given. Fortunately, Roger Martin du Gard offered his support to the company, and succeeded in pacifying the Commission.

With the public, the play was a success. From the critics, the response was sparse and unappreciative. One 'ordinary spectator' even wrote to the *Lettres Françaises*[15] after seeing the Parisian production, to chide the critics for their reactionary attitude. He praised the play highly for its 'realism seasoned with poetry', and summed up his feelings in a sentence which may well explain the play's success: 'There is finally a play in Paris at which one can laugh or cry without hearing about lavatories, without hearing about the introspective anguish of some good-for-nothing.' It would seem that socially, committed plays were a rarity on French stages at that time and, at least in some circles, there was a demand for them and a keen interest in the few that were put on.

Les Ames mortes (Dead Souls)

The Théâtre de la Cité de Villeurbanne presented Adamov's adaptation of Gogol's novel, under the title *Les Ames mortes,* in 1960. It was put on in Villeurbanne and at the Odéon in Paris. Jacques Rosner assisted in the direction of the play.

Gogol's novel follows the travels of a swindler, Tchitchikov, who attempts to make his fortune in pre-revolutionary Russia by acquiring from landowners the deeds to serfs who are dead, but whose names are still on the official census lists. In order to colonise the sparsely-populated south, the Tsarist government offered inducements to people who resettled their serfs there: they were given not only free land, but also a *per capita* resettlement subsidy. Tchitchikov could purchase 'dead souls' for very little from landowners glad to get money for nothing. As the souls were officially still alive, he could pretend to resettle them and make enormous profits from the government subsidies.

Adamov's background, education, and temperament, suited him very well to the task of translating Russian literary works. The dramatic adaptation which he made of Gogol's long and unfinished novel was a reduced version, but it remained faithful to the spirit of the original as Adamov saw it. Any dramatised version of a long narrative, and particularly of such an episodic work as *Dead Souls*, must necessarily be selective, and therefore stress certain themes. Adamov emphasised the sense of a social gap between Tchitchikov and the landowners: they are the establishment, and he is trying to enter their ranks; their complacency is opposed to his clear-sighted and energetic ambition. Adamov's text underlined the social issues because these are, in any case, the issues which strike a twentieth-century reader or spectator. What is described in the novel as part of a normal social system (characters are parodied for their greed and their vanity, but not for their acceptance of a slave-based economy), when it is simply presented onstage to a modern audience, becomes appalling.

Gogol's novel is filled with the poetry of unending plains, hills and open spaces, the beauty of the Russian steppes. This Russian background to the play was conveyed in several ways in Planchon's production. First, Planchon and Allio interspersed between the fifteen scenes two- or three-minute animated film projections of Tchitchikov in his troika, travelling endlessly along the roads of the Russian plains, past dreary towns and villages. The projections were of sketches by Allio, in sepia tones, and they showed not only Tchitchikov, but the people he passes; they were stylised so that a human profile merged into an animal shape, a lock of hair into the curve of a pathway. The sketches reflected the change in mood between the first and second halves of the play. The first part, as in the novel, simply follows the hero through various farmlands and towns as he goes about his business. The second part, however, portrays the spread of rumours about Tchitchikov once people have begun to suspect that his business is not altogether legal, and that he may have put some of them in jeopardy. For this second part, Allio used caricature more freely, and made the rhythms of the film sequences more jerking and unexpected.

Allio found other means of suggesting the constantly-changing settings as well. At the back of the stage, on a huge cyclorama (a background device with a rough surface, usually plaster or canvas, covering the back and sides of the stage and used with special lighting to create the illusion of sky, open space, or great distance at the rear of the stage setting), there was a fixed projected image of distant horizons. Above the set, and in front of the cyclorama, a new picture was placed for each setting, the town, the plain, the landscape immediately surrounding the inn, farmhouse, or road in which a specific scene took place. On each side of the stage, Allio projected slides meant to give social as well as topographical information, pictures of large official houses for the scenes at the governor's house, for example, and wooden houses and a wooden church for the scenes at the small land-owners' homes. The central set for each scene was realistic apart from a few 'transparent' walls. Almost as a part of the set, Planchon introduced onto the stage a world of serfs and servants, different for each master, who were constantly present and at work but always silent.

Claude Lochy composed an accompaniment for the play which, like the sketches, became more grotesque in the second half. The music was used to characterise different groups: a wind quintet for the petty officials, Russian folk music for the landowners and their servants, and, for the governor and those in power, romantic ballroom music played as though by a village brass band, in out-of-date French fashion.

Gogol's characters, self-seeking, smug, and stupid, are objects of ridicule. In Planchon's production, this burlesque side of the social picture was emphasised not only through Allio's drawings and Lochy's music, but also through another stage device: the actors wore ridiculous false noses. Adamov found the symbolism of the false noses redundant, as the characters seemed to him to be ridiculous enough in themselves. It seems that for the public, however, the false noses were a meaningful stage image, a physical deformity reflecting the moral ugliness of Gogol's characters. 'Class solidarity', as the critic Pierre Marcabru noted, 'becomes nose solidarity.'[16]

It was through the acting that Planchon created the sense of a thoroughly hierarchical society, in which the smallest difference in the social status of one person is marked by a corresponding difference in another's behaviour toward him. Gogol himself pauses in his narrative to comment on the class consciousness of his countrymen:

It must be said that if we in Russia have not caught up with the foreigners in some things, we have far outstripped them in the art of behaviour. It is quite impossible to enumerate all the shades and

Set for *Les Ames mortes*, Théâtre de la Cité de Villeurbanne, 1960

subtleties of our manners . . . We have clever fellows who talk in quite a different way to a landowner with two hundred serfs and to one with three hundred serfs; and to one with three hundred they will talk differently again from the way they will talk to one with five hundred, and in a different way again from one with eight hundred – in short, even if the number were to grow to a million they would still find different shades for it.[17]

Planchon, and Adamov, who attended some rehearsals, constantly reminded the actors that their character must be visibly conscious, at every moment, of the class to which he or she belongs. In a scene which takes place at the landowner Manilov's, for instance, there are several servants present as well as the farm manager. Here, Adamov indicated, '. . . the farm manager must be one rung above the other servants: he must bow less deeply than they to the master, and they must not laugh until the farm manager gives the signal by doing so himself'.[18]

Tchitchikov's victims, '. . . the grasping and gullible citizenry of a degraded feudal society . . .'[19] appear uglier and more foolish than he. Like many of Planchon's own characters, he is an outsider, trying to become part of a clan. Adamov liked him because his absolutely logical and businesslike use of the serf system for his own ends shows up the system itself. He saw Tchitchikov as the fallen descendant of literary heroes who set off on a quest:

Like Ulysses or Don Quixote, Tchitchikov travels tirelessly in pursuit of his goal. A grotesque and derisory epic, for this goal is mixed up with the most sordid of frauds . . . he [Gogol] had just invented, to put it simply, modern critical literature, the literature which denounces the established order by always showing the consequences of that order, the literature which, from deduction to deduction, sheds light on the absurdity of what one has got used to considering logical.[20]

Thus it was Gogol's 'modernness' which attracted Adamov to Dead Souls. It was one of Brecht's tenets that society, and especially accepted aspects of society, should always be shown to be alterable. What is accepted is neither necessary nor eternal. In Les Ames mortes, as adapted by Adamov and staged by Planchon, this is made eminently clear.

Adamov was, for once, unhappy with Planchon's work and even with Allio's drawings, although he found them beautiful in themselves. The staging as a whole may have appeared overdone to him; in any case he was disappointed. Critics who saw the play were impressed with the clarity and energy of the textual adaptation, but most of their praise centred on the remarkable work which Planchon had done with his company. The acting showed superb cohesion. Not only did the actors act in relation to one another, they performed totally in harmony with the stage sets, the special effects, and the music. Pierre Marcabru wrote: 'The Théâtre de la Cité is today what is most important for the future of French theatre, and its renewal.'[21]

A. A. Théâtres d'Arthur Adamov (A. A. Plays of Arthur Adamov)

After Adamov's death, Planchon created this collage which was intended both as a theatrical homage to the man, and as a stage essay on his work. The project was first conceived in June 1974, and the script which I use is dated December 1974. It is made up exclusively of extracts from Adamov's own plays and his memoirs and other writings. Thus, while it is 'written' by Adamov, it has been 'selected' by Planchon and his company. The basic framework is provided by the five tableaux of Le Sens de la marche (The Meaning of the March), with extracts from other writings inserted. The play is in twelve tableaux and it presents episodes from Adamov's childhood, interspersed with scenes from his adult life, as he himself revealed them in his personal writings and symbolically in his plays.

Planchon was motivated not only by his friendship for Adamov, with whom he had created several plays, but by a very special admiration for the playwright's work. In press conferences before the play, he compared the relation of Beckett and Adamov to the relation of Büchner and Lenz. Like Büchner's, Beckett's work is masterful and well-polished; his plays are already classics. Despite Büchner's mastery, however, it is the work of Lenz which has influenced younger writers to a far greater extent. Planchon believes that, in the same way, Adamov, whose drama is not as perfect as Beckett's, will be remembered and will be far more influential in fifty years' time than Beckett.

Planchon used Adamov's own work because he felt that it has a strongly autobiographical element. Adamov's plays emanate, as Planchon recognised, from a dream universe; the collage, too, was therefore intended to have a dreamlike

quality, to be a 'spiritual' portrait rather than a strictly bio-
graphical or aesthetic study. Adamov's personal obsessions
come out in his plays in the form of recurring images and
scenes, and it is these images, these scenes, which Planchon
incorporated into his play.

In the first and last scenes of *A.A. Théâtres d'Arthur
Adamov*, to the sound of old-fashioned Russian music, a
picture of the past in Russia appeared, recalling the world of
Les Ames mortes and the world into which Adamov was
born: one saw young women with parasols, elegant in white,
men in panamas, old servants, a landau . . . but they were
behind a transparent screen, as though they belonged in an

A. A. Théâtres d'Arthur Adamov, TNP, 1976. Laurent Tetzieff and Pascale
de Boysson

old sepia photograph, a faded memory, or a dream. The play begins with the first sentence of Adamov's *L'Homme et l'enfant* (*The Man and the Child*): 'My father owned a good deal of the petroleum in the Caspian area'[22] and with the child Henri/Adamov in bed, his father sitting on the ground surrounded by oil derricks. The mineral motif was everywhere, from the luminescent grey vertical panels on the lateral walls to the pit-coal colour of the back wall and the mound of bluish rocks on the floor. A series of repeated gestures (like those of Planchon's *La Remise*) created a feeling of obsession: three father-figures threw stones into the child's bed, the child went through a complex ritual of gestures before lying down on stones and sleeping.

There are recurring characters in Adamov's plays, a father/elderly servant who remains an interfering influence on the hero, as in *Le Sens de la marche*; a tyrannical, emasculating mother, as in *Les Retrouvailles* (*Meeting Again*), or *Comme nous avons été* (*As We Have Been*); a passive, servile sister/fiancée/wife as in *Le Sens de la marche* or *L'Invasion* (*The Invasion*). Woman is seen as a threat; the fiancée in *Le Sens de la marche* is desirable from afar, but frightening as soon as she becomes available; the wife in *L'Invasion* eventually leaves; the woman in *La Grande et la petite manoeuvre* (*The Great and the Small Manoeuvre*) finally reviles her crippled lover. The hero in this last play feels unworthy of love because he has lost his arms and legs. In *A.A. Théâtres d'Arthur Adamov* Planchon had the hero's self-deprecating passage spoken by a man with arms and legs intact. The scene's underlying meaning thus became clear: it is about impotence and a resulting fear of women, an ever-present motif in Adamov's plays.

The theme which Planchon used as the principal one in his production is that of a constant procrastination to make a political commitment which seems necessary and yet always premature. At the beginning of his career, Adamov wrote plays which were classed by the critics of the day as 'absurdist'. After the visit of the Berliner Ensemble to Paris, however, he began to see the possibility and the importance of socially-relevant theatre. *Paolo Paoli* in 1957 was the first of a number of plays which attack unacceptable facets of western society, from the dehumanising trade of Paoli, to the irrevocable escalation of the American war in Vietnam in the 1960s in *Off Limits* (written in 1969). Adamov was a critical supporter of the Communist Party, although he did not join. His wife became a member. He wrote in 1968: 'I too am thinking of joining the Party but I am hesitant. On certain problems I really do not agree with them. And then, Communist friends tell me that I will be more useful to the Party from the outside than if I belonged to it.'[23]

Le Sens de la marche begins with a scene, included early on in Planchon's production, in which Henri/Adamov's friends come to get him as arranged because it is time to go off and join the revolution. Henri/Adamov prevaricates, asks for time to prepare. Finally they leave without him to catch the train. The train is one image which Planchon culled from the many recurring ones in Adamov's work, and used in his production. A railway line sparkled at the back of the stage, and in the first and last scenes a life-sized train passed, complete with chanting revolutionaries, a machine-gun, and a red flag. The sets as a whole projected an uncomfortable nostalgia, the distance between the remembered world of childhood and the experience of a misfit adulthood. The need and the near-impossibility of commitment are summed up in the phrase *prendre le train en marche* (to board the moving train). It is in the early plays especially that the anguish of indecision is portrayed. Adamov writes in *L'Homme et l'enfant* of recurring dreams in which he is 'called', and admits that '. . . at bottom, I know very well that I am lying to myself, that I will answer *them*, join *them* as soon as *they* have called me' (p. 95). The future tense here is important; the call is a permanent and unrelenting exigency, and yet it is awaited as a moment placed somewhere in the future. His characters live an agony of guilty procrastination, and the agony is to a large extent his own.

The picture of Adamov which emerges from Planchon's production is that of a child unable to grow up, of a perpetual adolescent. The play, in fact, cites Adamov's reminiscences of his earliest fears; he was afraid of growing up, and of becoming poor. The real Adamov did become poor; his father's oil rigs are taken over in the play as they were in reality. Did the 'real' Adamov, however, grow up? The fear of impotence, the sexual perversions, the difficulty of committing oneself which Adamov reveals in his memoirs and in his plays may be evidence of immaturity. But Planchon's production is based only on Adamov's early plays, and it is therefore an incomplete portrayal of a man who, in his later

life, showed an obvious political commitment in his artistic
work and gave public and courageous support to the Communist Party. Patrick Chesnais's performance as Henri/
Adamov emphasised the uncertainty, the hesitations of the
character in every situation. In his interpretation he had,
apparently, the unfinished gestures, the mitigated protesta-
tions, the half-hearted rebellions, the ill-assured speech of a
vacillating man. Several critics, including Jean-Jacques Lerrant, objected that there was more to Adamov than this production suggested, although Lerrant went on to admit that
the show was overwhelmingly beautiful and persuasive.[24]

Planchon and his company were aware of the problem
from the start. They had decided to make the political side of
Adamov known through the press conferences and debates
around the play, rather than through the play itself. They had
also planned to present an Adamov 'museum' in the foyers
and halls of the theatre, including such things as a barricade
of cobblestones surmounted by two flags of the Commune (in
a reference to Adamov's play on revolutionaries *Le Printemps '71* (*Spring '71*). Unfortunately, fire regulations made
it necessary to withdraw these tableaux, and only first-night
viewers saw the production as it was originally intended to
be. It would have had the advantage of informing spectators
whose knowledge of Adamov was slight, and who may have
been confused by what is an allusive and somewhat elliptical
production. I think, however, that it would not have re-
dressed the balance which is weighted in favour of
Adamov's earlier, more 'personal' work. The bias is inten-
tional.

Planchon saw Adamov's difficulties as typical of the
lower-middle-class intellectual of the 1930s to the 1950s,
not only in his relationship with his parents, but also in
his political development. Adamov did not merely live
these problems with an extraordinary intensity; he integrated them brilliantly into his dramatic works. Adamov's
plays are a remarkable transformation of dreams, obsessions,
and neuroses into dramatic material. Adamov, like Planchon, was a surrealist; he was a friend of Éluard, Breton,
Artaud. Many of his plays are at least partially based on
dreams (*Le Professeur Taranne* is simply a transcription of a
dream); they have a dreamlike structure, and an often nightmarish undertone. Yet they take a definite social stance; it is
this combination of social rootedness and a very personal,

dream-like quality which makes Adamov an outstanding modern playwright. Arrabal is one of his most notable successors.

Planchon is fascinated by dreams and their structure and by madness, and he, like Adamov, went from surrealism to social commitment. But there is a more fundamental resemblance between Planchon and Adamov, and it is that likeness which explains Planchon's decision to create a play based on Adamov's early work rather than simply to put on one of his last plays. When one reads Adamov's memoirs, when one looks at his various incarnations in his plays, one is left with the sense that this man of remarkable intelligence and talent, through all his experiences of rejection, his years of professional frustration, his terrible illnesses, managed by some miracle to retain a kind of innocence. The last image in *A.A. Théâtres d'Arthur Adamov* is that of the two children, Henri/Adamov and his sister, side by side on a swing. Little wonder that in the childlike hero of *A.A.*, some critics saw a correspondence with Planchon himself. In Planchon's plays as in Adamov's, there is an innocence which survives despite everything, a certain tenderness which intrudes into even the most bitterly ironic, the most seriously contrived, of scenes. Both heirs of French surrealism and of Brecht, both politically committed, Adamov and Planchon meet also on this very personal and delicate ground.

4

English classics: themes for the twentieth century

So it is that in the second half of the twentieth century in
England where I am writing these words, we are faced with the
infuriating fact that Shakespeare is still our model.

Peter Brook

In order to produce the English classics in France, a director
must get over the difficulty of translating and adapting a
poetic text from another century for our own (or of finding a
suitable translation); he must also overcome the problem of
the audience's unfamiliarity with the history of England, and
with the conventions of the Elizabethan stage. Yet Shakespeare was included in the repertoire of almost all the
théâtres populaires of the fifties and sixties.

Roger Planchon had a long-standing admiration for
Shakespeare, but he chose to produce Shakespearian plays
for other reasons as well. He considered the form of the plays
well-suited to a popular audience. In Shakespeare the great
number of short tableau-like sequences creates a cinematic
effect far removed from that of classical French drama. The
rhythm of the plays was thus familiar to Planchon's company, as they were trained from the start to use film-like
enchaînements (linkages of one scene to the next) in their
production. In addition to this fluidity, the plays, written
when sets were reduced to a stark simplicity, had the directness necessary for productions aimed at the unsophisticated.

It was not only the form of the plays which led modern
young directors to choose Shakespeare as a 'popular' dramatist for the mid-twentieth century. The preoccupations of the
Elizabethan age – the nature of political power, the relation
of the private individual to his public role, the concept of
necessary violence – these are concerns of our own time.
Furthermore, these serious themes are treated in a way
which is never completely alienating; never, as so many
modern plays are, devoid of hope for the individual. Thus

Shakespeare, presented to a modern audience, needs little 'interpretation' in Planchon's sense, but rather a fidelity to the text and to what we can discover or assume about the spirit in which it was written.

SHAKESPEARE

Henry IV

Planchon decided to stage *Henry IV*, as we have seen (p. 8), after an audience survey indicated a widespread interest in Shakespeare. It was his first production at Villeurbanne, in the 1957–58 season. Planchon chose *Henry IV* specifically because he thought that his public would appreciate its fast pace and its sense of conflict. Furthermore, he decided to use the entire play: *Henry IV* was given in two parts, roughly following the two parts of Shakespeare's play, the first en-titled 'Falstaff', the second 'HenryV'. Each part lasted three hours. He was to find, in retrospect, that he had been right:

> . . . we put it all on, in its entirety: my work of adaptation consisted only of making the text clearer, more effective, than that of the French translations which we know – never to simplify it. There we were right: what pleased our public was the wealth, the complexity of the work, the fact that it takes place on several levels, that it tells several stories. Thus each spectator was able to see what interested him the most.[1]

Planchon's audience was unfamiliar, not only with English history, but also with the theatrical medium itself. Allio's sets, therefore, like the textual adaptation, were designed to help spectators disentangle a complex plot. The backdrop gave general historical and geographical information. It was a large hanging showing the maps of Shakespeare's day. Placards on each side of the stage gave the geographical setting of each scene, as did models placed beside them. A sloping stage was used to emphasise the backstage action, and to project the show towards the public. Between tableaux, in order to help the audience follow the plot, key sentences in the coming scene were projected on a screen. This was, then, the *présentation* Allio's sense. The props themselves, those things nearest the actors (the *représentation*) such as walls, furniture, tree trunks, etc., were relatively realistic and faithful reproductions of objects of the day. Planchon was nevertheless careful to keep these props and also the stage movements simple: a public square was created with a few pieces of wood, for example, or, in truly Shakespearian style, a huge crowd was represented by five or six actors.

The costumes were planned with great care to give the spectator leads into the social and moral position of the characters. Most of the costumes were reminiscent of both modern and medieval dress. Allio divided the characters into three groups. First, there was the proletariat, those who frequent taverns and who cannot afford colourful clothing; they were dressed in rough or limp fabrics in dull tones.

Falstaff, Théâtre de la Cité de Villeurbanne, 1957. Marie-Louise Ebeli as Mistress Quickly and Jean Bouise as Falstaff

Secondly came the footsoldiers, who were dressed in poor, shapeless uniforms, impersonal, ill-fitting, and cumbersome with stiff leather and metal. Thirdly there was the nobility, who wore well-cut clothing which looked warm, comfortable, and luxurious. There were distinctions amongst the nobles as well. The political figures (the King, Westmoreland, Northumberland) wore comfortable but sober dress; the 'tribal' chiefs (Percy, Glendower, Mortimer, Hastings) were decked out in rather aggressive-looking costumes; the professional soldiers (Walter Blunt, Mowbray, Warwick) were very soberly clothed; and finally the more frivolous characters (Gloucester, Clarence, Lancaster) were dressed with a little panache, rather elegantly. The Prince was dressed with a refined simplicity; his friend Poins wore a shabby imitation of the Prince's clothes. The Prince's costume changed as he did, from something like blue jeans, to a double-breasted jacket, to a smoking jacket, and finally to the robe of state, made deliberately heavy-looking so that he looked almost crushed beneath its weight.

The sound track, composed by Claude Lochy, was fairly complex as it reflected the turmoil of the play, set between two reigns, and in which each scene is balanced between the serious and the clownish. Lochy used traditional themes to suggest the past, more abrupt ones to suggest the present, and he superimposed on these, variously, the sounds of bells, of crowds, of horses, of lightning, the clash of weapons, etc. Music was used to connect the tableaux, to underscore certain themes, and to characterise different groups such as the Church, the Court, the People (in a manner which Lochy was to use again for *Les Ames mortes* in 1960). For scenes set in the old King Henry IV's palace, the accompaniment was courtly and vaguely religious; for the Prince's scenes, set more often in taverns, it was modern and harsh.

Jean Bouise played Falstaff, as he was to play Schweyk a few years later. Like Schweyk, Falstaff is an opportunist, whose very presence shows up the 'greatness' of the other characters as superficial and fortuitous. There was unanimous praise for Bouise's performance. Dressed in a tan buckskin suit, moving about with tender consideration for his great stomach, he had an animal-like presence which suited the role perfectly. Bouise created an ambiguous personage true to the Shakespearian model, full of raucous commonsense, not above making a profit from the war, but neverthe-

Falstaff (Jean Bouise) and cronies

less pitiable when he is abandoned by the Prince. He made
people laugh heartily, but at the same time he played the role
so that Falstaff gets a serious hearing occasionally. Falstaff's
famous speech on honour in act V, scene I, for instance, was
spoken as an insolent outcry verging on open rebellion,
rather than as a simple coward's self-justification. He was a
central image in the production, showing up both the feudal
concept of heroism on the one hand, and the hard
materialism of the new age on the other. Falstaff's last scene
was made unequivocally pathetic, in order to emphasise the
inexorability of the historical process and the ultimate vul-
nerability of such a character within it.

The presence of Falstaff made it impossible for Planchon
to stage the battle scenes as glorious, or to present the nobles
as superior or even honourable men. Planchon deliberately
showed the heroes, when they were off the battlefield,

engaged in gratifying their physical appetites, in eating for example, even as they discussed great political questions. On the battle field, he showed the crass brutality to which the defeated, nobleman and commoner alike, were subjected. The Archbishop of York was dragged on the ground; the rebels captured by Lancaster's double-cross were herded away like animals. There were mimed sequences added to the play, showing the trials and outrages to which common people and common soldier alike were compelled to submit.

Individual figures were also 'demystified' in a similar way. The old Henry IV was depicted as a political adventurer. His costume, a plain tunic with the occasional royal 'trinket' adorning it, suggested a king not secure in his position; there was no sense of the established monarch accustomed to luxury. The public was constantly reminded that he was a usurper and that his position was therefore precarious. Shakespeare makes it clear that Henry IV's policy was always to involve his country in wars abroad in order to stave off rebellion at home. His speech in the first scene, in which he dreams of setting up a crusade, was deliberately bereft, in Planchon's production, of heroic or idealistic overtones. It was shortened and spoken dryly, unemotionally; the King's motives could thus be assumed to be neither religious nor patriotic but simply a matter of political expediency.

The Prince of Wales was played as utterly ruthless, especially in his final, callous rejection of Falstaff. The change from the old King's reign to that of the young Prince is the change from feudalism to a more modern and more materialstic age. In the tavern, therefore, the Prince learns more which will be of use to him on the throne than he would at court. One can as easily cheat one's landlady as capture one's enemies in battle with false assurances; the plebeian wisdom of Falstaff in the inn parallels the ruthlessness of the noblemen at war. The Prince was played by Planchon himself in the 1958 production, and played as one whose ambition is present from the beginning, overlaid for a time with a youthful charm, but coming forth inexorably when opportunity allows. The characters as a whole were played on a realistic human scale, seldom sublime, often ridiculous, sometimes monstrous.

If Planchon loved Shakespeare, it was for a reason especially evident in *Henry IV*, because '. . . individual destinies are indissolubly tied to the collective destiny, psychology to politics'.[2] Hotspur, for example, is both an individual and the representative of a code of belief at a specific time in history: a medieval code of honour, in a hierarchical world. The Théâtre de la Cité production made this quite clear. In the scene of Hotspur's parting from his wife, Planchon had André Batisse, who played Hotspur, emphasise the sharp contrast between his tenderness to his wife as a loved object, and his sudden reassertion of his male superiority over her when she wants to know about the military concerns which he considers his preserve. Hotspur sees himself as possessor, his wife as a chattel. It was a scene in which his medieval outlook and his personal behaviour were shown to be inextricably and uncomfortably linked, a scene which, unfortunately, still has a modern resonance.

In Shakespeare, Planchon found the ideal sort of play for a new audience. At Villeurbanne, *Henry IV* was presented in bold, clear episodes, but it was not reduced. A true 'Brechtian', Planchon respected his spectators. He brought out, through the stage language, the historical content of the play, the picture of a society in transition and of the individuals within it. Claude Olivier thought this production had 'The magic of theatre which makes the spectator not a voyeur or an accomplice, but the witness of adventures in which he is deeply involved, but in which he finds he is both judge and accused, impassioned actor and intransigent critic.'[3]

Troilus and Cressida

Troilus and Cressida is a difficult work and was in the 1960s seldom played and little known in France. Planchon said that it was '. . . one of the least-known plays of Shakespeare. It has baffled people. Because it begins as a farce and turns sour. It seems to lack unity. It is a difficult play.'[4] In 1964, in a world concerned with disarmament, in a France interested in developing its offensive weaponry, the military themes of the play were extremely relevant. The resurgence of interest in the play in the 1970s shows that its themes remain topical.

Planchon said in an interview[5] that one of the features of the play which attracted him was the way in which the personal theme of love and the social theme of war were intermingled; he called it '. . . the story of people who make war well and love badly'. He went on to speak of Shakespeare's attitude to war, one very much in tune with that of the late twentieth century. In *Troilus and Cressida* men are in control of their own destiny; there is no fate; people make war of their own volition, even in some cases after a lucid appraisal of the worthlessness of their motives. 'Showing the tragedy or the absurdity of war has become banal,' Planchon said in the same interview, 'but making it clear that the choice of war or of peace is in the hands of men is a completely different morality.' The play lends itself well to a Marxist analysis.

Because the text of *Troilus and Cressida* is so virulent and powerful in itself, the aim of the Théâtre de la Cité was to use a translation as faithful as possible to the Shakespearian original. They aimed for a fidelity to the text which was at the opposite extreme from their free adaptation of *Edward II*. Seven people, including lecturers from the university in Lyons and Planchon himself, worked on the translation, which is almost a word-for-word version. The play's rhetorical quality makes its staging even in English problematical; writing any adaptation therefore was a particularly demanding task. Writing for a Villeurbanne public made it necessary to aim for clarity above everything else.

There were two major types of change in the Théâtre de la Cité version of Shakespeare's play. First, mythological allusions which have become obscure to a modern public were often suppressed. Boreas became simply *le vent* (the wind), 'Apollo knows' was rendered simply as '*Dieu sait*' (God knows). The very well-known mythological names, such as Neptune, on the other hand, reappeared intact in the adaptation. The second kind of alteration, and the more important, consisted of changing the sentence order, and making subordinate clauses into separate sentences; in this way the meaning of one clause could be absorbed before the next was heard. This was done only where the original passage seemed very convoluted or confusing (for example, in the case of Agamemnon's speech in I. iii. 1170–4).

The lyricism of some passages, and indeed the poetry of the text as a whole were inevitably lost in the translation. The incantatory frenzy of Cassandra's vision, for example (II. ii. 104–12), because it springs from the rhythm of the passage, and from a brilliant use of alliteration and vowel sounds, completely disappeared in French. Such a line as 'A moiety of that mass of moan to come . . .' (l. 107) in another language, can either be rewritten as new verse, or rendered straightforward and pale, as it was in Villeurbanne: 'Une

moitié des gémissements à venir . . .'[6] In the translation as a
whole, style and imagery were retained as much as possible
in a slightly simplified form, but the key themes of the play
were given as much importance as possible by paying close
attention to meaning rather than to sound.

Jacques Rosner and Yves Kerboul assisted Planchon in
directing the play. Planchon called the set of *Troilus and
Cressida* 'une machine à jouer' (an acting tool) as opposed to
the 'décor-commentaire' (the set which makes a commentary) of such productions as *Tartuffe*.[7] Designed by André
Acquart, the sets were meant to allow the play to speak for
itself. The objective was a very simple, linear *mise en scène*.
Differences between Greeks and Trojans were clearly shown:
the energetic but disordered Greeks lived in a jungle of tents,
panels, and folding screens, while the Trojan civilisation
presented to the enemy nothing but an enormous steel gate
which opened and closed in a stately fashion. Yellows and
browns predominated, although the steel also reflected
iridescent tones for the lovers' scenes, and finally became
blood-splattered in battle.

As befits a play about war, the sets were especially effective in the confused battle scenes. They consisted of panels
connected to a central axis, which could be raised or lowered
to divide the stage into constantly changing spaces. The
critic Dominique Nores compared them to an immense,
blood-stained deck of playing cards being shuffled as the
warriors attempt to find their way through them.[8] This part of
the set was certainly a commentary on the war theme in the
play: '. . . in the end, this set, by cutting up the battlefield . . . by sweeping through space on the demented
rhythm of an epic and derisory butchery, throws one upon
the other these rag-tag warriors . . .'[9] The costumes for the
warriors were half tunics, half modern battledress, and in
their movements they recalled twentieth-century guerilla
fighters, although this was never blatant.

Shakespeare treats all the characters in this play ironically,
as the stage language in Planchon's production made clear.
The Trojans seem innocent, cleaving to their code of honour
like Hotspur in *Henry IV*; but that code is outdated. They
were shown to be pompous and old-fashioned; the Council of Troy was like a family reunion, with little sister
Cassandra having her visions, and the brothers teasing one
another but finally showing fraternal solidarity. The Greeks

are more pragmatic but equally ineffectual. Their own council of war at the start of the play was staged like a petty electoral campaign, with old hands reiterating hackneyed political phrases. Even Ulysses's famous speech on the great chain of being was played as the attempt of a petty politician to gain support.

It was through the characters of individual warriors especially that Planchon debunked the concept of glory in war. The *démystification* was pitiless. Ajax '. . . resembled Maxie Rosenbloom and confirmed the resemblance by exercising like a prizefighter'.[10] Agamemnon was played as a mediocre, self-satisfied fool, and Nestor as a senile old wreck. Paradoxically, Thersites became a more serious figure in this production. He is a Shakespearian fool, whose perspective is abrasively cynical but sadly accurate. He was played by Gérard Guillaumat as a brooding, tragic character with all the bitterness of the outcast, the bastard, the disillusioned idealist. As a serious character he counterbalanced the buffoon-like imbecility of the other characters, the 'heroes'.

Even the great hero Hector was humanised in this production. Planchon saw between Hector's behaviour and his beliefs an inconsistency which is only one example of the play's grating, sardonic humour: 'Hector knows that Helen is not worth the blood which is being shed for her. Nevertheless he acquiesces to the battle; he even tries to find a value in it by the sacrifice of his own life. But here too it is said that the sacrifice of 100,000 lives does not justify an error and does not establish a value.'[11] Hector is a lucid man who chooses to follow the forms of 'honourable' conduct, even though he knows how meaningless the term is in a war-torn, decaying world; he fights, absurdly, to justify the deaths of those who have fought before.

The Théâtre de la Cité gave a sympathetic presentation of Cressida, much influenced by Jan Kott's analysis of her in *Shakespeare Our Contemporary*. Troilus sacrifices her because he believes in a warrior's code, a code which is shown to be worthless in the rest of the play. The motif of trade which runs through the play crystallises when Troilus agrees to have Cressida exchanged, and thus reduces her to the value of a piece of merchandise. Planchon doubted whether Troilus actually loves Cressida, as he was later to question whether Titus loves Bérénice. In Cressida's last appearance, she flirts with Diomedes, unaware of Troilus's presence and the anguish she is causing him. Colette Dompiétrini in the part brought out brilliantly Cressida's cynically rational subjection to reality: she has been bartered by the man she loves, and fidelity is no more than a shattered myth. Her pragmatism contrasted sharply with Troilus's desire for loyalty from the woman whose love he has willingly subordinated to military priorities. The critic Françoise Kourilsky considered this scene as the most successful one in the production:

Planchon, while respecting the changes in tone of the scene, brought out clearly the ambivalence of the situation. Cressida . . . is dislocated before our eyes, her very unity explodes: she is Troilus's Cressida, woman deified, and Diomedes's Cressida, woman as a vulnerable object of desires and of interests. Words and

Troilus and Cressida, the battle scene. Théâtre de la Cité de Villeurbanne, 1964

conventions are her sole remaining protection, and she uses them in all lucidness: surrendered from the start, she still lets herself be conquered with all due ritual.[12]

For Planchon, the interest of the play lies to a great extent in the difference between the ideals and the behaviour of the characters, between the heroic vision and the day-to-day reality. The theme has always fascinated him. In *Troilus and Cressida* it is so evident that it almost needed no emphasis, and Planchon said of the play: 'It shows men who make war very well, all the while insisting on the idiocy of war, and men who make love very badly, all the while emphasising the beauty, the miracle of love; this I find absolutely extraordinary and quite contemporary.'[13] Many critics who saw this production also commented on the modernness of the play; it seems written for our time, in its treatment of war, in its constant ironic twists of event and of character.

Because of this modernity, and also to make the play clear to his public, Planchon created a translation which was extremely faithful to the literal meaning of the original. The rather scholarly, stilted text which resulted provoked startlingly angry reactions. The translation was called '. . . clumsy, scholarly, crushingly complicated, falsely trivial, with no real polish, practically unintelligible', or again '. . . disastrous to listen to; knotty, elliptical to the point of amphigory . . .', and by critics normally open-minded and sympathetic.[14] The Villeurbanne text is no more complex than the Shakespearian original; if anything, it is slightly simplified. The Shakespearian text is very difficult, however, and the French translation conveyed most of the difficulty with none of the poetic resonance. Furthermore, several critics complained that the actors themselves seemed not to understand their lines or to enunciate them clearly, except for Gérard Guillaumat and Pierre Santini (who played Thersites and Diomedes, respectively).

The annoyance of the critics was motivated by more than the traditional Parisian hostility to provincial acting companies (*Troïlus and Cressida* was the first play in Planchon's second Paris season). Michel Vinaver saw the production twice. The first time he felt exhausted by the need to concentrate on the text, and it was only the second time, when he was able to understand without strain, that he appreciated the beauty and intelligence of the production. He thought that 'Most critics, for whom it is necessary to absorb a play every evening, slipped, understandably, from fatigue to irritation, and as a result there was an assortment of vengeful opinions which has few precedents in the history of Parisian dramatic criticism.'[15] The obvious problem is that most people see a production only once. Not surprisingly, it became clear in the discussions with audiences at Villeurbanne that *Troilus and Cressida* was one of Planchon's least understood productions.

Planchon is, as we have seen, increasingly reluctant to point out lessons in his productions, for fear of being 'impolite' to his public. He even put off staging *Troilus and Cressida* until the end of the Algerian war, to preclude easy comparisons. In his selection of plays, Planchon enjoys mixing the amusing works, the good draws, with the serious and the experimental. *Troilus and Cressida*, it would seem, belonged to the latter category. Despite its complexity, Planchon felt that to have staged it differently would have been a betrayal of this '. . . masterpiece of baroque structure'.[16] Furthermore, the play was so very relevant to the 1960s that not to have staged it would also have been a kind of betrayal.

Richard III

Planchon put on *Richard III* at Avignon in 1966 and in Villeurbanne in March 1967. The adaptation was once again written under Planchon's supervision and, like the *Henry IV* one, it combined a fidelity to Shakespeare with a desire for clarity. The changes made in the text were for the most part omissions or abbreviations of lengthy passages. The scene structure was largely respected, except that act II, scene iv, a conversation of some 70 lines, was omitted and its main points included in a few sentences at the beginning of the next scene. References to historical events antecedant to the history of Richard and not necessary to the comprehension of the play were suppressed in the translation. Stage directions included in the dialogue were also omitted, as they could be acted rather than spoken. Planchon also shortened and sometimes omitted Richard's monologues (for example I. iii. 324–38 was omitted). The envious villain glorying in his plots in an aside to the audience is an Elizabethan convention inherited from the Morality play, not a modern one. An audience bred on the cinema and television would find it less amusing than a sixteenth-century public might have.

Any asides which were superfluous in terms of advancing the action were eliminated. Nothing was edited which altered the course of the action; as always, Planchon's major concern was the *fable*.

Repetition was omitted except in scenes where it had a translatable poetic effect, for example act IV, scene iv, in which Queen Margaret, Queen Elizabeth, and the Duchess of York sit before the palace, side by side, bewailing the deaths of their sons, husbands, lovers. The losses of each woman are counterpointed by those of the other two (ll. 40–6). The passage was translated almost word for word, and it is as powerful in French as in English.

The set design for *Richard III* had three remarkable aspects: the use of lighting, the costumes, and the machine-like props. The designer was Claude Lemaire. The Avignon production was given in the courtyard of the vice-legate's palace, a vast open space, and costumes and lighting were planned to fit into this setting. The buildings which formed the background (built at the time of the historical Richard III) were lit up with a golden and pink glow; the costumes were in light tones of beige, white, and grey, so that the actors and even the props could 'disappear' into the walls despite the strong lighting. The decision to maintain a steady artificial lighting was a departure from the usual Vilar-inspired practice of using only the natural evening shadows. Although it was less effective in ghost or dream sequences, for most of the play it compelled the actors to play very forcefully in order to attract the public's eyes and ears.

The use of costumes of similar colours (in Planchon's words '. . . all the shades which one finds on eggshells . . .'[17]) was a way of negating class differences in the characters instead of pointing them out as in *Henry IV*. The corruption, as this sameness underlined, was general. As the play progressed, the colours became darker, with black armour and helmets indicating the imminence of war.

The idea behind the props was in line with Jan Kott's thesis[18] that in all the Shakespearian history plays, a machine-like cycle orders the lives of the characters: the inexorable cycle of history. Lemaire gave the set a mechanical quality which made it the perfect embodiment onstage of this critical view of the play. The props were all machines, 'killing machines', wrote Gilles Sandier,[19] 'sitting machines, eating machines, sleeping machines, torturing machines'.

Copied from paintings of the period, they were like large wooden toys, looking terrifyingly effective. The lighting emphasised the looming presence of these mechanical shapes; scaffold, giant cross-bows, even the furniture of state were silhouetted against the pink wall behind. The stage seemed crowded, not only with these large threatening forms, but also with actors, who moved in compact groups. The stage area was moulded into an apparently solid mass, the action became itself a machine-like ritual. The stage space, according to Gilles Sandier, although '. . . occupied by the insensate tumult of History . . .' took on the appearance of '. . . a solemnly arranged ceremonial, of a masquerade of buffoons conducted like a ritual . . .'; the stage was '. . . a space subjected by Planchon to a kind of elongation and distortion comparable to those which extend the faces and the bodies of El Greco'.[20]

The battle scenes were noted for their beauty and their irony. Instead of using the traditional sword fights, Planchon placed two 'armies' on the stage. To depict the battle of Bosworth Field, the same actors changed sides, with their armour and equipment, to represent first the soldiers of one army and then those of the enemy forces. The final battle was trimmed of any remnants of epic grandeur. It began with a great flurry of movement, of carefully orchestrated chaos as the two camps prepared. The actual encounter, finally, lasted no more than a few seconds: four actors gripped one another and then flopped to the ground like children playing dead.

Restrained for a smaller indoor stage, the 1967 production in Villeurbanne seems to have been all the more powerful. There was no longer a feeling of general tumult. The principal antagonists were starkly confronted, while the secondary characters remained frozen in the background. The battles here, both the verbal sparring and the physical combat, took place in a space made deliberately claustrophobic and inescapable: 'The stage is transformed', wrote Gérard Guillot, 'into an arena closed on all sides.'[21]

For the audience of Shakespeare's day, the word 'politics' connoted intrigue and evil machinations. Every one of the characters in *Richard III* is caught up in an atmosphere of plotting and of unrelenting violence, and the Théâtre de la Cité production emphasised this universal deceit and ambition. Planchon pointed out that all the characters are as

ruthless as Richard himself: 'It's just that Richard's plot is the
one that succeeds. In fact all the characters are potential
Richard IIIs.'[22] Planchon thought that there was no dramatic
reason for Richard to have a physical deformity, as his brand
of evil was not unusual. As he had done for his production of
Tartuffe, therefore, Planchon chose for the leading role a
young and attractive actor, Michel Auclair. The decision to
use Auclair, according to Planchon, made Richard's deception of other characters seem more plausible, and his seduc-
tion of Lady Anne more acceptable to reason; it was also
more accurate historically.

Planchon saw Lady Anne as a woman who accepts a young
attractive murderer because she is flattered by his attentions,
as well as for the sake of regaining power. In the rest of
the production, however, he emphasised the women's all-
excluding love of power. Was there any reason to make Lady
Anne less ruthless than the others? If she is to follow Richard
at all, there is little difference between her accepting a leer-
ing hunchback and a smooth-faced seducer: where moral
categories have been wiped away there is little room for such
aesthetic considerations. A monstrous-looking Richard who
succeeded at times in looking 'good' to the other characters
would have been more terrifying, and truer to the play
Shakespeare wrote.

Auclair played Richard as a complex and interesting
character. He was unquiet but politically suave, ambitous
but uncertain of the value of success, spurred on by self-
challenge and other people's fear. He also brought out, without the help of the soliloquies, the grimacing joy which
Richard takes in his machinations. Richard had two smiles,
the one a victorious gloating over defeated enemies, the
other his courtier's affability. Both were equally sinister. All
the characters, indeed, showed an unexpected graciousness
and courtesy. At the same time, their general unctuousness
was startlingly funny. The critic Guy Leclerc praised the
production, mentioning '. . . a beginning which was, for
goodness sake, comical, in which the merciless picture of the
acidulous hypocrisy of avid politicans made the audience
laugh . . .'[23] The picture was funny because it was recognisable – the smile was of those courting power, then as now,
and of those who gain it temporarily.

Richard's downfall is inevitable. Like Falstaff, like Edward
II, he becomes the victim of a system which he controls only

for a time. To a modern audience his defeat is not so much a
moral judgement as part of an ongoing historical cycle in
which power continually changes hands, often destroying
those who have held it. The vigour and directness of the
production brought out both the horror of the political world
of *Richard III*, and its bitterly comic relevance to our
own.

MARLOWE

Edward II
In November 1959, the Théâtre de la Cité was asked to create
a play for the July 1960 drama festival at Orange (a city in the
Vaucluse, north of Avignon, with ruins of a Roman
amphitheatre and theatre). They decided to do Marlowe's
Edward II, which they had already produced in a translation
by Adamov at the Théâtre de la Comédie in 1954. They chose
it partly because no modern play would fill the huge Roman
theatre at Orange, and partly because they liked its historical
approach. 'We no longer', they wrote in the programme for
Edward II (produced as *Édouard II*), 'feel interested in
psychological debates . . . unless they are set against a social
and historical background. Ultimately, this is the point on
which we differ most with the Cartel.'[24]

The production was put on as a genuine group effort, with
discussion and improvisation encouraged at every stage of
rehearsal. The troupe decided that they would use the text as
freely as if it were a film script, and make it their own
creation, as Picasso had done when he painted his own
original version of Velázquez's *Las meninas*. The first
rehearsals were simply improvisations on themes springing
from research notes, with no text, set, props, or direction.
The actors noticed that Marlowe deprives his king of any
aura of divine right; he shows that men, not principles, are in
conflict. The play would therefore require little '*démystification*'. On the other hand, they felt that they could present
historical events more clearly than Marlowe, and even
perhaps rearrange them. They admit in the programme for
their production that 'It is not under the reign of Edward that
the Renaissance was established, but to make our fable more
exemplary, this is what we show.' It is easy to see whose
influence was at work, especially when one considers that

Brecht himself wrote a version of *Edward II* (*Leben Eduards des Zweiten von England*).

After presenting the play in Orange in July 1960 and at Baalbek in Lebanon in August 1960, Planchon decided that they were going to start everything over again, text, sets, and *mise en scène*. The company discussed the play anew. Their summary of Marlowe's play at this stage (recorded in the later programme) foreshadows what was to become Planchon's essential preoccupation in his own plays: 'What does the fable of *Edward II* tell of? The march of history. *Men in the process of making history are formed by it*. In this play all of them (almost) are crushed by this colossus' [my italics]. With this key idea in mind, Planchon and his co-director at the time, Jacques Rosner, wrote a new translation of *Edward II*. It combined elements from both Adamov's and Brecht's versions.

The first difference which strikes one when one compares the Marlowe original with the Villeurbanne adaptation is that the latter is much longer. It is virtually a new play loosely based on the original. Marlowe's text provides the bare minimum of dialogue and monologue necessary to advance the action. Planchon and Rosner's text, ironically enough when one considers how much importance Planchon attaches to the *events* of a play, is verbose, slower-moving, full of self-explanatory lyrical outbursts by various characters. It is, in parts, very beautiful, in others, rather dull reading. It lays a much greater emphasis on the personal psychology of the characters, explaining at length what Marlowe is content to suggest in a line or two. Again, this is rather ironical in view of the troupe's professed distaste for psychological drama.

The political structure of England is presented very differently in Planchon and Rosner's play. In Marlowe's play the common people are present, but their role is extremely limited. The Mayor of Bristol and Rice ap Howel present their homages to the Queen and Mortimer, servants such as Spenser and Levune become the King's favourites, other commoners appear as guards or executioners. There is no class conflict; the conflict is between Edward II as a weak king and his rebellious lords.

In the Villeurbanne version, 'the people' are more in evidence. In one scene English soldiers at Blacklow realise that they have been abandoned to be massacred by the Scots; in

another the people's discontent after this defeat is men-
tioned, and we learn that the lords have destroyed the crops
and tried to impose a tax to reduce the people to helpless-
ness. There are moments, admittedly, in which the class
analysis is irritatingly simplistic: Édouard II, for example,
chats with the cathedral builders and elicits their sympathy
for his favourite, Gaveston, because of the man's stable-boy
origins. On the whole, however, the historical restructuring
is both effective and moving. In the Villeurbanne play a
powerful merchant class is seen to be emerging in the commons. It is they who support the King, in opposition to the
noblemen. After he is killed, when the people are said to be
rioting, it is not the lords, as in Marlowe, but the commons
who encourage the young Prince to have Mortimer arrested.
Thus in the Villeurbanne version, although it may be at the
cost of some historical accuracy, there is a sense of the
growth of classes, of the increasing power and conservatism
of the merchants and, as always in Planchon's work, a feeling
for the poorest, the most ordinary man, crushed in the power
games of the wealthy.

The Villeurbanne play unfortunately overdid the homosexuality of the King. Perhaps the company felt that a modern public needed to have everything spelled out. There is
one scene in which Spenser and other courtiers dress up as
ladies in order to amuse the King. The critic Pierre Seller was
right when he wrote that Edward's homosexuality may be
presented in a brutal way in Marlowe, but never in a vulgarly
shocking way, whereas the Villeurbanne production
occasionally recalled the gay nightclubs of Paris.[25] Indeed,
while Marlowe's Edward is opposed because his favourite is
dangerously powerful, Planchon's Edward is opposed
because the noblemen and merchants are prejudiced against
homosexuals! Planchon may have believed that this prejudice had not been emphasised enough in Marlowe; but
paradoxically it is Marlowe's king who elicits pity, *his*
weakness which fills one with terror, whereas Planchon's
version of the character seems comparatively bloodless.

The sets for *Edward II* were designed as though for a
modern play; that is, rather than suggesting a historical era,
they were meant to illustrate the main themes of the play.
The actors played on a circular platform about 40 cm (16 in)
high and 11 m (12 yd) across, with iron-red tiles on the top
surface and gold around the edge; it sloped towards the

audience so that the metallic surface acted as a mirror. At the outdoor theatre in Orange, this stage was placed at the foot of the audience, who were seated halfway around it in their amphitheatre seats. Large gilded panels around this central platform doubled as cupboards for props when these were not in use; the panels could also be moved about to suggest various architectural forms, now ruins, now a fortress, now a building site . . . The stage furniture and props were kept extremely simple and functional; consisting of a few seats, gates, screens, and platforms of polished wood, they could be combined, like the panels, in different ways in order to suggest an almost limitless number of areas and of objects. Iron, wood, and gold-like materials were used. When the

Edward II, Théâtre de la Cité de Villeurbanne, 1961. The King (Jean Leuvrais) and his favourites in 'decorated' costume, left; their opponents in 'expressionist' dress, centre; Michel Robin as Bishop of Coventry, right

play transferred to a traditional auditorium, Allio borrowed from the Japanese theatre the idea of using two runways on the sides on which the actors came onto the stage.

As in *Henry IV*, costumes were used to distinguish groups of characters. While in *Henry IV* the differences had been in cut, texture, and colour, here, however, the entire style was different for each group. The King and his favourites were dressed in a 'decorated' style, wearing highly colourful, refined, ornate costumes. The costumes of the rebellious lords were in an expressionist style; the colours were quieter, and shapes were altered with padding, in a brutal stylization obviously in contrast with the delicate finery of the king and his minions.

Just as Planchon was to use the revolving platform in cinematic style in *Schweyk im Zweiten Weltkrieg*, here he used spotlights as though they were cameras. He thus created a cinematographic effect in keeping with the company's intention to use the text as if it were a scenario. The spotlights, raised or lowered from the flies in full view of the audience (in proper Brechtian fashion), were used to follow one actor, to frame another, for 'close-ups' on characters' faces, to reshape and vary the stage area; they were used, in other words, with the freedom of a movie camera. The lighting helped to maintain the pace of the action, with quick black-outs between tableaux. Some critics complained, however, that these frequent black-outs made the production irritatingly choppy. Certainly in the text individual tableaux, although often intensely·emotional, are equally often cut off, so to speak, in mid-current. When this tendency was emphasised by the lighting, parts of the production must have seemed to be a series of anti-climaxes, making the spectator alternate confusingly between involvement and abrupt alienation, between Planchon's lyrical text and his Brechtian staging.

In the Villeurbanne play there is an offstage voice which comments on the action. It gives historical information (describing, for example, the coronation of Edward II, and later the battles of 1312), and it informs us about the progress of each side in the battles against Edward II. It points out for us that while Oxford was being built, wars were being waged; it describes the misery of the common people during the winter famine; it tells of the imprisoned King's suffering, but when he pleads for mercy admonishes him with the

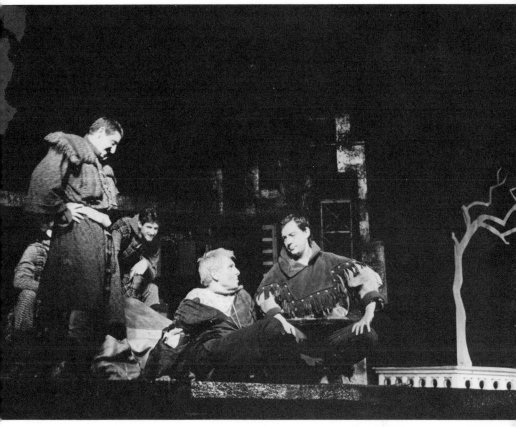

Edward II. The King (Jean Leuvrais) tortured by Matrevis and Gurney

reminder that he has himself shown none. In the reading it becomes, undeniably, a rather irritating *vox ex machina*; Pierre Seller called it '... *une surenchère pathétique*' (superfluous pathos).[26] The explanations which it provides could have been incorporated into the dialogue, and its comments seem unnecessary hints to the audience on how to react to the obvious.

The musical accompaniment, composed by Claude Lochy, was conceived, like the sets, as though for a modern play. The music was not, as in *Henry IV*, a historical reconstruction, apart from one clear allusion to Renaissance music at the moment of Edward II's short-lived triumph over his enemies (the troupe, as we have seen, had decided to give the play a Renaissance setting). The accompaniment was really a complement to Planchon and Rosner's very lyrical text. The play traces the life of Edward II as seen through his own eyes: it includes flashbacks, reminiscences, premonitions; it reminded Lochy of grand opera. As Claudel had done in his play *Christophe Colomb*, Lochy decided to experiment with the Wagnerian idea that text and music were interrelated parts of a dramatic whole. He wrote in the programme for *Édouard II* that 'The role of the musician was . . . to play a kind of filigreed reflection of the spoken text, to relate the passages from dream to reality in it, to fill out the understatements constantly used in psychological relationships, to create a continuous dialogue with the actors.' The music, played by deep-toned instruments and drums, included distorted sounds, and many unfinished phrases, reflecting the internal world of half-thoughts and incomplete dreams which the play depicted. To convey Edward's fear of battle, for example, martial music was played on the rhythm of a racing heart-beat, as the King remembered his own anguished reaction to war. The text, however, far from being understated, tends to be too wordy, and one wonders whether Lochy's attempt to 'complete' it may not have seemed another *surenchère pathétique*.

The critical response to the play was interested but not greatly enthusiastic. Many felt that the text was uneven, alternating between Marlowe's (or Planchon's) lyricism, and an analytical, Marxist approach to historical events. The *Times'* critic, who regarded the adaptation as Planchon's own creation loosely based on Marlowe, was able to take a more favourable attitude to the production as a whole: 'The loss of Marlowe's mighty line is not as great as it first appears . . . To make up for it, M. Planchon lavishes on his spectators a poetry that is seen rather than heard and so scores over most of his rivals, with whom the spoken word is traditionally paramount, the plastic stage picture of little or no account.'[27] The stage language seems indeed to have played as important a role as the text itself, but the text is undeniably verbose, and Pierre Marcabru was right to suggest that 'It would be necessary to tighten up not so much the duration of the events, but the language which stifles these events, drowns them in a flow of explanations, which are sometimes a little too candid, and often too definitive.'[28]

The general impression was that this was a promising but incomplete piece of theatrical experimentation. The reactions of critics ranged from irritation to confidence in the company's future work. Elsa Triolet summed it up: 'In short, here is, on the whole, a show whose defects are as obvious as is the talent behind it, and which appears to be the first draft of a work which we will one day be able to see and hear.'[29] It is understandable that after such a response to his rewriting of *Edward II*, Planchon should have felt it was time for him to begin his own writing career. His first play, *La Remise*, was originally written in 1962.

5

French classics: human beings and social beings

BEHIND Planchon's conception of the classic plays and their value for us, there lies his passion for history. Looking at the past helps us to understand that the present is itself no more than a historical phase. French classics, like the plays of Marlowe and Shakespeare, were presented on the Villeurbanne stage suffused with a sense of history. Although Planchon never neglected to find out all he could about previous interpretations of a play, his own productions, based strictly, he always claimed, on the text, often took quite a different direction. He believes that the classics are written on two levels, that of the permanent written text, and that of the stage language, which evolves, and which may change drastically in the space of thirty years. This attitude explains both his respect for the written text, and his translation of it in defiantly personal terms onto the stage. He has said that he has done his most original work with the classics, and indeed that '. . . great directors put on great productions only with classical plays'.[1]

MOLIÈRE

George Dandin
Planchon created *George Dandin* at Villeurbanne in 1958. In subsequent years the company took the production on tour in France, Italy, eastern Europe, and North Africa, and presented it briefly in New York (1968) and in London (1969).

Planchon saw the play as much more than the gross farce it often becomes on stage. He described it in the following terms in the Villeurbanne programme:

This cruelly amusing story of a newly rich peasant who has tried to escape from his class by marrying a well-born '*damoiselle*' [lady] – an inescapable situation – becomes more involved with the in-

82

laws, obsessed with etiquette and wishing to regild their armorial bearings; the gentleman from town (a small scale Don Juan) followed by his henchman, the village ne'er-do-well.

Seeing the plot in this essentially social light inspired most of the work done on the production.

When Planchon considered each character in turn, he was puzzled by the kind of costumes which have traditionally been given to them. The costumes at the Théâtre de la Cité were based on commonsense rather than on tradition. Dandin, a nouveau riche landowner, wore, instead of the traditional peasant's smock, an expensive-looking outfit, with a touch of the parvenu about it. The country aristocrats, instead of the usual elaborate court dress, wore clothes more suitable for the countryside. Clitandre wore a hunting-costume; the Sotenvilles were dressed in very good taste, as they pay attention to the rules of etiquette and propriety; Mme de Sotenville and her daughter wore simple dresses, light-coloured because of the summer heat. Even Lubin, who would want to play down his peasant origins, seemed to have consciously avoided wearing peasant clothing. Everyone was thus dressed not as a caricature, but as a believable person.

The Théâtre de la Cité had to cope for the first time in this production with the unities of classical French drama. René Allio, who conceived the set for *George Dandin*, was given the responsibility of creating a unity of place. In the programme at Villeurbanne, he dedicated the set to Le Nain, '. . . to this great realistic painter, to his colours, his subjects, but especially to his manner, at once objective and friendly, of describing nature and men in his day, of showing things as they are . . .' Although the set itself was realistic, Allio made a point of placing it in the middle of the stage, leaving a free zone between it and the sides and back of the stage, in order to remind people that they were in a theatre.

Allio emphasised the social division, not only between Dandin and Angélique, but also between him and the class from which he has tried to escape. On one side of the stage was a wooden barn, in which farmhands and animals lived; on the other Dandin's house, solid, sunbaked, a proprietor's dwelling. As it was to be in *Les Ames mortes*, the stage was filled with extras – peasants working for Dandin at haymaking, bringing in the harvest, preparing food, doing the unending chores required on a farm. They gave the set its feeling of an actual farm in the provinces. There was a cart-load of hay, a chopping-block with an axe stuck in it, a kitchen garden near by. The continuous hard work of the people around and economically beneath Dandin under-lined his new social situation. The programme, which includes quotations from La Bruyère and others, suggested that the peasants in the seventeenth century were the dispos-sessed on whom the wealthy depended to maintain them. The stage picture powerfully emphasised this idea. Each servant was somehow shown to be a total human being, even the silent toiling extras, an old wet-nurse, for example, fol-lowing Dandin about with tender looks and gestures. Colin, who has barely ten lines to speak, suddenly came to life and was a presence in his own right. Lubin and Claudine revealed a toughness well in keeping with that of the society around them: 'Lubin is the cock of the walk, and Claudine, Angélique's servant, a hardened girl who knows how much credit to give to young men's promises.'[2] The farmhands laughed at Dandin as they saw him being manipulated by his wife and her parents.

Some critics believed that the extras were there to rep-resent the poetry of work, the real values which lie in the peasant's toil. Planchon's vision was not so idealised, how-ever. Dandin's predicament is that he is no longer quite a part of a world which he can never leave behind altogether: each detail of the set said this eloquently – from the mud and dung which clung to his shoes, to his own thickset figure, walking about the farmyard with part of his attention always on the hay-making or the corn-grinding, pushing the farmhands about in his frustration. The more fully human the extras appeared to be, the crueller their lot and Dandin's hardness seemed. The world was the reflection, in a lower social sphere, of that of *Richard III*, with everyone out to take advantage of everyone else. Dandin himself was not unde-serving of pity, caught between the farm in which he is resented as the master, and the household in which he is duped and cuckolded by his wife and mocked by his in-laws. The set and the extras demonstrated the social no-man's-land into which Dandin has trapped himself.

George Dandin is a play constructed around five mono-logues, and in which there are frequent asides to the audi-ence. Planchon felt that these asides broke up the dialogue and seemed improbable; as often as the text permitted, characters therefore showed that they could overhear their interlocutor's attempt at an aside. Dandin's monologues introduce a different time level into the play and they are difficult to stage convincingly. Dandin's first monologue was spoken in a traditional straightforward way, except for one detail (as the Villeurbanne programme explains):

the character addresses the audience directly, a new time level is introduced, but to compensate we have placed him in front of a page of the *Petit Classique Larousse* [school editions of the classics] which, we hope, will show that the matter in hand is well and truly a classical play and not a Brechtian affectation in which the actor addresses the spectators directly.

Despite the tongue-in-check denial, it was an excellent little A-effect (alienating device), although even then Planchon would probably have felt embarrassed at using a term which has been so clumsily interpreted and over-used since Brecht. For the second and third monologues by Dandin, a different form of presentation was used. It is less clear, from the text, that these two speeches are spoken directly to the audience, and so they were presented as ruminations, almost *monologues interieurs*, or soliloquies, spoken by Dandin to himself. To show that these were not on the same time level as the action on the stage, that they were enclaves in the passage of time, the stage movement froze while they were being said, and resumed afterward as if no time had elapsed. Claude Olivier described the effect of this solution onstage:

George Dandin soliloquizes in the yard of his wealthy farm; the entire household is present, frozen for the moment, each in the attitude most characteristic of him or her. And, in the admirable sets conceived by René Allio . . . a whole universe looms up . . . it recalls miraculously and recreates innumerable paintings and engravings of the seventeenth century . . .

And when Dandin finishes speaking to himself, this whole little world comes to life, each works at his occupation, as he will not cease to do during the entire show.[3]

It was precisely these occupations which gave the production its sense of realistic time. Under a soft, changing lighting, the chores changed with the progression of the day; each hour, from dawn to dusk, had its appointed task, from the departure for the fields to the bell rung for mealtimes and for prayer. To counter the break in continuity caused by the intervals, at the start of each act the actors repeated the last moments of the preceding act. At the end of act I, for example, everyone from farmworkers to Sotenvilles quietly composed himself for the Angelus, then finished up the day, sweeping up, resuming interrupted quarrels, etc., and got into position for the next act. The lights went down, and came up again to reveal the characters at the Angelus once again; they then repeated their previous movements exactly. The concept of unity of time was thus not only observed (with the twenty-four hours almost individually represented), but used to considerable effect.

Despite the beautiful rural setting, the society depicted in *George Dandin* is a fierce one, in which characters' misdeeds are often mitigated by their situation. Angélique is sold to Dandin; as a victim of his social ambition and her parents' rapacity, her attitude to her husband is understandable. There is no marriage between them in any but a legal sense. Angélique was played, therefore, not as a hardened adulteress, but as a silly young girl easily seduced by the attractions of a younger and more sophisticated man than her husband. In Planchon's production, Angélique and Clitandre also retired to the barn long enough to persuade even a modern audience that they have had a toss in the hay. Molière's public was no doubt convinced by less.

Angélique's parents, in keeping with tradition, were presented as slightly ridiculous characters, but not in the usual way. Instead of being precious or over-exuberant, they were excessively stately and rigid. After all, they are poor provincial aristocrats trying desperately to keep up standards. Furthermore, M. de Sotenville prides himself on being a veteran, and so Mme de Sotenville showed the *savoir vivre* and good breeding of a former officer's wife. In Planchon's production, they were not entirely amusing. They have married off their daughter to a rough peasant in order to remake their fortune, and the mean opportunism and callousness of this action was brought out.

Planchon referred to Dandin as M. Jourdain [*Le Bourgeois gentilhomme*'s] country cousin, and he thought there were modern parallels to the story: 'The production of *George Dandin* must not show the drama of the cuckold. It must show the comedy of one cuckolded through snobbery. There are today, with the wealthy merchant who marries into the bourgeoisie, almost identical situations.'[4] It took Planchon's

The Angelus scene from *George Dandin*. Armand Meffre as Dandin, Colette Dompiétrini as Angélique

company, and Jean Bouise as Dandin, to make the bitterly tragic undercurrent of this comedy apparent. Instead of a banal farce about a cuckold, the play became, in the words of Jean-Jacques Lerrant, '. . . the story of ambition, of vanity in a caste society in which money was, however, eroding the barriers'.[5]

There were, of course, great differences between the fate of the parvenu in the seventeenth century and in our own, and Planchon made his actors well aware of them. During the American visit in 1968, this point met with sympathetic understanding:

The character of Dandin has been fixed for us as a particular social result of a particular period in a particular place. He is the recognisable ancestor of modern Dandins who have used their hard-earned money to gain social advantages which have proved more trouble than they are worth. Yet through this production we see the difference between Molière's Dandin and his modern counterpart, between the social attitudes of the seventeenth century and today's.[6]

87

Perhaps some spectators went a step further with Planchon, and understood the implications of this difference. Planchon had submitted the play to a Marxist analysis. Unlike Molière, whose ridicule was aimed at the folly of trying to change castes at all, Planchon had the benefit of three centuries' hindsight. He wrote in the programme for the Avignon festival in 1966, '. . . patience: the time will come when the Dandins will become conscious [of their class]. Their consciousness is for the time being negative: "We are not nobles."' Dandin was portrayed as a figure frustrated in his social ambitions for more than comic reasons, as Planchon made clear:

> . . . this form of society in which our characters move engenders its own contradictions; in this case, misalliance. By underlining with rigour and precision the form of this society, we are showing its particular and historical character. At the same time a solution appears which will be given by the evolution, the transformation, the mutation of that society.[7]

Planchon was following a Marxist-based precept, reiterated by Brecht, for staging the classics: society must be shown to be mutable. In Dandin's situation lie the seeds of social change, and they were made perceptible in the production.

There was no blatantly didactic intent in the Théâtre de la Cité's *George Dandin*, nevertheless. Dandin was comical as well as pitiable, neither a proletarian hero nor a totally-blamable clown. Jean-Jacques Lerrant, the Lyons critic who has long followed Planchon's work, probably best summed up the social message of the production: 'As in every one of Planchon's *mises en scène*, who has left didactic theatre far behind him, the relations between man and society are complex. Each is determined by the other without this process being reducible to a clear operation. Each being carries within himself his mystery, his alibis and his unfathomable justifications.'[8] The characters in Planchon's production of *George Dandin* were at the same time individual beings whose lot is determined for them by society, and shapers of that society for themselves and for others.

Le Tartuffe
Tartuffe was first put on at Villeurbanne in 1962, and in the following years in Moscow and Leningrad (1963), Paris (1964), Stockholm and various European cities (1966),

Avignon (1967), and New York (1968). In 1973–4, Planchon recreated the play and took it on tour in South America, and then in France. In November 1976 he put it on at the new National Theatre in London. The French government does not like touring companies to put on modern plays abroad, no doubt because the artistic merit of a classic is unassailable, possibly also because classics are thought to be politically innocuous. *Tartuffe* is therefore a perennial choice for tours.

Planchon based his analysis of the play on the question 'What does Tartuffe do?', rather than on the question 'Who is Tartuffe?' Looking at the events in the play, Planchon challenged the traditional idea that Orgon passively follows Tartuffe's lead: in fact, the play progresses because of Orgon's decisions. Rather than concentrating on Tartuffe in the production, therefore, Planchon gave Orgon equal importance. After studying Orgon's actions, he concluded that the man's attachment to Tartuffe, although he is himself unaware of it, is a sexual and emotional one. If one looks, for example, at the scene in which Tartuffe courts Elmire, whilst Orgon remains hidden under the table, it is clear from the text that Orgon stays under the table despite Elmire's repeated hints and cries for help. Although other directors have him pop out enraged, Planchon stuck to the text and left him under the table, passive, while his wife is subjected to Tartuffe's amorous advances. He pointed out, also, that two endings were possible to the relationship between Orgon and Tartuffe:

(1) The denunciation of Tartuffe as irreligious and a greater aspiration toward the saintly life on the part of Orgon;(2) the crumbling of the religious pretexts which make Orgon believe that it is they that attach him to Tartuffe and a clear realisation of the nature of their relationship.

But here, and it is far from meaningless . . . he rejects religion, along with Tartuffe, which is the unconscious but clear recognition of the sexual tie which links them.[9]

Reflecting on this phenomenon of a wealthy man fooled by infatuation, Planchon looked at his social context to find the reason. He wrote in the programme:

Why, in this society, does a great servant of the state . . . take refuge in an aspiration to mysticism, to the religious life in order to give . . . a new meaning to his life? Historians answer that after the Fronde, the monarchy established itself solidly, and that the power

of the social group to which Orgon belongs was reduced or disappeared altogether. Through these questions, we are referred back to
the *Grand Siècle*, of which Molière seizes a few of the important
contradictions by presenting a conflict incarnated by individuals . . . but formed by social phenomena, historical from top to
toe.[10]

Thus in Planchon's view Orgon's life is empty because he
can no longer exercise political influence, and his 'religious'
conversion is an attempt to fill a vacuum. It is a point of view
which is not in contradiction with the text of the play, which
is certainly in harmony with the history of the day and
which, most importantly, illuminates the play for a modern
spectator.

Rejecting as irrelevant the vexed question of whether the
play is pro- or anti-catholic, Planchon therefore concentrated
on the social situation of Orgon, on his power within his
family, and on the climate of thought which permits Tartuffe
to take advantage of Orgon's unconscious infatuation by
posing as his mentor. Planchon's intention was neither
didactic nor demonstrative, and he attempted to reduce the
inevitable subjectivity of his interpretation by sticking to the
events of the play. In 1962, it was one of the first productions
in which Planchon thus attempted to reduce the extent of his
interprétation.

The much-praised set of *Tartuffe* was meant to convey both
an abstract picture of the sensibility of the century, and a
realistic one of its daily life. Allio, who designed the sets for
the first production, explained that the set was a visual
parallel to Tartuffe's gradual uncovering. It was a three-sided
box made up of movable panels; as the play progressed, the
inner panels were raised so that the room appeared larger
and larger, the walls more and more schematic. Paintings
were chosen for the erotico-religious themes popular in the
seventeenth century. As the back panels disappeared, more
and more could be seen of an enormous baroque painting of
the deposition from the cross. An inlaid parquet floor
reflected the gold and light-brown tones of the woodwork
and the walls. The style of furnishing used was more Louis
XIII than Louis XIV, because in the time of Louis XIV, when
the play takes place, only châteaux would be up-to-date
enough to have Louis XIV furniture; Orgon's is a bourgeois
home. Lighting effects were planned to create a special sense

of time; there were to be no dark corners, and no feeling of a realistic passage of time.

Costumes, at least those of the men, were designed to look as modern as possible while remaining historically accurate. Trousers were in the Louis XIII style because that style is more similar to our own; some coats were strictly in a Louis XIV fashion, but those worn by Valère and Damis were very like those of elegant young men of the 1960s. The policemen's uniforms in the last scene were modern, as these have in any case not changed; the only anachronism was the addition of today's *ceinturon* (military belt).

Lochy's music was intended as a framework for the play rather than to sustain the action. An overture in a French

Tartuffe, 1962. Gérard Guillaumat (left) as Cléante, Roger Planchon as Tartuffe

Tartuffe, 1964. Orgon (Jacques Debary) betrayed

style was played by two string quartets, and the accompaniment as a whole was a decorative reinforcement of the atmosphere of religious sensibility.

The austerity of the sets in the earlier productions emphasised the well-controlled *mise en place*, which more than one critic compared to patterns of fencing. The flow of movement was conceived as in a film. Planchon felt that Molière was showing an entire society through this small family circle, and his production made this clear. The sets were both 'everyday' and representative; people's gestures, too, from temper tantrums, slaps, and tears, to hugs and caresses, from taking off an overcoat to putting on a dressing-gown, made the audience feel that this family was in the midst of its most ordinary life, and that this is how people might have lived in a seventeenth-century bourgeois home.

This historical accuracy of the production as a whole justified a scene often unfairly edited, that of the Exempt's speech in praise of the King. Planchon was very interested in the speech, because it is a rare instance of a character making a personal comment on his society and on his place within it. In Planchon's production, even Tartuffe's manservant Laurent, having waited in the wings for the past three centuries, finally came out of hiding to put away his master's hairshirt and whip. (In traditional productions he does not appear; Tartuffe calls him and throws the hairshirt and whip into the wings.)

The set designer for the 1974 production, Hubert Monloup, retained some elements of Allio's stage sets. As in the first version, the curtain opened on a detail of a baroque painting showing a deposition from the cross. In this production, however, the painting was then raised to reveal Orgon's house; it was almost a palace, its size suggested by echoing sounds from above and around the specific room in which each scene was set. This palace was filled with scaffolding and ladders; baroque religious frescoes and marble sculptures were partially hidden by tarpaulins; in one scene the covered shape of an enormous equestrian statue was in evidence, with only one hoof showing. In the production that I saw in London, the first scenes took place in an entrance hall, cluttered with boards, tarpaulins, etc., on which people perched or leaned uncomfortably as they spoke. The sky was visible over the hallway, and a statue of a troubled, seated Christ was suspended from the flies throughout. The house looked as if some work of renovation or redecoration had been begun and then interrupted. Meanwhile the family made use of the rooms as they were. Indeed, Planchon created the atmosphere of an intimate family existence not only by having characters put on coats when they go out and remove them when they enter, but by having them appear amongst one another in shirtsleeves and petticoats, combinations and nightdresses, innocently informal in their family setting. Once again there was an almost continuous movement on the stage: Dorine berated Mariane in a laundry room while busily folding sheets, the family continually ate snacks as they discussed Orgon's infatuation or their danger.

The feeling of a house in transition reflected the ideological uncertainty of the seventeenth century. The family live in their century as they do in their uncomfortable surroundings, compelled by the simple necessity of going on living; they contend as best they can with the disastrous effects of Orgon's delusion, itself made possible by the extent and nature of religious feeling in his age. In the second production more clearly even than in the first, Planchon showed the spiritual and social dilemmas of a century through the relationships of ordinary people in their day-to-day setting.

This microcosmic analysis revealed a society ruled by two powers, the secular monarchic and the religious, which might join together to impose an unbearable weight on ordinary people. More than a simple comedy of human error, this was a play depicting the way in which the ruling sensibility of a given society might be used to ill effect by an adventurer like Tartuffe. The message was clear. A group of farmers went to see the play and in a subsequent discussion, one of them said that he had compared what he saw on stage with his own experience of village life; asked if he saw only religious parallels, he answered, 'No; in the country people use whatever is highly regarded at the time. You could transpose without changing much except the costumes.'[11]

According to Planchon, social and personal forces interact to create events. If he constructed a picture of an age, in so doing he could not neglect the psychological forces at work in *Tartuffe*. Planchon admired the play precisely because the characters are so enmeshed in the action: 'No character analyses himself, each is caught up in the action, each expresses an "I" rather than the "he" disguised as "I" of demonstrative plays.'[12] Because the characters do not speak of their motives, it was the work of the production to suggest what these motives are.

Orgon, for example, is unaware of his love for his friend. His own behaviour to Tartuffe, Dorine's complaints of his excessive tenderness for the man, and particularly his public preference of Tartuffe to Elmire are indications of a love which is physical and emotional rather than spiritual. The production therefore underlined this attraction: Orgon's attitudes and gestures in the presence of Tartuffe were those of a lover. The stage language conveyed Orgon's self-delusion as well as his infatuation. The role of Orgon was played by Jacques Debary in the 1962 and 1964 productions,

and by Guy Tréjan in the later ones. Both brought out the
pathos of this man's situation, past middle age, neglecting
and even harming his family for a love which he has neither
the insight nor the courage to admit to himself. The later
productions emphasised Orgon's homosexual attachment
more, but both ended in a scene of emotional violence.
Orgon, as we have seen, reveals the true nature of his friendship by rejecting everything, even religion, in a rage. He was
played as a lover scorned and cheated, and he remained
bitter, empty, and too ashamed and defeated to look Elmire
in the face.

The early productions of *Tartuffe* at the Théâtre de la Cité
made Tartuffe both young and impenetrable. As the programme pointed out, the original production in 1669 had
used two young actors for the role, Du Croisy, then 34, and La
Grange, the dashing young leading man in Molière's troupe.
In 1962 Roger Planchon played the role himself; in 1964, he
chose the young and attractive Michel Auclair for the role,
thus making the character understandably attractive to the
older Orgon, and also understandably attracted to Elmire.
Dorine does describe him as repulsive (II. iii. 646–7), but
Planchon dismissed the passage as an angry exaggeration.
Auclair surprised audiences by the openness of his
demeanour; rather than being old, eccentric, and sly-
looking, he was good-natured and aggressive, at all times
confident of his power over Orgon. Auclair gave the audience no clues to his 'real' thoughts. This interpretation,
which made no concessions to the public, is fully justified by
the text of the play, but it was nevertheless a very unconventional one. Like a Hamlet or an Iago, he played his role so
well that the audience were left wondering whether it is
always a game or not, whether or not the character retains a
conscious control over his hypocrisy at all times.

In the production which was put on in London, Tartuffe,
played by Planchon himself, seemed neither young nor
attractive. No doubt Planchon had decided that Dorine's and
Mariane's contempt for the character was well-founded after
all. Orgon's blindness to his own love is more believable if
the object of his love is unattractive. This Tartuffe's movements had a certain reptilian quality; he tended to appear
and approach noiselessly, and furthermore he was blessed
with a shadow. Laurent (played by Michel Raskine) became a
younger and smaller version of Tartuffe, who dogged his

footsteps, listened behind doors and crept into corners in just the same way as Tartuffe himself has insidiously crept into Orgon's household. Not content to return to the recent tradition of an ugly Tartuffe, Planchon thus underlined the point by giving him a double. Planchon was probably motivated by a rereading of the text, in which Tartuffe's very speeches suggest an odious and evident deceitfulness. At the same time, however, this Tartuffe like Auclair's never gave himself away to the audience, for nowhere does the text justify a wink or a gestural aside from him.

Planchon established a delicate balance between Orgon and Tartuffe, the one attempting unknowingly to make a spiritual bond out of a sensual passion, the other using his own hypnotic appeal over Orgon to gain power and wealth. The ending of *Tartuffe* often seems a tacked-on conventional one, but in Planchon's production it follows very logically from the rest of the play. Orgon, formerly useful to the king, now powerless, seeks to fill his time and renew his self-esteem through a spiritual ascension and finds himself deceived by his mentor. Tartuffe's ends are purely secular; he wants Orgon's fortune, and the religious front which he assumes is merely the one most likely to succeed in his day. Orgon, as a wealthy property-owner, though he *has* become tangentially involved in plots against the state, is less of a threat to order than a cynical adventurer like Tartuffe, and it is therefore very credible that the King should pardon Orgon and arrest Tartuffe. In Planchon's production the intervention from the Sun-King was shown to be motivated not by a superior justice, but by political good sense.

Indeed, the later production emphasised the state's power in a series of violent stage images. A group of armed men entered Orgon's house as the family was about to sit down to a meal, and suddenly they were all 'trapped' in a waist-deep pit, on a platform lower than the stage level, like frightened prisoners in a cell. The King's men aimed muskets at them from a higher level all around. It was a striking stage picture of their powerlessness in the face of the state. In the end Tartuffe and Laurent were seized violently, and Laurent was stripped and hung up by the wrists. The King's power is absolute, his benevolence selective and dictated by reasons of state. This historical stage-statement was a far cry from the conventional interpretation of the scene as a paean to the forgiving justice of Louis XIV.

Orgon, his family, and Tartuffe all belong very obviously to a definite kingdom and to a specific era. Planchon made them individuals, powerfully moved by personal passions, and members of their society as well, whose power to act and whose motivation has a complex relation to the laws, the powers, and the ideology of their time and place.

MARIVAUX

La Seconde Surprise de l'amour (*Love's Second Surprise*)
La Seconde Surprise de l'amour was presented in 1959 and 1960 at the Théâtre de la Cité de Villeurbanne, directed by Planchon and Jacques Rosner.

Marivaux does not give a specific setting for his play, and because the text suggests several, the company decided to disregard the rule of unity of place in this production. Émile Copfermann in his book on Planchon explained very intelligently why Planchon had felt free to 'interpret' the play in this way: 'The extrapolation rests on this premise: the author, corseted by an inadequate norm imposed from the outside, attempts to transgress its rigour through subterfuge. It is up to the director to translate and in the process, to arrive at a modern reading.'[13] Thus, as Marivaux himself had tried to 'stretch' the convention of unity of place, Planchon felt that it could be discarded with all due respect to the playwright.

According to the text, the Marquise and the Chevalier are neighbours who share the same grounds, and so the play was set in their common gardens and in their two houses. Precise scenes were located where, in all likelihood, given the actions and the words of the characters, they would take place. The first scene, in which the Marquise has awakened but is too bored to dress was set, logically, in her bedroom; scenes in which she receives the Chevalier were set in her reception room; Lubin courted Lisette in the corridors, the most likely place where servants might exchange a few private words. The choice of setting also underlined themes. The first dialogue between the Comte and the Chevalier, for example (III. vi) took place in a fencing room, with the Chevalier idly practising his fencing because he has nothing better to do, and with the verbal duel paralleling the sword-play. In act II, scene viii, Hortensius gives a reading for the benefit of the Marquise. In Planchon's production it was set in her garden in winter, with the Marquise and Chevalier warmly dressed and sitting near a brazier, and Hortensius further off in the cold, blowing on his fingers to keep them warm. The Marquise would have organised a poetry reading without really knowing what it was, according to Planchon (although this seems highly unlikely) and so the venue was impractical. Furthermore the wintry scenery was a reflection of her own heart, which is still closed to love. In act III, scene viii, the Chevalier gives up the Marquise to the Comte, and the text suggests that she accepts the Comte's attentions out of spite. Planchon had the conversation end with the Marquise running off pursued by the Comte, and they were next seen both in her bedroom, en déshabillé and without their wigs. At the end of the play also, the Marquise and the Chevalier were shown leaning against their nuptial bed, as servants tidied busily around them. Gabriel Marcel, never one of Planchon's admirers, thought that this materialisation was 'absolutely contrary to the spirit of Marivaux'.[14] The point is of course that although in Marivaux's day the situation might have been understood without being shown, today we are accustomed to having things made clear.

René Allio designed the sets. He placed enlarged reproductions of Watteau paintings around the back and sides of the stage. The style of the various rooms, and particularly of the ceilings, was thought out with care. The most stylish, in eighteenth-century terms, was that of the Marquise's bedroom, for which Allio took his inspiration from a ceiling in the Hôtel de Villette. (In Paris, quai Voltaire and rue de Beaune; formerly the Hôtel de Bragelongue, it was transformed in the eighteenth century by the writer the Marquis Charles de Villette. Voltaire spent his last year there.) In her reception room a more austere and formal ceiling suggested not only that this room was used for formal calls, but also that it was not new. The Chevalier is a poor younger son, and so the ceiling of his reception room was less ornate and more old-fashioned, a simple panelled ceiling of the sixteenth century. For the outdoor scenes, two entrances were placed, one on either side of the stage. The Marquise's door was a copy of that of the Hôtel Matignon (constructed around 1721, rue de Varenne, Paris, and now the seat of the Prime Minister). The Chevalier's door was again more austere and old-fashioned. Furniture, especially that in the Marquise's bedroom, was designed after paintings of the day and looked

low, comfortable, and relaxing. Costumes were copied from
paintings of the period as well, especially those of Watteau.

Planchon pointed out that Marivaux's characters are narcissistic: 'The class in power try to be fascinating and truly
do fascinate. The others look on. But these completely idle
people whom Marivaux shows us, at whom can they look, if
not at themselves? They would like, as they look at themselves, to find the picture fascinating.'[15] As a comment on
this narcissism, mirrors were in evidence everywhere. In
one case this visual metaphor was refined. The Chevalier
practised his fencing on a life-size dummy with a mirror
instead of a head – giving thus a visual expression of his
masochism.

In order to emphasise this motif of narcissism, Planchon
also had the actors play to one another. The aristocrats struck
poses, while the servants stared at them openly, with a candid interest in their affairs. Done with subtlety, this added
another dimension to the social picture: the aristocrats
expect their servants to take an interest only in them, and do
not imagine that they may have their own lives to lead.
Planchon wrote: '. . . in the midst of a line [act II, scene vi] the

La Seconde Surprise de l'amour, 1959. Malka Ribowska as the Marquise,
Pierre Meyrand as the Chevalier, Jean-Pierre Bernard as the Comte

Marquise suddenly senses that Lisette exists as someone else: this irks her. In act I, on the other hand, she speaks to her without even supposing that she might be different and have her own problems, such as her love for Lubin.'[16] In Villeurbanne productions there is no such thing as a 'foil' who is not a character in his or her own right.

As in the production of *George Dandin*, the principal characters in *La Seconde Surprise de l'amour* were surrounded by servants, occupied by the daily tasks of cleaning, cooking, etc. These servants were on the lowest level, beneath Lubin and Lisette, who are immediately beneath the master and mistress. Like the farmhands in *George Dandin* they were silent, endlessly busy, and without power. Lubin and Lisette have a say in their lives, but it is limited by their social position. Lubin, contrary to tradition, was not a clown in the Villeurbanne production. If he is comical, it is because he would not be tolerated otherwise. It is the form and not the content of Lubin's lines which is funny, for he is seriously interested in Lisette. He is expected by his master to play the buffoon, and he does so in order to attain his own goal, which is no different from that of his master. Planchon liked the modern tone of Lubin's speeches: 'Let us look at the story. Lubin, like his master, has lost a mistress, but he does not make a display of his grief; all in all, he speaks of it as we like to hear grief spoken of, with delicacy.'[17]

Music for the play was composed by Claude Lochy, who decided to reflect through harpsichord music the extreme sensitivity of the characters to the spoken word:

we have chosen the most Jansenist [puritanical, austere] ensemble there is: a trio of harpsichords capable of reproducing with all possible inflexions the cadences of this pure classicism ... The extreme delicacy of the characters, their sincerity, their way of holding in the violence of their passions, all this seemed to us to be expressed in the inflexions of these harpsichords, so thin, so melancholy, so austere.[18]

Language and music thus complemented each other in conveying the sensuousness and fragility of Marivaux's characters.

Planchon felt that his production of *La Seconde Surprise de l'amour* was a turning-point. It was the company's first serious study of love-conflicts in and for themselves. It was the first time their treatment of the theme was not an ironic one; their analysis (for analysis there inevitably was) was less critical than usual:

Of course, we still give criticism its place in this production (example: the Lisette–Marquise, Marquise–Hortensius relations) but I notice that the zone of pure description has become more important.

Some people think that theatre can only be negative or at least that all description must be critical to the maximum degree, but, I repeat, at a certain point criticism gives way to description.[19]

The movement towards a more descriptive theatre is evident in Planchon's plays even more than in his productions. His experience as a writer has probably helped to bring about the change.

One of the signs of this increasingly descriptive approach was his interest in the psychology of Marivaux's characters, in and for itself. The characters lie to one another, and in traditional productions, the actors show clearly that they are lying. Planchon considered this 'over-signifying' and thought it looked unlikely. In his production, the actors lied very convincingly, so that it seemed possible that the other characters, who are equally intelligent, might be deceived. Planchon was first attracted to Marivaux by the fullness of the characters. Far from being the pretty puppets which school texts and many traditional stage productions suggest, they are sensuous and alive:

The debate which opposes Marivaux's characters to one another is not an intellectual game free of all sensuality . . . but rather, a striving after carnal agreement. All prudery or ingenuousness are excluded from it; Marivaux's women are not unlike those of Laclos; quite simply they are less knowing, less lucid, though more sincere.[20]

The masters' forms of conversation, like those of the servants, were determined by their social position: the aristocrats must be refined and polite because they are the masters. There is little room for directness in their necessarily conventional language; they must lie prettily, intelligently, and constantly, and yet their goal is sensual. Planchon saw '. . . a peculiarly modern tension between the characters in Marivaux, between their appetites and feelings on the one hand and their social code of behaviour on the other'.[21]

Marivaux's characters are as they are because of their position in society. By juxtaposing toiling servants to idle masters, by showing that characters are bound by linguistic and social conventions, Planchon was making a clear though restrained comment on that society. With the utmost charm and elegance, the characters denounced their own artificiality and their egotism at every turn; by their intonations and gestures, they revealed that the pursuit of love by devious and roundabout games was their sole occupation. Looked at in this way, wrote Michel Vinaver, 'Marivaux's theatre, from rosy-coloured, veers to black. It offers the vision of a humanity closed to any sort of redemption; of a humanity whose movement, as enchanting as it is, is completely without hope.'[22] Planchon was to describe a similar world in his collage *Folies bourgeoises* in 1976, a world of trivial pursuits engaged in for their own sake.

It is true, as Elsa Triolet wrote, that:

La Seconde Surprise de l'amour was not written to show the idleness of its heroes, or the dependence of the domestic servants, which is like serfdom, but nevertheless, *with our perspective today*, this is more than obvious, and the way of giving an entourage to the amorous intrigues of the Marquise, the Comte and the Chevalier makes this idleness and this dependence more flagrant . . . this third dimension makes the whole affair more palpable, more dramatic . . . and more comical as well.[23] [my italics]

The play was intended as a comedy, like many of the plays on which Planchon based his *Folies bourgeoises*. In both cases, however, because the picture is true to life, it has a bitter undercurrent: these people are trapped in a world of trivial games, a world, not so much of dead souls, as of wasted souls. Planchon's production of *La Seconde Surprise de l'amour* succeeded in bringing out both the comedy of the Marivaux play, and the harsher truths which surround it, which are perceptible 'with our perspective today'.

MUSSET

On ne saurait penser à tout (One Cannot Think of Everything)
In the same programme as Marivaux's *La Seconde Surprise de l'amour*, at Villeurbanne from February to March 1959, Planchon presented a version of Alfred de Musset's *On ne saurait penser à tout*. He was assisted in directing the play by

Jacques Rosner. Unfortunately, as it was presented only at Villeurbanne and for a short run, very little information is available on this production.

Planchon no doubt chose to present this short play with *La Seconde Surprise de l'amour* because of its resemblance to the Marivaux play. Musset's little 'proverb' is a light comedy about a young Marquis and a widowed Comtesse who really wish to marry each other, but who are too absent-minded to come to a firm decision. Victoire, the Comtesse's maid, finally brings matters to a close by writing a note to remind the Marquis to propose and to be certain to get a definite answer. As in Marivaux's play, the aristocrats hesitate and the servants act.

Planchon seems to have interpreted the play in the spirit of the knockabout slapstick shows which he had developed to perfection at the Théâtre de la Comédie. He deliberately pushed fidelity to the text to the point of absurdity:

'A living room in the country'; that is the setting given by Musset to his proverb *On ne saurait penser à tout*. Roger Planchon has taken Musset literally . . . and the piano is in the ferns, the sofa becomes a tree trunk, and the wardrobes come down from the branches.[24]

The stage properties included such items as two canaries (one in good voice), a cuckoo-clock in working order, two butterfly nets, a hunting-horn, a gun, a backgammon set, a croquet set, a deck of cards, a watering-can, a great quantity of artificial flowers, and a number of green plants. As in *George Dandin*, no detail of country life was omitted: but here the country setting was a caricature.

Claude Lochy played the role of the forgetful young Marquis de Valberg, Jean Bouise his servant Germain. Bouise had to be taught the subtleties of backgammon for the play; the humorous possibilities of such a fine comic actor as Bouise demonstrating his skill at backgammon, croquet, etc., are manifold, particularly in a production which allowed for improvisation from the actors. The critic Gérard Guillot said that although he found the 'proverb' written by Musset unbearable to read, he had laughed heartily, along with the rest of the audience, at Planchon's presentation of it. It became at Villeurbanne:

A burlesque show in the finest vein, a burlesque in which plants grow by themselves and visibly beneath the watering-can, in which the butler carries all the houseware in his pockets, from the salt-cellar to a tin of shoe polish, in which the piano plays with no pianist as soon as the lid is raised . . . And all is carried along in a rapid, irresistible, hysterical movement, destroying reality one moment to reconstruct it the next. It is no longer Musset, some morose souls will say. Never mind that! . . . We laughed, laughed uproariously.[25]

The Villeurbanne production of *On ne saurait penser à tout* thus seems to have demonstrated Planchon's talent for maintaining pace as well as his unerring sense of humour.

RACINE

Bérénice
Racine is probably the playwright most venerated by French critics, and Roger Planchon's productions of *Bérénice* in 1966, 1969, and 1970 provoked a shock wave among them.

By the mid-sixties, Planchon believed that ideally 'a dialogue establishes itself between the classics and the successive eras which put them on', and it is useful to compare this view to that of Brecht: 'The Socialist Realist performance of old classical works is based on the view that mankind has preserved those works which give artistic expression to advances toward a continually stronger, bolder, and more delicate humanity.'[26] There is a traditional view that the meaning of a text is immutably and eternally fixed, and that we should subordinate our own sensibility and experience to that meaning; and there is the diametrically opposed opinion that we can impose on a play, unilaterally, a meaning relevant to our day but perhaps superfluous to, or even in contradiction with, the text. Either approach cuts off the ideal dialogue between the classics and us. When he read *Bérénice*, therefore, Planchon tried to respect the play in itself while making it come alive for his own audience.

Racine presents a special difficulty for a director accustomed to reading a play through its events. Because the action is reduced to essentials, traditional interpretations have concentrated on the psychology of the characters. Planchon approached this psychology from a different direction. He looked carefully at the events which do take place in the play, not only the external riots, the delegations to the palace, but especially the decisions taken by Titus and his reversals of them. 'The chronology of events is important', wrote Planchon, 'because this is what throws the greatest light on the behaviour of the characters.'[27] We learn of these events only through the speeches of the characters, and the speeches are coloured by a given character's feelings at a given moment in the play. Planchon made it clear to the actors that characters must repeatedly redefine themselves to the audience and suggest that they never are completely accurate in their self-appraisals.

When Roger Planchon looked carefully at Titus's actions, he concluded, despite three centuries of productions showing the opposite view, that Titus does not love Bérénice. Roland Barthes wrote in 1960 that he thought Titus was attached to Bérénice not by love but only by habit, and that the play was the story of a leave-taking which Titus hesitates to initiate.[28] Rome, in the opinion of Barthes and of Planchon, is a pretext and not the reason for Titus's repudiation of Bérénice. Planchon wanted to present the play in a resolutely modern perspective, and it is true, as Gérard Guillot pointed out, '. . . that today love breaks through all barriers, all conventions, all traditions. That Titus does not overlook everyone else and marry Bérénice is admitting that he no longer loves her.'[29] In this instance, however, it would seem that Planchon overstepped himself. It is true that contemporaries of Racine (quoted in the Villeurbanne programme for *Bérénice*) expressed the opinion that Titus did not love her. On the other hand, it is disregarding the force of conventions in societies vastly different from our own, and, more importantly, it is disregarding the text itself to say that Titus is bored with Bérénice. Perhaps he does not love her enough, but he definitely loves her, and it is precisely this love which makes the act of separation so difficult to undertake.

Racine, although he used the figures of Titus and Bérénice, based his play on the love affair between Louis XIV (then prince) and Marie Mancini. Planchon tried in his production, therefore, to reconcile Racine's ideas of the classical age with the love conventions of the seventeenth century, and to put the whole into a modern perspective. The set was conceived as one which would represent both an idealised classical Rome, the court of France under the regency of Anne of Austria, and the world of Louis XIV:

an ideal society in which princes are at the same time admirable politicians, brave warriors and sublime lovers. War, love and politics, all sublime . . . The set therefore evokes a room in a palace belonging to an ideal society. This society is neither Rome nor the Versailles of Louis XIV. It is the past. A fantasy Louis XIII court borrowing elements from Rome (the armour), from Versailles (the mirrors), etc.[30]

The set was a greenish-bronze palace with sombre panelling. On one side was a dais decorated with billowing blue and white brocade draperies embroidered with a B and a T interlaced; on it lay luxurious creamy-white fur rugs. At the back was a very high cabinet of mirrors. The costumes were those of the court of Louis XIII, with a slight suggestion of Mantegna about them. A crowd of extras represented the court, made up of cardinals as well as Roman senators.

The mirrors, of course, were there to recall Versailles. As in *La Seconde Surprise de l'amour*, the characters are narcissistic, and watch each other and themselves; the mirrors emphasised this theme. Roland Barthes believes that in Racinian tragedy, each character wishes to *see* the other humiliated before him, to feel victorious by witnessing the other's defeat with his own eyes.[31] The mirrors in Planchon's set extended the possibilities for this visual possession of one character by another. The shifting reflections were also a scenic parallel to the misapprehensions and the indecision of the main characters. Their inflated gestures and movements were multiplied to infinity, and shown to be unreal in themselves, theatrical in all senses of the word.

Another feature of the staging was meant to point out this self-dramatising tendency in the characters: the sound of footsteps offstage. They were heard even before the lights went up, while the set stood empty, to suggest a distant crowd. They were heard again four more times in the course of the production, and Planchon himself explained their purpose. He gave as an example Titus's monologue in act IV, in which he decides to go and speak to Bérénice. He walks toward the door but stops on the threshold:

Then the rhythm of the steps is taken up by the sound, and the character (who has stopped) hears, along with the spectator, his steps continuing in the palace, sounding on the tiles, and then he hears the sound of his boots abruptly stopping as though his audible 'double' had just taken the decision not to continue any further.

This use of a sound effect is subjective, more than that it seeks to give an ironic clue to the subjectivity which is displayed before us . . . If the spectator sees the character standing still on stage 'hearing' the splendid echo of his footsteps (a disproportionate, inflated echo) continue and in a way duplicate his action because the steps in their turn stop, the spectator is forearmed to understand ironically what the situation is.[32]

The steps also increased the sense of a watchful world outside. Like the offstage echoes and sounds in *Tartuffe*, they suggested that there were people behind the walls; in this play, they were people ready to interfere. Titus does not make his decision in a vacuum.

To translate the strict constraints of Alexandrine verse into stage language, Planchon decided to impose a very rigid *mise en place* on his actors. They moved only in straight lines, or at right angles in simple, defined geometric patterns. There were no small movements, although a few curved movements were used, all the more important because they were few. This geometrical stage movement conveyed the rigid authority of the court and of Rome behind it, and increased the sense of unreality of the world presented. Moving within this strict pattern, the actors amplified their gestures and gave their *tirades* their full emotional force. They sighed, shouted, were ostentatiously 'brave', alternated between brutality and self-pity, joy and defeat. Racine creates a passionate intensity of feeling within a rigidly conventional verse form; Planchon demanded a verbal violence from his actors within a pre-arranged and rigid pattern of movement.

Planchon chose young actors for the main parts, Sami Frey as Titus, Francine Bergé as Bérénice, Denis Manuel as Antiochus; this further departure from convention was a significant one. Planchon chose young actors precisely because he felt that the behaviour of the protagonists, their prevarication, their vanity, their lack of moderation, was typical of adolescents. He said during discussions of the play: '. . . I would like . . . the public to have in the presence of the characters a critical attitude, while at the same time feeling sympathetic. We are all, we have all been a Titus or a Bérénice.'[33] Because of the youthfulness of the three principals, their *confidents* took on a new significance. They represented more than 'straight men' prompting long speeches; they were, rather, authority figures, older and more experienced, trying to put the three young people on the right path. Planchon was aware that in classical tragedy the lady-in-waiting herself is a princess or a great lady, who would not scruple to give sound advice, especially to a young girl.

The youth of the actors unfortunately robbed the play of its sense of a long-matured passion. Planchon found the characters immature because they are almost totally self-centred. He was disregarding the fact that Racine's characters are placed in a hothouse of passions separate from the 'real' world. The outer world exists only insofar as it helps or hinders their passion. In this case it (Rome) hinders it. Planchon overlooked Racinian conventions to some extent in this production.

It was, nevertheless, the youthfulness of the actors and their energetic performances which most startled and impressed the critics. Brecht, and Planchon after him, thought that an actor should always show how, at a given moment, he has the choice between the behaviour which he adopts and that which he does not adopt; in other words he should never give the impression of following a pre-arranged script, but rather of being free and unaware of the future. Francine Bergé as Bérénice succeeded very well in conveying this ignorance of the future, mainly through her delight in the present. She was, at first, a young woman conscious of her charms and confident in their power to hold Titus. Some of her early lines thus came alive with irony and coquettishness. Her insouciance gave way only gradually as she realised, little by little, and in spite of her attempts to deceive herself, that she is about to be rejected. A jesting Célimène at the beginning, in the moment of truth she was literally struck to the ground by the violence of her grief, and the true power of Racine's text came through. She left the spectator with a final impression of utter loss, of permanent grief.

Sami Frey's performance as Titus was fraught with emotion, and it made more than one critic question Roger Planchon's claim that Titus has become bored with his mistress and is trying to get rid of her. Frey's performance suggested not only cowardice and indecision but also shame and self-loathing, not weariness with Bérénice but deep and genuine grief at having to part with her. It was a performance of swiftly alternating moods reflecting a tormenting indecision, '. . . an extraordinary study in inner paralysis periodically breaking free into shuddering violence'.[34] Although Planchon the analyst of Racine may have concluded that

Titus was not in love, perhaps Planchon the director found that the play works best as a love play.

Even the usually dull Antiochus gained a new importance in this production. Denis Manuel played the role in a more traditional way than the other two principal actors. He shared the narcissism of the other two and their adolescent self-centredness. But his own painful if not desperate situation was made, for once, to seem worthy of concern. The critic Raymonde Temkine even wrote, amusingly:

That Denis Manuel was able to make endearing a role whose reputation for dullness, one believed, was justly acquired, is proof of Planchon's revitalising work and of the talent of the young actor. For the first time, no doubt, one was interested in this young man . . . to the point of wishing, against all logical necessity, trivially, that the repudiated queen would find consolaton in him.[35]

The characters of *Bérénice* do not exist in a specific historical world. Their context is an idealised world, in which nevertheless their sentiments appear both human and immature. The play does not lend itself easily to a strict Marxist analysis. That Planchon chose to do it at all is an indication of his increasing interest at the time in 'descriptive' rather than 'critical' theatre. He succeeded in giving it a vitality seldom found in new interpretations of the classics.

Bérénice, 1966. Titus (Sami Frey) seated, with his retinue

PART II

The playwright

6

Five musical comedies: the more the merrier

In Planchon's work as a playwright there are two distinct currents. First, there are the spectacular shows created with the collaboration of the entire company, and including many songs and dances: these are the five musical comedies. Secondly, there are the more traditional dramatic works to which Planchon claims individual authorship, namely the peasant plays and the two modern comedies, as well as *Bleus, blancs, rouges*. Planchon shows similar preoccupations in both types of production, but he presents them in a different way. The spectacular shows are openly satirical and ask questions explicitly. In the other plays, ideas are presented implicitly, within the fable, and are treated more seriously.

Five of the plays written at the Théâtre de la Cité were not signed by Planchon, or at least not by Planchon alone: *Les Trois Mousquetaires, O M'man Chicago, La Contestation et la mise en pièces de la plus illustre des tragédies françaises 'Le Cid' de Pierre Corneille, suivies d'une 'cruelle' mise à mort de l'auteur dramatique et d'une distribution gracieuse de diverses conserves culturelles, La Langue au Chat*, and *Folies bourgeoises*. These were plays for which the cast and the technical team often took an active part in the elaboration of the production, and even sometimes of the text. They are, more than Planchon's other plays, the product of constant group work. All five rely to a great extent upon music and dance, and upon slapstick comedy, and all five are satires. All these plays are about myths – literary, theatrical, social, or political.

Les Trois Mousquetaires (The Three Musketeers)
The play *Les Trois Mousquetaires* was a *création collective* first presented in 1958 and repeatedly recreated until 1969. The Théâtre de la Cité, as we have seen, first decided on the Dumas novel after a survey of their Villeurbanne public uncovered a general interest in Dumas.

113

The play had a predecessor, the slapstick cloak-and-dagger romp put on at the tiny Théâtre de la Comédie in 1954, *Cartouche*. By 1958, however, this kind of burlesque was no longer popular, and furthermore the 1500 seat Villeurbanne theatre would have been an inappropriate setting for it. The nineteenth-century play by Maquet and the 1951 adaptation by René-Maurice Picard were equally dated. The company therefore set out to create a new play based on Dumas's novel. Claude Lochy wrote a two-hundred page adaptation of the novel, and Planchon edited it until it was little more than an outline giving thematic indications. The actors then met to elaborate a playable text by improvising on this framework of ideas. They kept in mind, in the course of their work, the ideas prevalent in Dumas's day, and the historical background of the book. The resulting script was linear and action-orientated.

The troupe decided to add to the adaptation '*le petit grain de sable du quotidien*' (the little sand pebble of the everyday, the grating note) which would show up Alexandre Dumas's excessive romanticism. It was a method which the company was to use again, to debunk Al Capone in *O M'man Chicago*, and to make fun of the theatrical and political fads of the late sixties in *La Mise en pièces du 'Cid'*. In rehearsal, the trivial detail which would show up a serious scene might suggest itself in unexpected ways. Planchon told of the way in which one tableau, the courting of the Queen by Buckingham, took its final shape:

This show was conceived by the entire group of actors and by a few involuntary contributors; we were rehearsing the great love scene between Buckingham and the Queen, the classic adultery scene (all French theatre, from Dumas to Claudel, has applied itself to treating this scene) in which beautiful feelings unfurl themselves in deep, romantic undulations. Two workmen came into the rehearsal room with a ladder; the rehearsal, imperturbably, continued. The workmen left but the ladder stayed. Since then, we have a chandelier being cleaned during this love scene.[1]

In the production, much of the fun sprang from the juxtaposition of the grandiose and the trivial, and the very serious way in which both levels were presented.

The set designer in 1958 was Jean-Louis Bertin. The set was designed to permit a fast flow of movement, to present necessary background facts left out of the text, and to suggest

Les Trois Mousquetaires. Comic love scene between Buckingham, perched
on a stepladder, and the Queen

a slightly old-fashioned atmosphere, the flavour of a child's
storybook. All the action took place silhouetted against a red
semi-sphere, which reminded the audience (the regular
theatre-goers, at any rate) of Vilar and of Brecht. The costumes were in white to brown colours, and were carefully
copied from engravings by Jacques Callot and Abraham
Bosse (painters and engravers of the seventeenth-century).
Styles of furniture and architecture for each scene indicated
the social origin of the characters onstage; for Aramis,
Milady, and the convent, the decor was inspired by Louis
XIII fashion, that is, the bourgeois fashion of the day; for
royalty these styles were romantic, and indeed Wagnerian.
As in Vilar's and Barrault's productions, props were reduced
to a stylised minimum, like toys improvised from everyday
objects. Two bits of cloth at varying angles to each other were
used to suggest the narrow lanes of a still-medieval Paris,
allowing characters to run down a 'road', appear around a
'corner', etc. Characters came on on foot, tapping their heels,

on 'horseback' on a white stick, or in a 'carriage' made up of two pieces of cloth held by stagehands. D'Artagnan returned from England on a ship which was a piece of fabric 'floating' on the undulations of three large strips of cloth moved by black-clad stagehands. When Allio became set designer, he used a sloping stage, with the aim of giving the actors' movements an epic, three-dimensional quality.

As the show based much of its appeal on the dance sequences, the musical accompaniment was very important. Lochy composed an accompaniment for small band, which was more flexible than a large orchestra. The music was sprightly and had a strong rhythm, which helped to maintain the pace of the production. It complemented the realism of costumes and acting, but it also included the occasional discordant note which paralleled the use of the *grain de sable du quotidien* on the stage.

The structure of the stage adaptation was modelled on that of the novel, and so long periods of time had to be telescoped into a few moments on the stage. Taking his inspiration from sources as diverse as American slapstick films and the Peking Opera, Planchon devised many theatrical abbreviations to portray the adventures of Dumas's heroes. The play was a succession of brilliant shortcuts. It began with a series of rapid tableaux, unified by an actor who occasionally called out the number of the page or the chapter which was being enacted. The central adventure in the book, the race to retrieve the Queen's diamonds from Buckingham for her, became onstage something between a dance, a game of 'goose' (played with dice on a board, and formerly common in England and France), and a football match. The stage was divided into a large goose board, and the Queen and the Cardinal cast the dice in turn, controlling the movements of the musketeers from square to square. The point was thus made that the musketeers are pawns used by the Queen and the Cardinal; the excitement of the chase was also maintained without its melodramatic overtones. The return of the box of diamonds to the Queen was played for fun, with the musketeers displaying a fine passing style as they threw it across to one another.

Most of these techniques were not only shortcuts, but also a way of debunking Dumas's romantic vision of the events. Battles and duels especially were very impertinently treated. Planchon no doubt knew of the 1945 production of *Antony*

and Cleopatra at the Comédie-Française, in which Jean-
Louis Barrault had made his actors *dance* the battle of
Actium. The Peking Opera also performed in Paris in 1955,
and its use of dance and symbolic gesture certainly influenced Planchon, in the same way as the Balinese theatre had
impressed Antonin Artaud in 1931. Many of the battles in
Les Trois Mousquetaires were changed into dance numbers,
from flamencos to cha-chas. At the battle of La Rochelle, for
example, with standards swirling, heels tapping, and a drum
beating, the French and the English took turns treading upon
one another's feet, occasionally 'killing' one another with the
flap of a flag, and calling each other names:

De Winter: Messieurs les Français, you will never be anything
but . . .
All the English: Pa-pists.
Jussac: Messieurs les Anglais, you are nothing but . . .
All the French: Hu-guenots.
The English: Feti-shists.
The French: Here-tics.[2]

Walter Kerr the New York critic described some of the fight
sequences. Some were absurd and hilarious: 'Somehow or
other an entire contingent of Cardinal's guards and King's
musketeers manage to squeeze themselves into a free-
standing picture-frame, where they fight at such close quar-
ters that they wind up in each other's arms.' Others acquired
grace and beauty: '. . . the lights go out to reveal a pitched
battle being fought by orange rapiers and purple plumes in
the abstract . . . '[3] Often duels ended on an anti-climax. The
famous duel between d'Artagnan and the three musketeers
was interrupted by an absent-minded passer-by asking for
the way to Chinon, and then setting off in the opposite
direction! In another instance, when the musketeers were
creating a row in the street at night, attacking one another
with noisy slaps in the face, an old lady intervened from her
window: 'Have you finished making such a racket? Can we
get some sleep now? Myself, I work in the daytime!'[4] Death
scenes in the production were never frightening, but usually
succinct, and sometimes elegant. Killed by the musketeers,
five Cardinal's guards 'died' by putting a black hat or a black
glove up to their faces, as in the Chinese theatre.
   The characters in the play were all placed in irretrievably
commonplace situations which made any pomposity on

their part seem ludicrous. Richelieu, in a scene which enraged so many spectators that it became famous (sc. 19), fried himself an egg while he plotted with Lady de Winter; wearing a white apron over his shrimp-coloured surplice, he looked less the history-book statesman than a simple gourmand. Buckingham was killed trying to ward off his assailant by splashing bathwater on him. Not even the King was spared, appearing every now and then to ask for directions in his confusingly large palace, the Louvre; at one point it was clear that he wanted directions to the lavatory.

The love scene between the Queen and Buckingham was staged to show up nineteenth-century styles of dialogue and romantic notions of love. Buckingham had to make his impassioned declaration beneath a shaky ladder (an idea genuinely, if unconsciously, contributed by the working class), on which two workmen perched trying to dust the chandelier. Isabelle Sadoyan as the Queen acted in strict Comédie-Française style, carrying her hands before her like precious objects, as in the famous Velázquez painting of Anne of Austria. Her completely serious tone underlined the silliness of her lines, as in this speech about her previous meeting with Buckingham:

Alone? No, we were not alone, there was a Cardinal's man in every thicket. I have not forgotten what followed, the outburst of the King, no doubt encouraged by Monsieur le Cardinal, Madame de Chevreuse my only friend, condemned to retirement. Myself deprived of dessert for four months.[5]

The lovers, attempting high-flown imagery, finished by using inelegant and even coarse language, and their dialogue was punctuated by the even more colloquial speech of the workers. As Buckingham is disguised as one of them, they eventually call out to him, 'All right, Gustave-Françoué, or whatever your name is, why don't you come and hold the ladder?' and 'Hey you, if you're not happy down there there's plenty of work up here.'[6] Finally, the hapless Buckingham is compelled to go up and help, and to try being a romantic lover while dusting a moving chandelier on an uncertain ladder. Critics were completely delighted with this inventive and hilarious scene.

Planchon debunked not only Dumas's romantic mystique of greatness, but also the fierce misogyny of his novel, as it comes out in his picture of Lady de Winter. In order to make the public aware of it, the production emphasised the men's brutality to the women. Mme Bonacieux narrowly escaped the unwanted attentions of the four musketeers by appealing to their patriotism. Athos squashed Lady de Winter's hand in a drawer, and pinched her gleefully when she was over-powered. Her death was staged for all its gory fun, with the ghosts of her successive husbands coming to gloat at her beheading. Before dying, she removed her mask to reveal, not evil incarnate (as Dumas would have us believe she is), but an innocent and beautiful young girl. Instead of the well-deserved punishment which it seems in the novel, her execution thus became what it really is, an act of brutality perpetrated by a group of men on one woman.

Much of the fun of the production lay in its pastiches of every conceivable form of theatre. It mocked everything theatrical, in France and abroad, from Claudel to Ionesco, Barrault to Vilar, the Comédie-Française to the Berliner Ensemble. Comic and dramatic effects were borrowed from almost every source imaginable; music hall, circus, the Marx brothers, Bob Hope, Jerry Lewis, Russian ballet . . . The gags were innumerable. A musical staff walked onstage with singers' heads instead of notes; Richelieu contacted his aides by walkie-talkie; a periscope emerged from the floor and surveyed the action. When the Queen was ordered to undress to be searched for a love letter (sc. 16), the scene was hidden at the vital moment with a panel saying 'censored', and followed immediately with the letter being handed to the King. At the end, d'Artagnan was lifted up to the heavens in a final triumphant whirl, like an Olympian god.

Entire scenes were obvious pastiches. Mme Bonacieux's escape from prison was played like a scene from Claudel's *Le Soulier de satin*, as staged by Barrault. Not only did her speech take on a mock-Claudelian lyricism; she also offered one of her shoes to her jailer, just as Dona Prouhèze leaves hers with the statue of the Virgin. Nothing was sacred: even Brecht was mocked. Rochefort, the jailer, decided to stage the scene of the arrest of Mme Bonacieux, for the benefit of Richelieu, with alienating device. The tall dark rubber-faced Jean Bouise stood forward pulling a child's wagon inscribed 'Mutter Bonacieux', and declared coldly, 'I represent Mme Bonacieux. I am a young person twenty-five or twenty-six years old. I have a peaches-and-cream complexion, a slightly turned-up nose, I have no moustache . . .'[7] After his speech he sang a little song, in the Lehrstück (didactic play) tradition, a parody of the songs which Brecht included in his plays as a means of expression equal to the spoken text.

Planchon borrowed from whatever medium would be most expedient and appropriate. The perfect sense of timing for which he was to become recognised gave even such an apparently disorganised production the smooth flow of a film. Indeed it recalled Hellzapoppin for several of the critics; it certainly had the same chaotic rhythm. In one scene (7, p. 32), d'Artagnan stopped speaking in mid-syllable. The actors looked at one another in silent dismay; d'Artagnan tried to speak again but still there was no sound. A stagehand then appeared carrying a placard apologising for technical difficulties. For a few moments the action continued as a pantomime, with stagehands carrying in balloon-shaped signs for the next few lines of dialogue. Suddenly a tape recorder squealed out some speeches at chipmunk pitch, and then the 'sound' returned to normal. The use of balloons for speech brought the comic-strip world on to the stage. The technique was used very cleverly in some productions abroad: on opening night on Broadway, for instance, the actors suddenly went silent, and a team of stagehands carried in balloons with the English translation of the lines just spoken.

In the course of the play's long career from 1958 to 1969, the production was renewed so many times that only a fraction of the gags and pastiches could be shown in any one presentation. The play made fun of new styles as they came into fashion. One senses the influence of such television programmes as The Monty Python Show or the American Laugh-in in the gags used in the late sixties (for example, a giant fist coming down from the flies to punch characters, a hand coming out from the floor to be stepped on . . .). Occasionally unintended changes were made. In London in 1960, an English stagehand heard so much laughter he thought the play had ended and so brought down the curtain – in mid-scene. The audience, thinking this was yet another gag, laughed all the more. Planchon said that the reason for making modifications in the production was '. . . to overcome the boredom of . . .doing it again and again; we would remove a portion, add on a piece. Thus from beginning to end it would add up to an eight-hour show.'[8]

Although each presentation was thus a selection from a large number of gags, some critics, and especially the Americans, found that the jokes were too numerous. Walter Kerr complained that the show lost sight of Dumas completely: '. . . there were no scenes from the novel substantial enough to serve as true targets for the jest; we were improvising about a cipher'.[9] There was a Dumas aphorism quoted in the programme: 'It is permissible to rape history, but on condition that one get it with child.' One critic, Paul Morelle, asked '. . . can one, in turn, get with child the child of history?'[10] Morelle also complained that the show was too erudite, and aimed at well-educated theatre-goers rather than at a popular public. *Le Monde*'s Poirot-Delpech, too, sensed that the innumerable allusions in the production might be too esoteric: 'Planchon will be criticised for having organised his "gags" a little too much for the benefit of the professionals.'[11] This was a serious charge, and somewhat startling when one considers that Planchon thought of the play's international success as that of a good-natured romp, and was even somewhat embarrassed in later years at its lack of sophistication. The fact that the play was successful internationally was in itself evidence that its slapstick fun appealed to people who could not grasp all the textual references or the visual allusions to theatrical styles. The very wealth of gags which annoyed some critics, as well as the unrelenting gaiety of the production, made the show entertaining for audiences of all kinds. Each person could enjoy it at his or her own level of sophistication.

Planchon did not approve of Dumas's philosophy, but he admired the cloak-and-dagger excitement and youthful adventurousness of the novel. Because he succeeded in capturing onstage this sense of a rapid, joyous, all-enveloping movement, some reviewers thought that Planchon shared Dumas's kind of patriotic fervour. They were mistaken. The Théâtre de la Cité set out from the start to avoid identification with Dumas's values. Indeed the programme stated that they had systematically cut out or ridiculed passages which extolled patriotism or virility. The play was deliberately anti-heroic, deliberately anti-militaristic. According to the Moscow critic, Vadim Gaevski, Planchon had produced a comédie-ballet, in which the dance sequences were a poetic expression of opposition to bourgeois order:

In the show the element of dance enters everywhere; it seems that here precisely is that elusive internal enemy which is feared above all by the 'intrepid' military and the 'perspicacious' politicians. And in fact the main conflict of the show is expressed by plastic means; it is the conflict between dance and military drill.[12]

The great battles were depicted as children's games, the duels were derided, the noble musketeers were depicted as hired killers. The political actions of those in power were shown to be taken for trivial or evil reasons. Thus *Les Trois Mousquetaires*, created and put on mainly for fun, made its point too about the shibboleths of patriotism, honour in battle, of glamour and virility, and of the evil influence of womankind. Dumas's novel was its target and provided its structural basis but, continually renewed, it remained a witty and unrelenting demystifier of contemporary myths.

O M'man Chicago (Oh Ma Chicago)
Planchon wrote *O M'man Chicago* in 1963 with the avowed intention of creating another play with the immense popular appeal of *Les Trois Mousquetaires*.

When Planchon read accounts of the Al Capone story, he found that the facts of his career were as distorted by writers as the historical realities of the seventeenth century had been by Dumas. He was dealing with a legend quite similar to that which Dumas had created, a glorified picture of gangsters. Whereas every Frenchman knows his Dumas practically by heart, however, few people in France have a clear idea of the Capone story. Lacking a specific narrative around which a satire could be built, Planchon had to write the story of Al Capone rather than parody it. He did, however, make the gangsters into buffoons; unlike Brecht's *The Resistible Rise of Arturo Ui*, this was not intended as a historical tract.

The play was not to the same extent as *Les Trois Mousquetaires* a collective work. It was written by Roger Planchon after considerable research into the period. The play centred on two main themes, the study of Capone as a person, and the study of the circumstances which allow him to appear as a 'great man'. Planchon created around the figure of Capone three dream figures; the first, M'man Chicago, representing both Capone's mother and the city of Chicago; the second, Fool Daddy's Fog, a symbol of the misty city itself; and the third, Pottawattomie, a crippled Indian, the last survivor of the extermination of his people by the white man's civilisation. Asked in a university discussion about the presence of

M'man Chicago in the play, Planchon said by way of expla-
nation that '. . . according to some of Freud's analyses, gangsters have an obsessive affection for their mother. Thus, Al
Capone projects, in his imagination, a figure which is at the
same time his mother – the city of Chicago – and the woman
he loves.'[13]

The play is divided into nineteen tableaux, with many
song and dance sequences. It follows Capone's own reminiscences about his career. He enters at the start feeling that he
has failed, and wondering how to tell his life story. The three
dream figures then appear and lead the cast through a
number of scenes, dances, and songs, up to a final trial scene.
The main conflict throughout is of course between the
Sicilian criminals led by Capone and their Irish competitors
for the illegal trade in alcohol. In the course of his career,
Capone decides at one point to become honest. In order to
succeed in business, he needs capital, however, and so he
must continue his criminal activities until he has saved up
enough money. He becomes prosperous by organising his
underground business efficiently, but the 1929 stock-market
crash ruins him. At his trial (as really happened) he is eventually sentenced for income-tax evasion.

In order to meet the challenge of recreating in French the
American underworld slang of the 1920s, Planchon invented
almost a new language, rich in imagery, and full of witty
comparisons reminiscent of westerns, old gangster films,
and Hollywood scripts in general. It is deliberately artificial,
sometimes convoluted (especially the song lyrics), and full
of the cliché as well as the unexpected. It is almost impossible to translate its flavour back into English. Typical sentences are: 'They will serve you up on a platter, as an hors-
d'oeuvre, a massacre that will make the War of Secession
look like a picnic' (sc. 10, p. 59), and, 'Al, your little guy is
rusting my spurs with his ethical remarks' (sc. 1, p. 1).[14]

Despite the extent of his personal work on the script,
Planchon refused to sign the play, except as its co-director
with Jacques Rosner. It was, he insisted, the work of a group;
fifty people had participated in creating *O M'man Chicago*.
Song and dance were extremely important; indeed the story
was seen as a pretext for creating a kind of ballet, a comédie-
ballet. Claude Lochy composed music for Planchon's songs,
which was based on the tango and Charleston of the twenties, but transposed and recreated, like ballet music.

A quick glance at the songs gives an idea of their importance in crystallising the conflicts within the play, and in
marking the various stages of Capone's defeat. They are as
important as Brecht's songs for his own plays, and in fact this
play recalls Brecht's *Threepenny Opera* much more than it
does *The Resistible Rise of Arturo Ui*: it is lively, bright, and
generally light-hearted. Near the beginning the *Chant de la
Prohibition* (*Song of Prohibition*, sc. 1, p. 7), sung by the
gangsters, expresses their gratitude to the leagues of virtue
for banning alcohol and creating such possibilities for organised crime. The *Chant des vierges de Chicago* (*Song of the
Virgins of Chicago*, sc. 4, p. 25) is a belligerent warning to
lawbreakers. When Capone's empire begins to crumble,
Garibaldi, one of his followers who is insane, sings a little
song entitled *La Ménopause chez le racketeer* (*The Racketeer's Menopause*, sc. 13, p. 74). The last song, *La Cale
prend l'eau* (*The Hold is Leaking*) (sc. 16, pp. 95–6), is performed by the assembled gangsters; it expresses the passing
of their reign and the birth of a bureaucratic era in which
even vice is tied up in red tape.

As in *Les Trois Mousquetaires*, dance sequences were used
in battle scenes, with gangsters shooting one another to the
rhythm of a fox-trot or a Charleston, or dying in a kind of
jerking tap-dance. Dance was also used in the dream
sequences. In a scene entitled 'La Pluie' (The Rain), for
instance, all Capone's murder victims are standing under
umbrellas on a rainy day in the cemetery. M'man Chicago
arrives and they begin to carry her train; the march becomes a
dance, the dance a tango, until M'man Chicago takes a broom
and sweeps all the others off the stage. The scene ends with
Capone and M'man Chicago waltzing together to a syrupy
and funereal tune.

André Acquart designed a simple and quickly transformable set appropriate in a production made up largely of dance
numbers. It consisted of several panels and doors which
could pivot around, a few tables which were lowered from
the flies, and lighting which varied to change the atmosphere of the set completely from one moment to the next.
The costumes were stylised and flamboyantly reminiscent
of the twenties. At one point (sc. 16, p. 69) Capone wants
to redecorate his headquarters for a party. He begins by
ordering a pistachio-green decor with heart-shaped settees,
mirrors in the ceiling, and pornographic frescoes. Imme-

O M'man Chicago, Théâtre de la Cité de Villeurbanne, 1963. One of the song and dance sequences, with M'man Chicago on a cart

diately painters, plasterers, and removers enter to change the set. A few lines later he wants the decor changed to a pre-dominantly red one with white leather, polished wood, etc., and the set was once again transformed immediately. It was no doubt possible to suggest this instant redecoration with a few simple props, careful lighting, and a carefully choreographed bustle of extras.

Many of the gags in the show were a part of the Théâtre de la Cité's repertoire: coffins on wheels, suburban picnics, cigarette butts picked up and eaten, etc. The use of dream-figures, and the constant changes from dream to reality, as well as the *Ubu-Roi*-like interpretation of Capone and his gangsters, showed the surrealistic strain in Planchon's work. As we have seen (p. 2), he, like many of his generation, came to the theatre through the surrealists, and this first influence came out especially in the musical comedies. The 'analysis' of Capone is not taken seriously in the play, but the idea of staging his 'unconscious' at all, even for fun, was surrealist-inspired.

The critics were impressed by Planchon's production, but

many were dismayed by the text. In an attempt to make his characters' artificial speech sound as though they spoke it every day, Planchon had his actors speak quickly. Unfortunately the text, even in reading, is not an easy one to follow, and much of it was lost in the actors' fast delivery. The response of the critics was almost like that which they were to have to the difficult *Troilus and Cressida* in the following year. Fortunately, in this case (and one gets this impression even from reading the play), it was a production which came to life through the staging, in which dance and movement and song were the important elements, because the main intention was to create an evening's fun.

Of course, the ironies of the Capone story were brought out, too: virtue (prohibition) favoured vice (bootlegging); notorious murderers were eventually sentenced for income-tax evasion: as the programme pointed out, 'This relentless-ness of the law in recovering illegally gained money made the killers indignant.' The comparison with Arturo Ui imposes itself: Planchon showed Capone as Brecht showed his Hitler/Capone figure to be no more than a petty, power-hungry ruffian. As in *The Resistible Rise of Arturo Ui*, there was a strong criticism of the society and the government which allowed such a gangster to rise to power, but in Planchon's play the criticism was implicit, and it was subordinated to the comedy. There were numerous references to Capone's power over the authorities of Chicago through bribery and intimidation. When a police inspector declares that he will never be bought, Capone answers unperturbed: 'No fear, Inspector. My job is to buy the guys who pay you.'[15]

In spite of these allusions to corruption, people saw the play as an entertaining spectacular which debunked crime fiction and the Al Capone legend in a very amusing way. More than one critic saw in the show an example of 'total theatre' in the Wagnerian sense of a fusion of the arts of music and poetry. From reading the text, one gets the impression that the songs, dances, and the sheer fun of the production were more important than its 'message', and that comparisons to Wagner were perhaps a little too grand. It was an intelligent spoof, and Gérard Guillot concluded his review of the play by calling the production '. . . an authentic engine of war against today's intellectual stultification'.[16] In this, *O M'man Chicago* was clearly a forerunner to *La Mise en pièces du 'Cid'*, in which the attack on intellecutal stultification (*la décervellisation*) was to be made explicit in the concrete form of a 'culture machine'.

La Mise en pièces du 'Cid' (The Tearing to Pieces of 'Le Cid')
The Contestation and Tearing to Pieces of the Most Illustrious of French Tragedies 'Le Cid' by Pierre Corneille, Followed by a 'Cruel' Putting to Death of the Playwright and by a Gracious Distribution of Diverse Cultural Preserves is the English version of the title *La Contestation et la mise en pièces de la plus illustre des tragédies françaises 'Le Cid' de Pierre Corneille suivies d'une 'cruelle' mise à mort de l'auteur dramatique et d'une distribution gracieuse de diverses conserves culturelles*. It is the full title of a play which became known as *La Mise en pièces du 'Cid'*. Like *O M'man Chicago*, it was created with *Les Trois Mousquetaires* in mind. Just as the Dumas novel had been used as a pretext for making fun of fads in the theatre, television, and the cinema, so Corneille's play, chosen because it is the best-known of French classics, was used as a starting-point for a play about theatre in the 1960s. The very long title was itself a parody of Peter Weiss's play known in Britain as *The Persecution and Assassination of Marat as Performed by the Inmates of the Asylum of Charenton under the Direction of the Marquis de Sade*.

The play was created as a collage by the entire company, in 1969, when the events of May 1968 were fresh in everyone's mind. The text is made up, variously, of excerpts from Corneille's prefaces, from *Le Cid*, from women's magazines such as *Marie-Claire* and *Elle*, from popular newspapers, etc. The text was put together, edited, re-edited, reassembled, and rewritten, and the process continued even after the first few presentations. Jean Bouise who played the main role had to relearn his part a good ten times in a different order.

The main concern of the production was the problem of theatre: its situation, its role in relation to the other arts . . . questions which had been asked by young people during the events of May 1968. Because these questions had been put in the context of an all-encompassing revolution, it was impossible to recall them without bringing in political and social issues as well; in any case theatre has never existed in a vacuum. The main concern, however, was to deal satirically with certain theories of drama and art which had become fashionable in the 1960s. The farcical treatment of the themes of the play, far from being a sign of unconcern, was a safeguard against excessive seriousness: Planchon felt deeply worried by the impasse which theatre seemed to have reached in the sixties, and which the public had eventually sensed:

> in my opinion, around 1963, a certain number of shows reached a point of perfection, for example those of Strehler or Brook's *King Lear*. Directors then asked themselves questions, a few [Jérôme Savary, for example] abandoned the text completely ... one sensed that something was finished, and one didn't very well see how we were going to renew ourselves. It is these latent discussions that the public discovered a year and a half ago.[17]

It was this crisis which had led Planchon to begin writing his own plays, and in *La Mise en pièces du 'Cid'*, he gave vent to his worries about it.

The characters of the play can be divided into five groups: Fafurle and his two wives Germaine and Émilie, the actors of *Le Cid*, Bourdolle the literature teacher and his pupils, the theatre director M. Pierre and his assistants, and a team of Affreux Enzymes Gloutons (horrible greedy enzymes) led by a girl student, Bip-Bip. The unifying characters of the play are Fafurle and his wives. Fafurle is the French 'man in the street', full of commonsense and prejudice; played by Jean Bouise, wearing short, wide trousers revealing striped socks and white tennis shoes, he was as much a clown as a Frenchman on holiday. His two wives are the two sides of the average domesticated Frenchwoman: Germaine an elegant, beautiful, brainless vamp, Émilie a dowdy housewife, her head full of true-romance stories. The play begins when these three burst through a 'classical' stage set with their car, interrupting a rehearsal of *Le Cid* (just as in the TNP–Chaillot's 1967 production of *Maître Puntila et son valet Matti*, Puntila drove into the living-room with his car).

The actors of *Le Cid* appear only in a few brief sequences, and in their first scene they are reduced to a few lines of the famous dialogues, followed by a pantomime of their rehearsal, as the Fafurle group begin to make their own comments on the play. Corneille's Alexandrines were mercilessly chopped into near-gibberish, and they were interrupted when Germaine, reacting angrily to Elvire's lines, slaps the actress. Making fun of his own tendency to introduce a

crowd of extras into his productions of classical plays, Planchon added a number of useless extras to the cast of *Le Cid*,
and then had them shot by the student Bip-Bip. Because
Émilie wants a happy ending, *Le Cid* ends with Don Gormas
returning alive and Rodrigue and Chimène reunited over a
plate of paella. The unfortunate Chimène, however, later
enters pregnant, and angry not only at Rodrigue: she carries a
banner reading 'Merci Paul VI'.

The actors re-enter en masse just before the interval to ask
Fafurle, just as the theatre directors asked themselves in
1968, '. . . is it possible to continue putting on plays if the
barricades are running with blood; should we continue to
play Corneille?'[18] They are told that from sheer decency they
should stop, as the show takes place elsewhere in such circumstances. This may have been a reference to Günter
Grass's play *Die Plebejer proben den Aufstand* (*The
Plebeians Rehearse the Uprising*), put on by the Schiller
Theater in West Berlin in 1966. The play dealt with the 1953
East Berlin riots which were quelled by Russian tanks, and
brought up the question of Brecht's attitude to the incident.
The play, and Planchon's allusion to it, broached the issue of
the responsibility of theatre people in the face of social and
political upheavals, a question which was agonisingly topical in the wake of the events of 1968. The peripheral role of
the actors of *Le Cid* in *La Mise en pièces du 'Cid'* illustrated
the position of the theatres during the events of May 1968.
They were full of good will, but they became aware of their
powerlessness. At Avignon in 1968, the Living Theatre tried
to present their production of *Paradise Now* in the streets of
the city, free, after seats in the Cloître des Carmes had been
sold out. They were opposed by the mayor, and finally left
Avignon altogether. They accused Vilar, at the time the festival's organiser, of cooperating with a repressive authority.
Vilar's answer to the charge illustrates well the distress
which many liberals and theatre people must have felt in that
summer of 'events':

the festival [of Avignon] has never been revolutionary. How can
one deny that it is the prisoner of the bourgeois capitalist society
with which we are fed up! But it is precisely its ambition to find
within this framework a slightly less bourgeois, slightly less
capitalistic ground.[19]

In Planchon's play, M. Pierre the theatre director, although he has less claim to being anti-bourgeois than such people as Vilar, suffers a similar anguish. He is basically a traditionalist, breaking down at the sight of people picnicking in the theatre (as the occupiers of the Odéon in 1968 actually did), and extremely upset at interference from the uneducated public. When he is provoked by a revolutionary, however, he defends his career in the self-righteous tones of a veteran: 'I've been a revolutionary. Yes, in *La Mort de Danton* with Vilar in '56. I've played Brecht, O'Casey, and Gatti.'[20] In this litany of revolutionary playwrights Planchon cocked a snook at the popular theatre directors like himself whose repertoire, by the mid-sixties, had become rather predictable. M. Pierre reveals the limits of his radicalism when he protests against street theatre because in the streets there are no footlights. He is so innocent that he puts Corneille on a pedestal (literally) to save him from the revolutionaries; the symbolism was deliberately obvious. He finally stabs himself, with a literary flourish, and his suicide is followed by the appearance of a toilet, in mockery not only of lavatory symbolism (as in Arrabal's *Le Labyrinthe*), but also of theatre as a whole, flushing itself down the drain in its desperate desire to be popular, revolutionary, or shocking.

La Mise en pièces du 'Cid'. Fafurle (Jean Bouise) admires '*l'auto-censure*'

Bourdolle the teacher first appears as the archetypal scholar, for whom culture is a preserve, and art belongs in a museum, carefully guarded. Bourdolle leaves Fafurle a series of composition topics on *Le Cid*, which have appeared in actual baccalauréat (university entrance) examinations. At this point in the production, the house lights went up, and the audience found these questions, in all their academic irrelevance, being fired at them. Using real examination questions may have been meant as a parody of document plays of the sixties.[21] Fafurle, as he questions the audience, becomes an earnest and tyrannical examiner:

No toilets when one is sitting one's baccalaureate.
    What are they saying at the back of the hall? They are contesting. They are contesting the baccalaureate? (Fafurle picks up a telephone.) Monsieur le Ministre, the examination cannot proceed, they are contesting the baccalaureate.[22]

Fafurle's shocked tone is a measure of the universities' rigidity and their unpreparedness for the attacks which students made on the educational system as a whole in 1968.

    Bourdolle embodies the absurdities of the academic whose professional detachment has barred him from involvement with real people. When, at his own request, he is brainwashed by Fafurle, he turns into an anti-intellectual with ideas at the other extreme from his previous ones. Through him, it is clear, Planchon wished to debunk the rebels themselves as much as that which they contested. Bourdolle the revolutionary throws little red books of the *Thoughts of Chairman Mao* at the actors of *Le Cid*, and argues against his former beliefs with the same convoluted logic which he formerly used to defend them. When he encounters Corneille, a dialogue of contrasts ensues:

Corneille: Those who have hurried to the representation of my works oblige me immensely; those who do not approve of them can spare themselves the trouble of coming and getting migraine from them, they will save money and please me.
Bourdolle and the aesthetes: We want a disgusting, filthy theatre which stinks, which repels, which is afraid of neither mud nor dung, theatre which isn't afraid of getting its hands dirty ...
Corneille: Each to his method, I do not find fault with that of others and keep to my own.[23]

Bourdolle makes his final entrance in an extravagant hippy costume, and sets off a sequence in which 'mystical' couples dance, holding LSD sugar cubes between their foreheads and chanting 'Love, love, love' in English. There is little doubt that Planchon was poking fun at a scene in Jean-Louis Barrault's 1968 production of *Rabelais*, in which at one point hippy couples danced, embraced one another, and repeated in English the phrase 'Make love not war'. Bourdolle is equally funny as the fussy schoolmaster dusting the sets of *Le Cid*, as the advocate of kitchen-sink drama, and as a drug-taking hippy 'rebel'. No one was safe from this play's mockery.

The last group, that of Bip-Bip and her followers, the Affreux Enzymes Gloutons, are partly comic-strip characters and partly the creations of television advertising. During the demonstations of 1968 in Paris, the police claimed to be protecting the real students from the trouble-makers whom they referred to as *les affreux* (the horrid ones). Planchon's term would thus have had a precise meaning for those who had lived through the events. Bip-Bip is a student in rebellion against everything, and in pursuit of Doctor Mabuse, the only man horrible enough to attract her. When she mistakes Corneille for Mabuse, and finds that he responds to her sexual advances only by quoting from his prefaces, she gets her revenge by leading the stripping, whipping, torture, and killing of the playwright. The violence was, of course, a parody of the trend of showing physical cruelty onstage (as in Arrabal or Grotowski). Planchon even aimed a glancing blow at Samuel Beckett: Corneille is finally stuffed into a dustbin.

Two characters who delighted public and critics alike were the two identical policemen Albert and Albert, inspired by the Dupont and Dupond of the French comic-strip series *Tintin*. The conflicts of May 1968 had brought innumerable complaints of police brutality, and these two characters provoked a satisfied amusement in those who had been spectators or activists in the demonstrations. Albert and Albert appear whenever the dialogue begins to sound political, and they chant a couplet which critics quoted with relish: 'Subversion – no subsidies . . . Subsidies . . . no subversion' (pt I, p. 50). (Subversion pas de subvention . . . Subvention pas de subversion.) It was, and is, the most concise statement possible of the government-subsidised theatres' fear of censorship through economic pressure.

Theatre groups were worried that even without direct intervention from their sponsors, they tended to limit their repertoire in order to make it acceptable to them. In December 1968, the government banned a production of Gatti's play on General Franco, which Georges Wilson was to put on at the TNP-Chaillot. As the government acted at the very last minute, the theatre suffered a financial loss as well as a loss of freedom, and theatres all over France joined in issuing a protest on the matter. It was inevitable that other subsidised theatres would be made nervous by this kind of censorship, and would be tempted to put on nothing too controversial.

Planchon incarnated this idea of self-censorship in a concrete image on the stage. Using a punning link with the French word for self-censorship, *l'auto-censure*, he had the actors of *Le Cid* construct a car called *auto-censure*, while the Fafurles give a bitingly ironic commentary:

Germaine: Look at them, Léon, they're going to build it themselves, these theatre people are so ingenious. Look at them get through their problems! They cut a scene here and there, they split a line into two, they patch up an act or two and presto, the *auto-censure* is built!
Fafurle: Your old rattle-trap is a bit of alright! It looks a little more like a wheelbarrow than a racing car, but I must admit the cushions are very plushy. The clutch is automatic, it reverses beautifully. It leaks quite a bit, but you can't have everything![24]

Claude Lochy's music for the play was itself a collage, made up of innumerable borrowings from very well-known sources including, for example, parts of the soldiers' march from *Faust*, of the Toreador song from *Carmen*, and even Bach's *Song of Joy*. Lochy also tried an experiment. He suggested themes and rhythms to the assembled actors, and called on their musical talents and their sense of humour to help him compose the score. In its way it was a small rebellion against specialisation.

The sets were designed by Jim Leon, a young English collage artist. The props were varied and so numerous that Jacqueline Cartier filled her entire theatre column by simply enumerating them.[25] They included such things as an entire classical set for the rehearsal of *Le Cid*, a fifteen-metre (just over sixteen-yard) length of string to symbolise the thread of the story, a bag of flour and two cream tarts for throwing at policemen, two coffins, whips and a dustbin for poor old Corneille, etc. Many of the props had to 'perform', many were parodies of extremes in contemporary theatre. A gigantic golden phallus, for example, inflated itself in full view in mockery of countless productions which had used such a prop in the late sixties.[26] Furthermore, the very abundance of objects on the stage reflected not only the mayhem of the 1968 revolution, but also the consumerism of the industrial west, burying itself under piles of useless 'goods'. The sets in this respect looked forward to those of Planchon's 1973 play *La Langue au Chat* in which Europe is depicted as living under waste-heaps of its own industrial products.

In the final scene, a large coin-operated machine appeared which, in return for money, gave canned advice to everyone in a soft artificial voice like those of airline announcements. Asked for culture, it immediately mixed together the various ingredients needed to create a perfect blend of culture (a dash of Bach, a touch of Vivaldi, etc.), which came out of a tap as a pink gummy substance, and which the actors kindly distributed to the audience (just as the Bread and Puppet Theatre had broken black bread with their audience, and the Open Theatre had given out apples). The machine may have been inspired by that in Gatti's *V comme Vietnam*, which symbolised both American military technology and American society (dispensing some Texan music when a dime was inserted). As the final image in Planchon's play, the culture machine was important, and to many people it was a depressing indictment of contemporary European society, with its prefabricated, premasticated ideologies and art forms. By leaving it onstage, Planchon was crying out for all theatre people, 'Where do we go from here?'

The critics, although they enjoyed the fun and appreciated the masterful staging of the production, complained that it attacked too many things at once. Some felt that the play had been created for the benefit of theatre experts. Gilles Sandier, for example, wrote:

In a show with no real aggressiveness, he [Planchon] lampoons but covers his tracks; though he lampoons himself, the game is not without some narcissistic complacency; this show is for the friends, the mandarins that we are, and for the bourgeois on the borderline of the bourgeoisie, intelligently enamoured of the theatre.[27]

It is clear, however, even from a simple reading of the text, that like *Les Trois Mousquetaires* the show could be taken on different levels, from that of a slapstick spree to that of an intellectual satire. The Villeurbanne public, eighty-five per cent of whom came from unions and organisations, and most of whom were inexperienced theatre-goers, if not working-class spectators, enjoyed the show thoroughly. The Parisian audience, for their part, many of whom had lived through the events of May 1968, readily recognised the social and political allusions in the production; those of them who were regular theatre-goers would also have appreciated the countless references to the recent fads in the theatre.

Another recurring criticism of the show was that its light-heartedness made it seem like a school variety show whose 'in' jokes, however cruel they may seem, are a harmless way of letting off steam. Planchon was accused, in other words, not only of writing for initiates, but of making light of serious subjects, of transforming major social and artistic upheavals into an evening's entertainment for snobs. Yet Planchon's own feelings about the 'revolution' of 1968 were serious enough, and they even showed through the fun of the staging once or twice. Colette Cosnier, a critic, wrote:

there is a moment when the laughter ceases: a group of young people invade the stage, brandishing red and black flags, covering the walls with slogans, and we no longer feel like being ironic, as though we knew that imagination would never be in power again, as though we were dreaming of what the theatre could have become, as though May 1968 had already been transformed into a myth.[28]

The point of the production was just this, that the 1968 revolution was now entering the realm of myth. It was over, and it had left only questions, not answers. Not everyone had the courage of Planchon, who saw this and said so clearly.

In *La Mise en pièces du 'Cid'* a long discussion by several characters on the question 'What is theatre?' finally leads to the conclusion that theatre is anything, as long as one succeeds in making it dramatic: 'Le théâtre c'est . . . N'importe quoi si on réussit à le rendre théâtral' (pt. I, p. 49). This production certainly illustrated a great number of the possibilities which this *n'importe quoi* opened up. Planchon considers the stage as the perfect arena for stark confrontations of opposing ideas. Here ideas were shown to be extreme by juxtaposing them with their opposites. Myths both political and theatrical were constantly demolished as soon as they had been set up. Planchon even made fun of the terms which had come out of the Villeurbanne conference of popular theatre directors in June 1968: Bourdolle asks of the three Fafurles: 'But who are these people? Actors, spectators, the non-public?'[29] 'Non-public' was a word which the directors had coined for the public which they had failed to attract to the theatre. In many ways the Fafurles were the non-public, and Planchon's production did not suggest a way of reaching them. When Bourdolle asks the director M. Pierre why the workers are not at the theatre, M. Pierre has no answer. The events of 1968 had made Planchon and his colleagues realise that no one, even himself, had attracted a representative number of working-class people into the theatre.

Was it time for suicide? In his play, Planchon invented, in a veritable firework display of ironic references, an appropriate death for each of the great men of the contemporary theatre:

– Mr Ionesco died a victim to duty.
– Mr Adamov died crying: long live stiletto heels and social unions.
– The mysterious Mr Beckett has always been dying, there is no end to his being in the throes of death.
– . . .
– . . . The good Mr Beck ate raw meat, Sir. He died a pacifist, of a violent death.
– Mr Grotowski crucified himself, yes he did, Sir, swearing all the while that he was an atheist.
– The exquisite Mr Strehler died onstage, like a diva in Damiani's white sheets.
– Mr Brook had a car accident, his Shakespeare overturned in a London suburb.
– Planchon died an old dotard, Sir, he was buried in the Ardèche.
– The hot-headed Chéreau heroically climbed to the top of a barricade but he is already mortally wounded.[30]

In his own comments on the play as well as in this memorable passage, Planchon made it clear that it was time, if not for suicide, certainly for rebirth. The production was Planchon's way of clearing the ground for something new, but it did not propose at the time to define that something. Critics complained about the lack of a positive standpoint in the play; Planchon had simply refused to substitute for outworn modes of expression a new one which would soon be as outdated as those which it replaced. The new approach, the new standpoint would have to be discovered painfully and step by step in the rehearsal rooms of those courageous enough to start again.

In Planchon's own case the direction was to be an ever more personal, ever more poetic approach to the human dilemma. There were, however, no glib answers and no formulae for the future which could be provided in 1969. Planchon wanted only to give people a perspective on theatre and on the events of '68. He has always felt that the role of theatre is to ask questions (and in this he is a 'committed' dramatist like Adamov, like Gatti, like Benedetto) but not to give answers. In *La Mise en pièces du 'Cid'*, he was stripping away the myths born of the *événements*, which many of his critics had not yet abandoned. It is not surprising that he met with only partial understanding.

La Langue au Chat (The Cat's Tale)
La Langue au Chat is the successor to Planchon's three first musical comedies: it relies on song and dance and spectacular effects, and it openly asks questions about the preoccupations of French society. It was first put on in Marseilles in October 1972.

La Langue au Chat is a play about mass deception. Planchon said that he was inspired whilst reading Ben Jonson's *The Alchemist* to find a modern equivalent to Subtle the impostor. Planchon's master deceiver is a guru-figure who calls himself Le Chat, the Cat. The play is set in the year 2000 in France, after a civil war in which half the population has been exterminated. The government decides to save the remaining half from committing suicide by giving them a new spiritual leader, Le Chat, a big television personality. The play consists of a series of television programmes, hosted by Le Chat and his two compères Aphrodite Bretzel and Louis, in which a succession of guest personalities appear. Off camera, Le Chat and Louis fight for Bretzel's favours, Le Chat has visions, and occasionally visitors from another planet (Les Transparents) appear, unperceived by the other characters, taking notes on the strange world in which they have landed. As well as the studio, the set revealed, in one corner, a chintzy flat belonging to an extremely commonsensical old lady, La Grosse, whose world is on a completely different level from that of the studio, but who occasionally communicates with Louis by telephone. Eventually, Le Chat is denounced to the authorities as a fraud. In the final scene, all his viewers, at his signal, set off sticks of dynamite 'to celebrate spring', and the play ends to the sound of modern society blowing itself up, followed by that of waves lapping and seagulls crying.

The atmosphere of the studio was that of an air-raid shelter. The walls, camera, microphones, spotlights, everything, was made of brass covered with peeling black paint. Following precise directions from Planchon, the set designer Max Schoendorff deliberately emphasised the claustrophobic feeling of the underground studio, not only by limiting the

La Langue au Chat, Villeurbanne, 1972. Colette Dompiétrini as Bretzel, ready to share the favours of her two admirers Le Chat (Roger Planchon), and Louis (Pierre Vernier)

number of exits, as Planchon suggested, but also by filling
the internal space of the studio with bulky machinery and
props. For each television programme a small set was
brought in on a wheeled platform and placed in front of one
or two of the cameras. The studio set was dreadfully effective, and suggested almost a concentraton camp. For the
visions of Le Chat, the back wall of the studio literally split
open with a horrible metallic grinding noise, carrying us into
the borderline world of Le Chat's mind, filled with uncon-
trollable images of violence, sexual fantasy, frustration and
death. Suspended in mid-air outside the left wall of the
bunker was the apartment of La Grosse, a room complete
with wood stove, pink linoleum, and yellowing photographs, and which Schoendorff described as a '. . . set within
the set', as a '. . . window floating outside time, an outlet for
tenderness . . . in a decaying world'.[31]

In this play Planchon wished to take people's fears about
contemporary society and bring out their funny side. The
society which he depicts is one exhausted by wars, suffocating in its own produce, and devoid of hope. News and
weather broadcasts give physical details of life in the year
2000:

Bretzel: The putrid winds which are moving from east to west will
not succeed in lifting – and we suspected as much – the leaden
cover over our heads. Therefore we will live today as we did
yesterday, under fluorescent lighting.
Le Chat: . . . the zone of depression is spreading westward and into
all hearts. The foul mists will lift at midnight. But then a rain of soot
will fall over the entire region.
Louis: Factories are pouring out torrents of green juice onto our
lovely cities. This morning all reinforced concrete surfaces are
covered in chemical foam.[32]

While Louis is reading a news bulletin about the wars, Le
Chat sees his first vision, entitled 'Les Poubelles de l'histoire'
(the dustbins of history). Two large dustbins appear, one
containing the rubbish of our consumer society, the other
blood-covered fragments of human bodies. A bell tolls and a
searchlight revolves over the dustbins. In an over-populated,
over-industrialised, and polluted world, human lives are of
little value, and corpses are thrown out as so much waste. It is
not surprising that despair is rife both in and out of the
studio.

It is a world in which there are no more solutions possible.

The politician who introduces Le Chat to the television audiences at the beginning of the play, the 'Ministre de la Culture et de l'Information pour un environnement aux petits oignons' (the Minister of Culture and Information for an apple-pie environment) shows signs of decay and senility even as he promises a new era. He sucks his thumb, plays with his hair, and his words gradually degenerate into nonsense. In his second appearance he refuses to admit that the experiment with Le Chat has been a failure even if, he tells the television audience, 'A few of you are still stupidly committing suicide, fools will be fools.'[33] One television programme deals with the problem of 'political leukaemia', an illness which is said to affect all the political personnel of the western world (including, most certainly, the Minister of Culture . . .), as well as journalists and revolutionaries. Le Chat explains their illness: like Beckett's characters they collapse with the demise of their language:

These men had a way of explaining the world in their speeches, in their editorials and suddenly the world has galloped away . . .

The world, having galloped away, left questions without answers and these questions without answers secreted insidious microbes which made their ideologies decay. The ideological blood which irrigated their brains decomposed, decayed. Now their arteries are going.[34]

The problem, treated in a ludicrous way here, is the inadequacy of predetermined thought systems, whether political, philosophical, or religious, to keep pace with events. It is a preoccupation which has developed from Planchon's original fascination with ideology and behaviour, and which is more evident in his later work.

Professeur Balotin, an expert on the disease, is powerless to help the sufferers of it. Indeed he is generally impotent. He is juxtaposed in the play with Docteur Braun, a woman ready to reform the world. She opposes Le Chat and scoffs at the bumbling Balotin in aggressively scatological language. The double act of these two characters was made even funnier in Planchon's production by the fine acting of Jean Bouise as the conciliating old Balotin, and of Michele Marquet as the uncompromising Docteur Braun. Even she, however, is overwhelmed by her task. Her solutions to the world's problems cannot work. She announces, for example, that the government will tax drug manufacturers and traffickers, and use the money to set up research institutions to find ways of fighting drug addiction. The financing of reform would thus depend on the profits of those creating the problems, and for whom reform would be financially disastrous. Docteur Braun eventually collapses physically under the strain of catering to the abysmal tastes of the masses.

The other major opponent of Le Chat's brand of spirituality is the young capitalist Neyron. During the rehearsal on 30 September 1972 at Villeurbanne, Planchon told Philippe Clevenot who played the role: 'When Braun isn't there, Neyron is the opposition. Braun's opposition is obvious in the text, that of Neyron has to be shown.' Neyron speaks in clipped phrases, using business anglicisms. He classes himself amongst the *'révoltés, désespérés, mais adaptés à la société'* (those in revolt, in despair, but adapted to society) and dreams of a 'new society *industrielle, jeune, dynamique, fiable, où tous tirerions dans même sens'*(new industrial society, young, dynamic, trustworthy, in which everyone would pull in the same direction). He is undeterred by Le Chat's riposte, *'Tirerions quoi? Pour aller où?'* (Would pull what? To go where?, sc. 4, p. 3), but it is a key question in the play. As in *La Mise en pièces du 'Cid'*, Planchon was asking where are we heading, although in this case the 'we' includes all of us, not only theatre people.

When Neyron first appears, Louis asks him how he has succeeded in reaching the studio through the mounds of rubbish which lie everywhere; has he used one of the tunnels which the boy scouts are digging through the waste? Neyron proudly announces that he owns the first *'turboaerotrain-flottant. Muni à l'avant d'une balayette japonaise en platine qui repousse saloperies sur côtés.'* (Turboaerohovertrain. Equipped in front with Japanese platinum brush which pushes rubbish to sides.) Louis immediately turns to the cameras to add, *'Vous trouverez bientôt ce gadget dans des magasins attrape couillons-à-succursales-multiples.'* (You will soon find this gadget in all rip-off-chain-stores. sc. 4, p. 2.) Too many consumer goods have transformed the cities into impassable waste heaps, and instead of clearing the rubbish, industry creates another gadget to get people through it. The gadget is a symbol of accommodation to intolerable conditions, and of Neyron's myopia as the advocate of industrial expansion at all costs. The cost is obviously social self-destruction.

In the world of *La Langue au Chat* political power leads only to decay; the power of religion, however, is non-existent. On one of the television programmes (in the series entitled 'Un homme, un passé' – One man and his past) the Pope makes an appearance. It is one of the funniest scenes, and was one of the most appreciated by the audience in the Maison de la Culture de Reims where I saw the play. The Pope describes how he now lives in lodgings in Rome because Fiat has bought St Peter's as an exhibition hall. Only one priest, indeed only one person, l'Abbé Comac, still believes in religion. Planchon called the Pope a 'lost character. He starts off in despair'.[35] The contrast between his station and his circumstances, and even more the contrast between his despairing tone and his hilariously inappropriate vocabulary make the scene irresistible. He says:

(of his schedule) Then we have some eats. Little siesta. Religious exercise. More eats. Telly. Prayer and sleepy-byes. Our sacerdotal life has become simplified.
(of his priests) All married. Nibbled away by psychoanalysis or politics. The last Spanish obscurantists have turned militant. Revelation has been replaced by Revolution.[36]

Comac, the one believer left in the world, begins by trying to revive Catholicism with a little advertising. Eventually, however, he turns to drug-inspired religion, much to the Pope's disgust: 'One little LSD sugar cube and Jesus goes boom in your head.'[37] Planchon generally presents Catholicism as a dead ideology, a thought system beyond redemption: eighty-four per cent of French people still call themselves Catholics, and Planchon wishes to give people a perspective on their professed faith by invalidating it onstage.

The only other believer in the play is *La Grosse*, the old-fashioned lady living in a flat suspended beside the studio. Her attitudes like her flat are anachronisms in the world of *La Langue au Chat*. La Grosse believes that the world's ills will be cured when the Martians come, and her confidence in this future salvation is touching. The Transparents, other-worldly beings, do come, but they come as observers and their efforts to help are even less effective than those of the three gods in *Der gute Mensch von Sezuan*. Innocence in Planchon's play lies with La Grosse, who is deluded, and with Les Transparents, who come from another world and are mystified by this one.

It is a world in which people self-consciously set out to find their 'self', their '*moi profond*', individuality, soul, something indefinable and constantly elusive, which they sense has been lost. L'Abbé Comac, involved in spite of himself in one programme, stands sweating for several hilarious seconds, as the metronome ticks away, trying to find an answer to the question 'Qui êtes-vous?' (Who are you?, sc. 8, p. 4). The point is that in a world of superficial quickly-changing images, aptly represented in the artificiality of the television medium, anything more profound becomes lost; the very terms 'meaningful', 'profound', 'soul' have become more than faintly amusing. Aphrodite Bretzel crying out for '*Les mots qui m'appartiennent*' (the words which belong to me), and '*ma vraie personnalité*' (my real personality, sc. 6, p. 7); Neyron, dreaming of returning to '*L'authenticité champêtre*' (rustic authenticity), and finding his '*assiette morale*' (moral foundation, sc. 9, p. 3), are both indulging in a nostalgic search for a kind of individualistic and personal reality which has been asphyxiated in the world of the year 2000. Louis, whom Planchon defined as a chameleon who changes personality with every new show, is perhaps more in tune with his era.

This world has destroyed love relationships as well as individuality. Certainly the desire for tenderness exists, and Aphrodite Bretzel once confesses almost affectionately to Louis: 'This evening I'd like to cuddle up to you for a little breath of tenderness', but she adds, knowingly, 'Tenderness today costs the earth, doesn't it, M. Louis?'[38] Aphrodite wants not only the tenderness of a great passion, but also dozens of sexual liaisons. In an outrageously amusing scene, she stands between her two colleagues, trying to convince them to share her favours, and making a symbolic offering: 'Take my chewing gum. A little piece each. It's been nibbled at slightly, but it's kept all its flavour.'[39]

Planchon said:

In the play, people know that television is a fantastic means of communication, but at the same time they sense that it is always falsified. In life it is the same. It happens, one day, that they want to pierce through the artifice but this too is integrated into the show. They want to blow up the falseness, as though the truth could break out.[40]

In the play, two of the people who try to penetrate behind the sexual 'freedom' of the year 2000 are Alligator and his sister Dorothy. Alligator is a writer of pornographic novels who has tried every conceivable sexual experiment and cries out '. . . sexually, am I really liberated?' (sc. 3, p. 6). He gets no answer. Dorothy, a vamp complete with skin-tight sheath dress and blonde wig begins by stripping in front of the cameras and ends by staging her own suicide; no amount of exhibitionism will upset the world of La Langue au Chat – the theme looked forward to that of the film Network. On television, behaviour is judged solely on whether it is good or bad for the ratings. The tragedy of Aphrodite, of Alligator, of Dorothy is not merely that they find the barriers to self-expression already broken down; it is that given complete freedom to speak they find they have nothing to say.

During the rehearsal on 30 September, Planchon said that he wanted all the news bulletins, even the most horrendous, to be read in a euphoric tone of voice. Indeed, despite the widespread despair and the horrifying state of the cities and people's souls, the world of the studio is a resolutely cheerful one. Through the television studios, despair is fought with constant injections of gaiety, often in the form of a song and dance. One of Le Chat's cheery addresses to the viewers shows how basic human appetites have been regulated by social necessity to be satisfied with synthetic substitutes: 'It is now 8.00. All families are gathered round the nice synthetic soup. Neon lights are glowing above your heads. It's super! Guzzle down your soupy-soup quickly. And slip into the asepticised pussy of your wives.'[41] Even death is pictured as no more than a slightly ludicrous process of decaying gradually away. To avoid epidemics the dead are cremated and to save space their ashes are put into jam jars; a government official has a bright idea: '. . . dear producer; on the funerary jam jars put coloured labels. It introduces a little gaiety'.[42] Repeated again and again the word gaieté becomes gratingly ironic. When the chorus sings a song to cheer up the despondent Pope, their song is an ode to empty joy; Karel Trow who composed the music found an intentionally and irritatingly catchy tune for it. The deformation of reality by television is crystallised in this image of a brave empty smile over a world of horror, a world whose final aspiration is self-annihilation.

The central character, Le Chat, is, like Schweyk, an ambiguous figure, neither collaborating totally with the authorities

La Langue au Chat, Villeurbanne, 1972. Michèle Oppenot as Dorothy (with blonde wig) stages her death as Doctor Braun (Michèle Marquais) looks on

nor resisting them absolutely. Planchon played the role himself. Le Chat's speeches include sheer nonsense, cheerful
obscenity, and sudden flights of poetry. As a television personality and self-styled guru he has some power over the
viewers. While he maintains his pose as a visionary, however, he constantly tells the audience that they are being
fooled, and some of his outbursts have an anguished cyni-
cism:

Yes, everyone is making fools of you and always has done. Today a
completely delirious man is speaking to you. A lunatic is smiling a
smile of complicity at all the nut-cases in the world. At the saints,
the mystics, at the imbeciles baying at night in the passages of the
underground. At all the madmen who throw themselves head first
against the walls of their cell. This civilisation is going to founder,
but I don't care a damn, I'm a cat.[43]

Le Chat is not altogether in control of his words' repercus-
sions. He has, in the course of the play, eight visions which
the other characters do not see. On the one hand they show
his lucidity, for they are images of the horror beneath the glib
world of publicity in which he lives. On the other hand their
content is often obscure or frightening to him, and he has no
control over them. They are intuitive and not intellectual, a
truth sensed but not rationally grasped. The visions reveal
his doubts, not only about society, but about himself and his
role. In one, a naked girl lies on an unmade bed, a portable
television set between her thighs, and Le Chat bewails the
cheapening of relationships by the over-exposure of sex (sc.
14). In another, a scientist studies a miniature replica of the
studio with the inscription 'Prehistoric television studio
with, taking himself for a cat . . .'[44] Planchon here succeeds
in thumbing his nose not only at himself and his play, but at
future critics of it. The last vision, which was used for the
posters, is an image of the frustration which leads the world
to self-destruction. Two men with cat's faces, blindfolded,
gagged, and wearing straitjackets, face each other across a
table with a chess board on it. They strain forward as though
they want to play, but they are held back by chains. The
vision stayed as the television viewers, on a word from Le
Chat, blew themselves up with dynamite, leaving nothing
but the sound of seagulls crying and waves lapping – a return
to nature without man.
    The production was made up of such a lengthy and com-

plicated series of events, shows, gags, and characters, that many critics, faced with the task of reviewing it, ended by summarising it instead. Indeed, the play is so profuse that it is impossible to digest in one sitting. (Planchon, one might recall, dislikes 'digestive' theatre!) Planchon was aware of the play's over-abundance, but he found that writing it freed him from many barriers and enabled him to write the more poetic *Le Cochon noir* afterwards.

While they were in Rheims putting on *La Langue au Chat*, Planchon and some of his actors took part in a discussion, which I attended, with the students of the acting school there. A student actress objected that *La Langue au Chat* did not give spectators any stimulus to take action about an unacceptable society, but allowed them to watch passively. Planchon replied that he did not intend to make people take direct action, but only to make them think: 'The play gives a perspective, a way of reacting, no solutions.'[45] This is one polite meaning of the title of the play, from the expression *Je donne ma langue au chat* (I give up, I don't know the answer). It gives no answers, but asks hundreds of questions. After seeing the play, one can no longer accept, no longer view television conventions, the current nostalgia craze, modern pornography, the idea of 'finding oneself', etc. in the same way. It explodes the myths which we prefer to accept half-consciously; by carrying our worst anxieties to extremes in an imagined future, it makes them seem ridiculous – and yet that future is just believable enough to be alarming. Like Planchon's production of *Richard III*, like Tom Stoppard's *Every Good Boy Deserves Favour*, this play succeeds in making you laugh right up to the moment when your hair begins to stand on end.

Folies bourgeoises (Bourgeois Follies)
Folies bourgeoises was first produced in April 1975 at St-Étienne. The play is a collage taken from *La Petite Illustration*, November 1913 to July 1914; this was a weekly publication giving the texts of all the boulevard successes of the day. *Folies bourgeoises* is made up of lines from twenty-five plays, put together in a vaudevillesque succession of songs, dances, and short scenes. Planchon's avowed purpose in creating this collage was to cull material from the plays in such a way as to go beyond the personal idiosyncrasies of each playwright and bring out recurring

motifs. It was, like *La Mise en pièces du 'Cid'*, a collaborative effort.

Planchon believed that the themes repeated in the plays revealed the underlying attitudes which made up the collective unconscious of the theatre-going public in France immediately before the outbreak of World War I. It is a surrealistic enterprise; Planchon was looking for a *surréalité* beyond the actual lines spoken. The lines are trivial in their original context, but juxtaposed with pieces from other unrelated plays, they often reveal a recurring idea, a similar attitude, a surprisingly general belief, and finally a pattern of thought. Planchon said of the plays:

> How can one speak such platitudes and have them accepted? The form corresponds to something real in the mind of the spectators, to ways of thinking which exist, which are reproduced on the stage, just a little, as one expects. Everyone likes to be simultaneously a little disturbed, a little reassured.[46]

Despite its apparently disjointed logic and Ionesco-like use of clichés (every one of them from the orignal plays), this is not an absurdist play. Its purpose is not to set out before us the absurdity of our own condition, but to unveil the public's attitudes in a specific time and place: France in 1913–14.

After reading the original plays one is left with a sense of unease, an impression of a society steadfastly closing its eyes to impending war, a society going headlong into a holocaust with its party hats on. One feels doubly uneasy after reading Planchon's *Folies bourgeoises*. The amount of jolly stage business and good knockabout slapstick makes it excellent entertainment. It pokes fun at the bourgeoisie which unconsciously considered its own *mores* as the ultimate standard; at its snobbery, its sexual coyness, its political naïveté. Like *La Langue au Chat* it deplores the triviality of popular entertainment, here the bourgeoisie's theatre, there the masses' television. Like *La Langue au Chat*, also, it ends in an apocalyptic destruction. Here, however, we are not in an imaginary year 2000, and the reality revealed at the end is a historical reality. As the play is a collage, and not a rewriting, we must accept that the gaiety of the lines is actually that of the era, and yet we know the outcome, and we know that the cataclysmic last scenes (set in a battlefield) are a true representation of that end. The general myopic jollity is all the more horrifying.

The techniques which Planchon uses in this play are familiar ones. He has certain lines repeated either for their own comic effect or for the added value of hearing them once more after some intervening business. He deliberately juxtaposes incompatible speeches, and equally deliberately has them spoken by the most inappropriate characters. The stage language for the production was of course Planchon's, and as in his earlier musical comedies he used it to debunk the lines spoken or the sentiments underlying them.

The use of repetition begins with the list of characters. Each of the six main female characters is called Rose. The name was popular in the plays of the day, but Planchon also uses it deliberately to point out that women on the stage in 1913–14 were represented as a breed, sharing a similar nature different from the male standard. 'That era,' Planchon remarked, 'showed an appalling misogyny.'[47] The characters were put together by taking the main prototypes (wife, husband, maid, lover, etc.), and then choosing, for instance, the maid's scenes from several different plays and collating them to produce an archetypal maid character.

The play begins with Mlle Rose, a large, ageing lady in a shortish lace shift, sleeping on an armchair in front of the safety curtain. In a glass case beside her is her own decomposing corpse. The period which we are about to see will be present before us in its deteriorating state, and also in its wish to ignore its own deterioration. Mlle Rose reappears to introduce various scenes, and acts as a guide throughout the play, occasionally clinking glasses with a mysterious sad-looking rabbit in evening dress, walking on stilts and acting as a silent master of ceremonies.

Throughout the play, Mlle Rose appears with a camera, and each time characters are delighted to pose for her. Photography at the time was a recent invention, one which could fix people's images for posterity. Evidently the characters of *Folies bourgeoises* feel that they are admirable and their activities worth recording. The Duchess has her photo taken with Le Valet (the Footman), the Parish Priest is photographed spanking La Bonne (the Maid), a girl called Christine is willingly photographed with three men in her beach hut. Indeed, in a technique typical of Planchon (as we have seen in *George Dandin*), bits of scenes are rerun – in this case whenever Mlle Rose appears with her camera. Gustave, Paul Léonard, and the Lady, three characters in a love triangle, happily repeat their jealousy scene for her; the Footman and the Duchess willingly recreate their lovers' quarrel, verbatim; and La Cantatrice (the Soprano) even redoes her own 'death scene' for the camera. As in *La Langue au Chat* the camera is hypnotic and central. The social stasis of the age is represented in this constant self-conscious freezing into poses. The photographs are in a sense a symbol of the theatre itself, recording more than a superficial image, and changing completely in meaning and value when set, out of context, before the eyes of people a few decades later.

The verbal clichés of the era are pitilessly mocked, both as expressions and as attitudes. '*Très chic, très moderne*', says Mlle Rose when the Soprano in a wheelchair embraces a man so passionately that he falls to the ground, then asks to be taken to the chapel.[48] '*Très chic, très moderne*', says Paul Léonard when Gustave appears in underpants, his wife in a corset, and insists that they go home to perform their conjugal duty (I, 10, p. 21). '*Très chic, très moderne*', says Mlle Rose when the Soprano boasts that men who buy her for a night end up sleeping in a chaise longue (I, 13, p. 28). In the original plays the 'chic' and the 'modern' consist of slightly daring or unconventional behaviour, but here Planchon applies it to completely absurd sequences, while retaining the original tone of shocked admiration.

Another oft-repeated expresion is '*Ma vie, c'est un véritable roman*' (my life is quite a saga). It is spoken by Rose the maid when she tells her life story to the Minister for the Fine Arts (II, 18, p. 42); again as she disappears behind a screen with him (III, 10, p. 19); and one last time as she plays her final scene to a film camera (IV, 9, p. 18). Many in the audiences of the original plays may have wished to be able to say that they had really lived exotic lives full of sin and luxury.Time and time again in the collage, references are made to a time of luxurious idleness and decadence, as in this speech by the Soprano (and it is to be noted that Mlle Rose makes an almost identical speech in the prologue!):

Ah! The days of syphilitic assemblies and the suppers to music at the Rotonde. The days of the Admiral Godefroy Meyronay de Saint-Gril. The sumptuous days when the beautiful Madame Meyronay de Saint-Gril demonstrated her Spanish ardour by taking two lovers at once.[49]

The dream of aristocratic wickedness and pleasure is a recurring motif in the original plays. No doubt seeing and hearing these unexpressed fantasies on the stage was the safest way of indulging them, as it brought no personal, moral, or social dangers.

Many episodes in the original plays recur in a similar form from play to play, and Planchon had great fun using these, often stringing them one after another in order to devalue them. In act II, scene 16, for instance, all the characters in turn have a *crise de nerfs*, a fit of hysterics. The temper tantrums are not only hilarious when they occur in such quick succession; they also show up the childish unreality of the characters in general, and possibly hint at a hysteria not far below the surface of the lines. Whole scenes are also repeated, sometimes simply to set a mood and then laugh at it: act III, scene 1, in which four gentlemen in evening-dress smoke in a garden and the Minister for Fine Arts sighs, '*Ah, fumer une cigarette à la lueur des étoiles*' (Ah, smoking a cigarette by starlight) is repeated in all its utter banality two scenes later. Even funnier is act II, scene 7, in which Gustave gets the news of his own death, exits, returns, and starts the scene again because he has spoiled his exit – an A-effect if ever there was one! In fact there was little danger of forgetting one was at the theatre while watching *Folies bourgeoises*.

One of the most vaudevillesque uses of repetition in Planchon's play is that of the pursuit of a woman (*la poursuivie*) by a *petit homme* (paltry little fellow). He chases her onto and off the stage at every turn of the 'plot', and in varying states of dress and undress. He pursues her, at different times, with secateurs, a butterfly net, a lasso, a piece of bread and jam . . . and eventually he appears Pozzo-like, led by her on a lead. A similar point is made by Gustave's repeated insistence that he and his wife perform their conjugal duty, until they are eventually provided with a bed and allowed to get on with it. The ridiculous pursuit, the many scenes of adultery and jealousy, the absurd persistence of Gustave, all these sequences suggest that marriage was a simple social convenience, and occasionally a sexual convenience for men. In the original plays as in this collage (although of course Planchon takes the point to extremes for the fun of it) marriage is seldom allowed to interfere in people's amorous dallyings.

As we have seen, Mlle Rose's camera incites several

characters to repeat their words and gestures for her. Other scenes, too, are interrupted and started again a few minutes later, like a reel of film rewound. One scene which is constantly interrupted is that of the Minister for Fine Arts' visit to Gustave to admire the Watteau which Sansonclair is donating to the nation, in the hope of becoming a member of the Legion of Honour. The sequence of events is turned awry so many times that one begins to think of the never-begun meal in Buñuel's *The Discreet Charm of the Bourgeoisie*. The Minister is first announced in act II, scene 18, as the guests try to remember the title of a volume of poetry which he wrote as a young man. Just as he arrives there is a demonstration by some peasants offstage, which the Minister calms with a speech full of impossible promises (retirement pensions for farmers, reducing the number of civil servants without touching currently-held posts, suppressing the army except for the garrison stationed nearby . . .) The incident typifies the general attitude to politics in the plays of the *Petite Illustration*: strikes and demonstrations are an unwelcome interruption best handled by a professional. The Minister's arrival is then again announced, the poetry book again alluded to in exactly the same dialogue as before. Just as the Minister is beginning to praise the Watteau, Gustave and the Lady enter fighting and go to bed to perform their conjugal duty. Sansonclair and the Minister begin their conversation again, speaking very quickly. After one last interruption by the Maid, who gives the Minister a bouquet and then tells him her life story, we sigh with relief as Sansonclair finally gets his decoration. Unfortunately, he dies of the emotion, and the others decide to stab him to death to see if he is alive. Mlle Rose stabs him, all take a bow, the curtain falls, the Minister and Mlle Rose take a bow. Mlle Rose takes out a sign saying BIS(encore) and the scene is repeated word for word, ending with a champagne toast. We are definitely in a world similar to that of *Les Trois Mousquetaires* and *La Mise en pièces du 'Cid'*.

The scene of the Minister's visit is taken from Lucien Gleize's *Le Veau d'or* (1913), although the outrageous intrusions are from several other plays. Behind the purely and undeniably comic effect of the interrupted sequence, we begin to see the scene as it really is: a ritual in which even the attitudes are clichés, even the highest decoration a trivial mark of esteem for money. The 'realities' are more basic, and they intrude in the form of a mass demonstration, a violent sexual encounter, and an equally violent stabbing. True to the general rule, however, even these realities are trivialised. The demonstrators are gulled in an instant by implausible promises, the couple retire to bed to perform their duty, the stabbing is of a corpse, and to make doubly sure we understand its meaninglessness, we are treated to an instant replay. In *La Langue au Chat*, Planchon accused the media of trivialising serious issues; here he points a finger at the theatre of 1913–14 in Paris for performing the same soporific function.

The obvious comic advantage of a collage is that one can juxtapose speeches and scenes in the most unexpected and absurd way for effect. Planchon uses this technique in a masterful way in *Folies bourgeoises*. In Brieux's *Le Bourgeois aux champs* (1914) the hero, Gustave, dreams of the country life, and tries to persuade the Maid to follow his household into the countryside:

How many leeks per hectare do you think one can cultivate? . . . Three hundred sixteen thousand. Three hundred sixteen thousand. Won't you follow us into the country? You'll see, we'll lead a generous, happy, healthy existence there.

The Maid, reasonably enough, and as in the original, replies, 'I'm afraid I'll get bored, in the middle of all those leeks.' Planchon has Gustave exclaim, using a line from another play: 'You third-rate hooker, you bar-room slut, you music-hall harlot', and, even more inappropriately, after the Maid's unmoved retort, has him spout reflective lines from a religious melodrama, Georges Rivollet's *Jérusalem* (1914): 'It's amazing how little it takes for the hereditary mire which we have at the bottom of our soul to come back up to the surface.'[50] The absurd over-reaction and the obvious changes in tone are the key to the humour. The scene recalls *Les Trois Mousquetaires*, in which silly lines were spoken in a dramatic and solemn tone. Here there is a constant jump from the down-to-earth to the melodramatic. The play is full of such dialogue, coherent in content but discordant in tone. The technique not only allows Planchon to make full use of the original fun of some of the plays (Brieux's dialogue is highly amusing in itself), but also to point out the all-too-frequent melodramatic exaggeration of the less well-written plays.

Planchon is, of course, not above inserting a little stage business to alter the entire conception of a scene. Act III, scene 6 has dialogue straight from Pierre Weber and Marcel Gerbidon's *Un Fils d'Amérique*, but the stage business is Planchon's:

Gustave: . . . (*He takes out a pistol. He aims. Fire. A scream is heard offstage*.) Ah! Robert Pascaud is dead. Poor old chap.
The Priest: Dead? You're sure?
Gustave: I'm afraid so. He's dead. Poor old chap.
The Priest: Poor old chap.
Gustave: Yes. Pascaud died, a month ago, in Buenos Aires.[51]

In *Folies bourgeoises* as in *La Mise en pièces du 'Cid'* and *La Langue au Chat* characters appear silently onstage, passing by in a number of disguises, sometimes on a wheeled platform, as a comment on the proceedings or as an incarnation of someone's fantasies. Here we are treated to the sight of Mlle Rose passing in the distance, stretched out like a siren; there of the Minister for Fine Arts in evening dress going past on a water-bicycle, and later on a tricycle. A vision of an oriental setting complete with giraffe, palm trees, and a local inhabitant, passes to illustrate Sansonclair's nostalgic memories, and appears again and again until he eventually goes by on the little set himself. The rabbit in evening dress, chased by Gustave in hunting dress, inverts a bucket over Gustave's head. At Deauville, beach-hut doors open to reveal any number of people in different groupings and states of undress, and shut again just as quickly; the huts shake with the goings-on within. Three girls cross the stage with skipping ropes, and later cross back again pursued by three ratings. At one point two characters meow *La Marseillaise*. At another Gustave appears on skis praising the beauties of May and the garden-party he has just attended. The President of the Republic, like Corneille in *La Mise en pièces du 'Cid'*, is dragged onstage in a dustbin. Obviously much of this stage business was just for fun, as in Planchon's other musical comedies. It also gave the production a certain feverish rhythm appropriate to the period and typical of boulevard comedy.

As in *La Langue au Chat* the characters are constantly in motion and something is always happening. As the play progresses there is a sense of mounting confusion and tension, of increasing violence with a corresponding increase in the desire to ignore it. The surrealistic element in the play is a strong one, and Planchon uses dream sequences more liberally and imaginatively than in *O M'man Chicago* or even *La Langue au Chat*. Each act includes a dream sequence not unlike Le Chat's visions. In act I the dream is fairly gentle and comical, with ladies blowing bubbles, gentlemen walking like marionettes with their hands tied to their feet, etc. (scene 14). In act II (scene 17) the ladies take seashells from the flies of the gentlemen, who howl in protest; the ladies, holding the shells to their ears, go and kneel among cabbages. The image of the cabbage patch as the source of babies (the French version of the stork story told to children is that babies are found under cabbages) recurs throughout the play. This dream sequence ends quietly, with everyone waltzing. Act II as a whole has a waltz in every second or third scene, and this dream sequence even includes a delicate exit by the poet Corciadès, taking baby steps and stirring his lime-blossom tea.

As fever mounts and war approaches, the rhythm of the play changes; the waltz belonged to gentler days: act III is played to the beat of a tango. Events become more violent: a monster in evening dress appears, Mlle Rose explodes some dynamite, Gustave makes everyone strip at gunpoint. There is a sense of impending doom; clearly the atmosphere is that of Europe just before the First World War, with society becoming more and more frantically hedonistic as people sense that the end is near. Monsters appear in the dream sequence entitled '*Le Tango monstrueux*' (scene 14), and one of them later begins to shoot people; as he does, characters push two balls up to a large tube, forming a superb phallus, in an equation of violence and virility. To emphasise the point, Gustave then enters patriotically dressed as a cockerel. The symbols become more explicit and the language deteriorates into clipped phrases as the last act approaches. At the end of act III, all the characters are dead drunk.

Act IV opens on a deserted battlefield, with everyone exhausted and fed up, wearing bedraggled clothes, much as in the last scene of *La Langue au Chat*. The characters insult one another, repeating fragments of their former dialogues (as the actors of *Le Cid* did in *La Mise en pièces du 'Cid'*), as though they are too exhausted to speak in complete sentences. They discuss the disappearance of Mlle Rose, for example, in these terms:

Folies bourgeoises, St-Étienne, 1975. Pascale de Boysson as Rose, the Duchess, in the foreground, with admirers and beach huts behind

The Priest: 'ppaling
Gustave: Scandal. Run. Catch up.
The Minister: Where. Where.
All the ladies, entering on crutches: Rose disappeared?
All the men: Disappeared.
All the ladies: Dis?
All the men: 'ppeared.
Gustave: 'ppeared. 'ppeared. 'ppeared.[52]

This failure of language, like that in *La Langue au Chat*, is a failure to cope with a suddenly transformed world – with the death of an era. The conventions of the plays in *La Petite Illustration* were already petrified, obsolete even as they were being applauded; the plays did not have a language adequate to face the cataclysm beginning in 1914.

156

The dream sequence in act IV (scene 10), although it begins hilariously enough with the President of the Republic dancing in wearing a tutu, is filled with more sadistic fun; props are red-coloured, and gestures have become jerky and unbalanced. Despite the obvious despondency and growing fear, when Mlle Rose enters and instals a film camera, each of the women in turn is delighted to tell her life story to the camera (as characters did in *La Langue au Chat*); in fact, in the penultimate scene, they fight for the camera's attention. The last scene is entitled 'La guerre est déclarée' (war is declared). In a little erotico-poetic ballet, the men's guns, decorated with tricolours, are fondled lovingly and obscenely by the women, who eventually get down in the cabbage patch and produce babies. 'Mes compliments, messieurs,' says the Minister, 'c'est travailler pour la patrie.' (My compliments, gentlemen, that is really working for your country – act IV, sc. 13, p. 23.) Shells are heard exploding closer and closer, the babies are handed up to the Président, the battle mounts, one baby is impaled on a bayonet, the others are thrown at the enemy. With everyone dead, the President of the Republic in official dress, but with a skull instead of a head, salutes, ladies throw roses over the dead, and the lights go dim. Mlle Rose and the rabbit have a last toast. Before the background of doom, their tone is quite light and unconcerned: 'Champagne', they cry (act IV, sc. 13, p. 25).

7

Two modern comedies

PLANCHON wrote two plays set in the present, *Patte blanche* and *Dans le vent*. In both these plays the characters live partly in a fantasy world which reflects their reality but gives it another dimension. In both, the actions of the characters seem determined not so much by individual psychological characteristics as by social circumstances. In neither play is there a conventional plot. In *Patte blanche* one moment follows another and we are left not with a feeling of progression but of day-to-day repetition. *Dans le vent* is constructed like a boulevard play on a series of situations. In both plays Planchon did his utmost to avoid a tragic or a lyrical tone: despite the undercurrent of sadness in each of them, and their basically serious themes, Planchon insisted that they were comedies.

Patte blanche (Password)
Patte blanche, Planchon's fourth play, was written in 1965 and produced in that year with Jacques Rosner directing, and Planchon assisting. It was the first time that one of Planchon's plays was directed by someone else, and the collaboration was useful to Planchon as a playwright:

> I retouched my play and I gave it its definitive form after Jacques Rosner had read, studied and sharply criticised the first version . . . Then he did the *mise en scène*, and his way of looking at the play made me look at it afresh . . . All this forced me to make the aims of *Patte blanche* clear, it compelled me to acknowledge certain more or less hidden meanings in the work.[1]

Years later, Rosner was to read Planchon's *Le Cochon noir* in a poetic way quite different from the author's own interpretation. In the case of *Patte blanche*, Planchon resisted a strong temptation to leave everything to Rosner and see the play for the first time on opening night. He attended rehearsals and attempted to explain his text, but he respected the indepen-

158

dence of Rosner who had the ultimate authority over the stage language.

Planchon had intended to write about the Algerian war, and he found no way of doing this except by presenting it through the eyes of children. The play presents not the war itself, but the way in which most of the French lived through the war. Set in a large provincial town, the play refers to Algeria only intermittently: a young soldier returns from the front, an Arab boy is murdered . . . The killing of Arabs in France was a common occurrence in the days of the Algerian troubles. The programme for *Patte blanche* includes a montage of actual newspaper cuttings from the dailies of cities and towns all over France with such headings as 'Shooting at Drancy: Five Algerian Muslims Killed'; 'A North African Shot Down in Saint-Chamond'; 'Body of a North African Found in the Seine', etc. In the play this sort of news, like the war itself, attracts little attention or interest. The play is in fact about this very indifference.

The plot revolves around three young boys, nicknamed King, Al Capone, and Ben-Hur. They meet regularly in a wooden shed in an empty lot, a refuge which they have named *L'Igloo-planque* (the igloo-hideout). They have a strict rule that in order to enter the *Igloo-planque* one has to show (literally) the white paw (*patte blanche*), present one's credentials, that is, to be accepted by the three of them. Each boy's dreams, and their games, are depicted alongside real situations at home. Their parents and families and all the adults in the play go about their business in a way which is both familiar and mysterious to the children. King's older brother, Gilbert, returns from the Algerian front embittered, boastful, and unwilling to settle down. Their father, M. Blanchot, is a widower thinking of remarrying. Ben-Hur's parents, the Prévieux, keep up a marriage which is no more than a convenience for both of them. Capone' uncle sells the *pension* which he has been running with his sister and buys the café across the street; he and one of his lodgers decide to marry; he sends Capone off to boarding school. Just before Capone leaves, a young Arab who sold peanuts in a café near the *Igloo-planque* is shot and killed near the shed, and his death frightens the boys more than they wish to admit.

There is thus no central line of action. In one of Planchon's talks with the actors after a rehearsal, he emphasised that the play merely follows a number of situations:

This play was written like a musical score. The dialogues are like a
background music, from which themes sometimes arise, racism,
war, old age . . . Almost as soon as they appear, these themes disappear in the flow of words. I ask you therefore to play the moment:
as in life, one word brings another, the individual moment is as
important as the historical moment. The word, as soon as it is said,
is lost, forgotten, left behind . . . Nothing stays, nothing is resolved, everything remains in suspense. No structure holds the
play together, no dramatic progression carries it forward. There are
children with their dreams, there are adults with their problems:
the whole makes up a fragment of everyday life. Everything looks
normal, and yet it is within this normality that there are all the
problems.[2]

The boys' fantasies, although they can be quite sadistic, are
not tragic. Planchon wanted these fantasy scenes to be
played as realistically as the others, and Rosner solved the
problem of setting them off slightly by using a subtle lighting
change. The boys' dreams are inspired by their real lives.
King, whose real name is Jean Blanchot, has lost his mother
and baby sister in a fire five years previously. He creates for
the benefit of his two friends a fictitious older sister who is
both beautiful and popular. Capone, Georges Chausson, is an
orphan being brought up by his aunt and uncle; his fantasies
make up for their lack of generosity to him. In reality he steals
money in order to buy himself something; in his dreams the
adults bow to his every request. Of the three boys, Ben-Hur
(Gérard Prévieux) has the most 'normal' home, at least in the
sense that he has both father and mother. His father, however, is a philanderer, and his mother relieves her boredom
by indulging in a Lesbian relationship with an old friend.
Ben-Hur's dreams are the most far-fetched; like his friends he
compensates in his imagination for an inadequate reality. As
in an Apollinaire play, and in many of Planchon's own plays
(notably La Mise en pièces du 'Cid'), for Ben-Hur a word
immediately calls up a vision. When he tells his friends that
his mother is an 'abandoned wife', he imagines her, and the
audience sees her, shooting his father. When he tells them
that his father reasons like a Jesuit, he and we see M. Prévieux
dressed as a Jesuit and protesting that he is an atheist.
    During a party the three boys get drunk together and have a
collective fantasy in which they avenge themselves on the
adults. The scene is completely surrealistic. The adults enter
looking threatening, until they are suddenly cowed by the

sound of a pirate ship's trumpet! The children thereafter take
command, ordering the adults to row, and then to put on a
variety show. One sings a song, another blows up furniture
with dynamite, a third does vocal imitations, and someone
else juggles plates. After a sea-storm in which everyone gets
sick, all the adults join in singing a mock-Wagnerian song.
The sequence has the amusing absurdity of Vitrac's *Victor ou
les enfants au pouvoir*, a play which Planchon produced in
1955 at the Théâtre de la Comédie. It looks forward to *La Mise
en pièces du 'Cid'* and *Folies bourgeoises* in which Planchon
gave his surrealistic bent full sway.

The boys in *Patte blanche* of course share in the ordinary
games of childhood. Planchon specified in the script that
some aspects of these games should be dramatised, although
not as seriously as the fantasies. When the boys take off in an
imaginary rocket, for example, the audience was to hear the
portholes clap shut and the engines start up; by exaggerating
the boys' own sound effects, the staging created a comical
perspective on their games – their imitation of motors for this
sequence, for instance, was amplified to suggest a superb
model of a super-rocket. Planchon succeeded in entering the
child's world of fantasy, both the personal fantasies born of
individual fears, and the collective imaginary games which
all children play. The adults in the play, except for Sophie,
the servant in the *pension*, remain indifferent to this aspect
of the boys' lives.

The boys, for their part, cannot understand the adults'
complicated world. Capone's uncle persistently courts one
of the lady lodgers in his *pension*; Tayssière, another
boarder, makes Sophie his mistress; Capone's aunt constantly invents tall stories of family crimes in order to get
attention. The adults' petty rivalries and jealousies are too
complex for a young boy to understand. King rightly says, at
the beginning of the play, 'Sex, that's for old perverts of
twenty.'[3] In every case the adults' conversations are unsuit-
able for the boys or inaccessible to them; they are too intellectual or too frighteningly salacious.

Between the world of the adults and that of the children
there is only one common ground: the boys have already
begun to acquire their elders' prejudices. At the beginning of
the play, the boys discuss the possibility of introducing a
young Arab boy, whom they have nicknamed 'Salut-mon-
Z'ami' (Hello-mine's-friend, no doubt from his greeting to

them) into their igloo-hideout. The two arguments in his favour are that he sells peanuts, which are very good, and that he seems nice. Capone declares, however, with the full conviction of received opinion, that no Arab can be trusted; he has heard from his aunt and uncle that they go about with razors in their pockets and attack Frenchwomen. The prejudice against Arabs is shown to be so deeply ingrained that it is nearly unconscious. 'North African' is itself a term of contempt. Algerians in general are called by the derogatory name *bicots*, a familiar term for a young goat; the boys use this term as frequently as their parents. The general attitude to the war itself is also very cynical. Most people simply ignore it. They place the responsiblity for it squarely on the shoulders of the government, and make no connection between their own racism and the imperialistic policies of their country.

'Salut-mon-Z'ami' is shot one evening very near the igloo-hideout, and a terrified Capone hears the shots from the shed. The killing gets little news coverage. Ben-Hur manages to find it: 'Capone, have you seen it, the newspaper talks about the death of "Salut-mon-Z'ami". Only you have to be very clever to find it; there are only three lines and his name is Mohammed-something-impossible-to-pronounce.'[4] Evidently the newspaper's readers would show little interest in this sort of killing.

It is this type of indifference which attracted Planchon's attention. His play shows how the questions of war and of reprisals on French soil could be ignored even as they went on. In *Patte blanche*, as earlier in *La Remise* and later in *Le Cochon noir* or *Bleus, blancs, rouges*, the characters see history in a fragmented and distorted way; it seems to take place *beside* their lives. Without insisting, *Patte blanche* made it clear that there is a continuum between the children's easy and unconscious assumption of the racism around them and the adults' eventual apathetic assent to war. Because the Algerian war had taken place quite recently (1954–62), the play had immediate relevance for Planchon's public. In Britain in the 1960s and 1970s it would be necessary only to change the word 'Algeria' to the word 'Ulster', or perhaps 'Arabs' to 'Asians'. Planchon was trying to make people aware of their own tendency to dismiss as irrelevant to them historical events which their attitudes have helped to bring about.

Because the action of the play alternates between the realistic and the fantastical, the stage sets were stylised and yet gave the impression of a realistic setting. They were designed by Michel Rafaelli in a pop-art style. The *Igloo-planque* was litte more than the silhouette of a shed, placed on wheels. It was easily moved out, to be replaced by a few symbolic elements of the lower-middle-class homes in which the children live. Around the stage was a neon panel, and its lighting changed to indicate whether a scene was fantasy or reality. Within the fantasy scenes, the costumes were quite realistic, if far-fetched: they ranged from a Jesuit's robe to a hairy Frankenstein disguise.

Critics, although many complained about the lack of a clear story line, were impressed by the delicate way in which the play brought out the themes of racism and the lack of communication between parents and children. *Patte blanche* is representative of many of Planchon's tendencies both in the theatre and in his writing. The play has a strong surrealistic element in its attempt to portray both the real and the dream worlds of the children onstage. Planchon loves the theatre for its life-like transience: in *Patte blanche* he captured a sense of the ephemerality of childhood. By using children in the play he also created a new perspective on superficially banal events. The children do not understand the adults or their ideas, and yet the audience sees the events of the play through the eyes of the children; compelled to share this fresh vision of the 'typical' adults on the stage, they are provoked to judge them and their typical values as well. Planchon had been worried at first about putting children on the stage. When the play was produced, he found that the adult level of the play did not work, but that the children's scenes did.[5] It is true that the grown-ups' reasonable discussions in the play are far less interesting than the comical, absurd, and sometimes quite moving fantasies, games, and conversations of the children.

The play was meant, as always with Planchon, to raise consciousness; to show, in this case, how easy it is to ignore the larger problems, such as the Algerian war, and to allow trivial problems to become the substance of one's daily existence. It was intended as a description of reality so authentic as to be in itself a call for change.

Dans le vent (*Trendies*)
Planchon wrote *Dans le vent*, his sixth play, in the winter of
1967, and presented it in Villeurbanne in 1968. He wrote two
versions of the play, and finally used the first, slightly modified according to the actors' reactions to it.

Jacques Rosner and Gilles Chavassieux assisted Planchon
in directing the play. *Dans le vent* has all the makings of
a boulevard play: slick modern sets, people falling in and
out of love, slamming doors, sudden exits, surprise entrances . . . In fact, Planchon found after he had written it
that it was somewhat like Vitrac's theatre in that it used
boulevard conventions, although it was not a boulevard
play. Planchon's purpose was to describe a certain social
class in contemporary French society. He described the
play's characters as '. . . a group of middle-class young
people who frequent cafés, who dance the jerk in fashionable
nightclubs and who repeat (with a little bad faith) "Hitler?
Never heard of him".'[6]

The figures in the play belong to a privileged social group.
Like the characters of Marivaux's plays, they have no financial worries, and therefore they have time to think about their
personal problems. They are apparently frivolous, but their
idleness and boredom has a tragic undercurrent. Planchon
insisted that his play was neither a tragedy nor a satire. It was
simply a love comedy set in the modern world.

The characters' eagerness to be fashionable makes them
vulnerable to prevailing ideas. Through them, therefore, it
was possible for Planchon to touch on the current climate of
thought in French society. One of the modern trends which
interested Planchon was the tendency in France as elsewhere in Europe to adopt American ways of thought:

It seemed important to me to see how the modern world is integrated into the bourgeoisie. Europe is being assailed by American
mores. Along with these, we are swallowing puritanism and a
kind of anguish which used to be foreign to us. We make fun of
the Americans, we enjoy seeing them lose face. At the same time,
we are influenced by them. The play speaks of this change in
mores.[7]

It was a theme which Planchon was to attack once again in
his production of Michel Vinaver's *Par-dessus bord*. Planchon saw this process as the inevitable historical domination
by an economically and politically stronger power over

small nations, an insinuation of the American super-
structure into the French mentality.

The play revolves around several interconnected groups of
people. Jacques the businessman and Mackie, the girlie-
magazine photographer, both wish to marry Anne, a reporter
who is already Mackie's mistress. Charles, Mackie's personal
assistant, is supposed to provide models willing to pose in
the nude; he meets Lou and Jojotte, tries unsuccessfully to
persuade them to pose for Mackie, then kidnaps Jojotte.
Frédéric, a rich idle young Oxford graduate, visits Mackie's
studio while Charles and Jojotte are there. Jojotte runs off
with Frédéric and they spend the night together. Frédéric's
family is in a turmoil. His widowed mother, Françoise,
wishes to remarry, with a politician, and his sister Lou has
left home because she is against the marriage. Régis, Françoise's father, insists that Lou's opposition to the marriage
is political. Lou meanwhile meets a drop-out, Joë, who is
Jacques's cousin, and Joë takes her to Jacques's apartment.

Anne spends a night with Jacques, is discovered by Mackie, and then leaves both of them. Jacques experiments with
LSD, and buys a toy guillotine to play with. Mackie, rejecting
Geneviève, an old friend who wants to marry him, leaves for
Alaska. Joë abandons Lou and she tries to kill herself; meanwhile her grandfather Régis has succeeded in finding her by
questioning Charles.

Frédéric plans to marry Jojotte, who is expecting his child.
Joë and Anne leave together for Cuba, but Régis dies as he
accompanies them to the airport, and they return to tell the
family. Lou finally accepts her mother's decision to remarry.

When he directed this play, Planchon stuck to his principle of putting the *fable* before interpretation of character.
Repeatedly, during rehearsals, he asked actors not to make
value judgements about their character at first.[8] He wanted
them to play each scene in and for itself: the spectator's
judgement should be based on the sum of a character's actions
and attitudes throughout the play, rather than on his appearance in the first few scenes. The play was meant to reflect the
unpredictability of life, and therefore a character must not
give away his future behaviour. As the characters' only con-
sistency lay in their inconsistency, continuity had to be
created by the *mise en scène* rather than by the acting. The
characters simply adapt to their circumstances as these
change. Planchon made the pace of the production alternate

between very fast, eventful sequences in which everyone takes action, and slower scenes during which little happens and the characters hesitate to make decisions. He thus created a sense of instability and uncertainty within the *fable* as well as in the characterisation.

The sets created the atmosphere of a boulevard comedy. René Allio and Planchon created an elaborate *machine à jouer* (acting machine, a term which Planchon first used to describe the sets for *Troilus and Cressida* in 1964). Like Rafaelli's design for *Patte blanche*, the style was strongly influenced by pop art. The sets consisted of three movable boxes which could be joined or separated to suggest telephone booths, a nightclub entrance, or an ultra-modern apartment. The furnishings for the various interiors were simple and also ultra-modern; they were wheeled in on trolleys or lowered from the flies. For the airport scene, for example, one saw two clocks and the silhouette of the tail of an airplane; in Mackie's studio, there were two huge enlargements of scantily-clad women, and a cut-out silhouette of a nude, her back decorated with a huge flower. All these movable elements (clocks, photographs, etc.) were visible, slightly illuminated, even when not in use.

The sets gave a visual background to the kind of mentality which the play describes. The innumerable gadgets which Jacques accumulates were the material equivalent of the ironic speech behind which he hides, and a symbol of the inadequacy of words for him; at the same time they were examples of Americanism creeping into Europe. When Jacques wants to seduce Anne at the airport, he takes out an inflatable sofa and almost asks her to join him on it before deflating it again. Middle-class preoccupations, shaped by and reflected in modern advertising, were expressed on the stage by the neon-lit nightclubs, the posters exploiting women, etc. The looming presence of the props suspended from the flies created a slightly oppressive atmosphere, that of people about to be submerged by consumer goods. The set recalled that of *Richard III* in 1966, in which instruments of torture and of warfare remained menacingly visible throughout the production. It was also the forerunner to the overcrowded pandemonium of *La Mise en pièces du 'Cid'*, and finally to the claustrophobic and infernal vision of *La Langue au Chat*, in which humanity is literally suffocating under piles of industrial waste.

As in boulevard plays, in *Dans le vent* coincidence follows upon coincidence, and chance meetings are the rule rather than the exception. Characters meet, love, pursue, and leave or marry one another with astonishing speed. However, instead of creating the reassuring atmosphere of an ordinary boulevard play, *Dans le vent* fills one with a growing unease. Planchon deliberately eliminated from the play one of the basic ingredients of boulevard theatre: the feeling that all will come right in the end. The play gives the impression that the events and situations really are succeeding one another in a haphazard way. Already in *Patte blanche* Planchon had captured (particularly in the scene of the boys' drunken fantasy) this Vitrac-like sense of unpredictability; in *Dans le vent* however, it is the premise of the entire play. Even Planchon's collage *Folies bourgeoises* was not to leave the spectator so uncertain at one moment of what was to happen the next.

The text of the play is full of the fantasmagorical. The characters express their dreams in fashionable clichés and in self-consciously clever terms. Although they are less likeable than the children of *Patte blanche*, the characters are never totally ridiculous. Their dreams express human inadequacies too believable to be completely laughable. They seem unable at times to distinguish between their private truths and the reality around them. Language is for them an unreliable means of communication, and they use it with suspicion. Each character is turned inward upon himself or herself; during one rehearsal Planchon even suggested that 'The actors must not look at one another, but each must try to find out if the other is looking at him . . . the characters play their own caricature.'[9] In Planchon's production of *Bérénice* the characters, surrounded by mirrors, often looked at their own reflection as they addressed other people. In *Dans le vent* they were surrounded with reflections of themselves as a social group rather than as individuals (the gadgets, the photographs, the slick furnishings . . .); the stage picture was one of class narcissism.

Planchon emphasised the characters' diffidence about words in two ways: in the written text, he had them express their feelings only in extravagant metaphors; in the production, as he had done for *Bérénice*, he emphasised the silences. Characters 'spoke' through their silences and their physical attitudes as much as through their words. Planchon

was to say, almost ten years later, that he thinks of most of the
speeches in his plays as '. . . coming out of a huge well of
silence and subsiding back again as soon as the impulse has
passed'.[10] The characters can express neither love nor pain
directly. Jojotte, for example, from the moment of her first
meeting with Frédéric, disguises her feeling for him in fairy-
tale language; she tells him '. . . a prince has entered into my
life. You are my prince, my knight . . .',[11] and Frédéric
responds by calling her Miss Mustard Seed.

The grandfather, Régis, uses fantasy as a game, in which he
opposes to a sordid and depressing political reality (that of
France in the 1960s) the ideal of a Greek republic which will
someday be re-established:

> it is not the young who are dangerous, it is all those who hope to
> brainwash me, who want to extirpate my singularity. I have the list
> of all those who belong to this plot, a gigantic international machi-
> nation which is determined to liquidate the last Greeks in order
> that there be nothing left, in front of the television set, but depoliti-
> cised and aseptic *petits bourgeois*.[12]

Régis's vision looks forward to the world of *La Langue au
Chat*, and his belief in the eventual triumph of the Greeks (of
the individual), is as touching as La Grosse's faith in the
coming of the Martians.

Just as the dream sequences in *Patte blanche* were played
realistically, so the poetic fancies of the characters in *Dans le
vent* were delivered with an emphasis on the literal meaning
of the words. Just as in Planchon's productions *Les Trois
Mousquetaires* and *La Mise en pièces du 'Cid'*, the actors
carried each figure of speech to its logical conclusion. When
an intoxicated Jojotte decided that she could walk on water,
she went into the bathroom to attempt it. When Frédéric said,
'I have a nail stuck in the back of my head'[13] he bent his knees
under the blows, looked up to see where they were coming
from, etc. Thus the concrete rather than the symbolic meaning of the words was constantly emphasised. In this way,
according to Jacques Blanc, poetic or fanciful lines became
more powerful because they ceased to appear as a paren-
thesis in the action and became part of the living character.[14]
The effect justified Planchon's long-standing mistrust of
over-pathetic interpretations of poetic passages.

Planchon's calculated misuse of the boulevard conventions surprised and interested critics, who persisted, despite

Planchon's claims to the contrary, in seeing the play as a
satire. Although it is not a satire of the middle class, nor
of the kind of characters presented, the play does offer a
pastiche of a genre, and it does so very well. Many critics
complained, however, of the puppet-like quality of the
characters, and felt, justifiably, that the lack of plot and the
deliberate superficiality made the play seem pointless. One
after another, they said that Planchon should have taken a
more definite stance in relation to the characters.

Certainly Planchon had set himself a difficult task: to portray people who were fashionable and upper-middle class,
who were at the same time caricatures of fashionableness,
and to show up the falseness of their values without making
them seem either worthless or dull themselves. Even his
critics had to admit that he had not failed entirely. In a few
isolated scenes, the tender irony behind the comedy came
out -- it is evident in the reading throughout the play, but in
the staging it seems to have come out particularly in those
scenes which were fanciful. There is one, for instance, in
which Charles, tired of persuading girls to pose in the nude,
dreams of giving it all up and becoming a shepherd in Provence. It is in their dreams of innocence, in their desire to be
loved, that the characters of *Dans le vent* are most human and
believable. For even such characters as these, Planchon
showed a sense of compassion. 'We well know,' wrote Jean-
Jacques Lerrant, 'in any case, that beneath an attitude and
a tone which are sometimes cynical, there is always in
Planchon a secret tenderness and a passionate interest in
beings and in their behaviour.'[15]

Even the usually sympathetic Lerrant, however, thought
that this play belonged in Planchon's career to a period of
'ascetic irony' which he, Lerrant, did not understand. The
play was written at the beginning of 1968, the year which
was to be that of the *événements*, and the year which was to
inspire the company to put on *La Mise en pièces du 'Cid'*.
One of the charges levelled at that play was that it lacked a
positive basis for its satire. Perhaps this lack of a definite
viewpoint was merely the culmination of a process of standing back and taking stock, which Planchon had begun long
before 1968. Planchon had tried to depict a social class in
such a way that people would take a fresh look at it and at
themselves in relation to it as they watched the play. Unfortunately, the picture was not in itself interesting enough. The

play was not a success with Planchon's audiences. Nevertheless, it is important as an ambitious experiment to use an old
comedy genre as the medium for a basically serious examination of our society.

In each of these two plays, a sense of the transience of
human existence gives the text a tinge of ironic sadness. The
boys in *Patte blanche* eventually leave behind not only the
igloo-hideout, but also the childish sense of protective
camaraderie which it gave them. In *Dans le vent* relationships begin and end, and people reject or accept one another
with a painful suspicion that even superficially-made decisions may have irredeemable effects. They do not control
their own destiny because, like the children of the first play,
they are not fully aware of the forces which help to shape it.
Of the two plays, *Patte blanche* is the more moving; it is set in
the provincial milieu which Planchon knows well, and the
characters are therefore more believable.

Neither play was a success in terms of audience response.
Planchon once said[16] that he always knew when he had
failed to achieve his aims in a play: he felt like rewriting it
immediately after it had been presented. Possibly *Dans le
vent* was an attempt to do more successfully what he had
tried to do in *Patte blanche*: to reduce the emotional and
psychological importance of the characters, while at the
same time refusing to write a linear plot. He had succeeded
in doing both these things in the musical comedies, for they
were almost revues; he had succeeded in *Bleus, blancs,
rouges* because the audience's knowledge of the historical
events of the Revolution gave the play a structure external to
itself. The *fable* needs to be more than a succession of unpredictable, incidentally connected events; even a slice of life
needs careful cutting for the stage. These two plays are interesting because they show Planchon experimenting with
something other than the intense human portraits of his
peasant plays or the slapstick fun of his musical comedies.
They are, however, experiments.

8

The provincial plays

La difficulté est de trouver le point de rencontre entre le
quotidien et le mythe.

Peter Brook

A deep-seated provincialism links Planchon's four peasant
plays, *La Remise* (1962), *L'Infâme* (1969), *Le Cochon noir*
(1973), *Gilles de Rais* (1975), and his play on the French
Revolution, *Bleus, blancs, rouges* (1967).

All the plays are set in the provinces, *La Remise* and
L'Infâme specifically in the Ardèche, *Le Cochon noir* in a
very similar small remote village, *Bleus, blancs, rouges* in
provincial France and the émigré routes of Europe, *Gilles de
Rais* in medieval Brittany. Characters commit atrocious
crimes in the apparent hope that their geographical remoteness will protect them – and indeed in some cases it does, for
a time at least. In four of the plays there is a war going on
'outside', a term which includes Paris. However, and this is
the essence of their provincialism, it is never quite 'their'
war, for all the sons it sends back maimed or mad. The
provincialism in these plays is that of people who sense that
all political initiatives are taken elsewhere.

La Remise (The Return)

La Remise was the first play to which Planchon admitted
authorship. It was first put on in 1962 at Villeurbanne, recreated in November 1963, and taken to Paris in April 1964. It
was published with *Le Cochon noir* in 1973.

Planchon found his first attempt at writing very difficult.
In an interview in 1974, he was to recall his early problems: 'I
had two handicaps: I was a director, and therefore someone
who thought in pictures, and I could not be naive. I knew
what a good play was . . .'[1] When it came to directing his own
play, the problems increased:

I could not bring myself to sacrifice, for the sake of the show, what it had cost me so much to write; to emphasise one aspect of the text to the detriment of the other. And especially the more I reread it, and the more I rewrote it, the worse I found it. It took me three years to get over the problem.[2]

La Remise is a semi-autobiographical work written at least partly for reasons of the heart. Planchon felt deeply attached to the wild and deserted region in which his father grew up, and he admired the grandiose character of his grandfather, on whom he based the figure of Émile Chausson. He placed the portrait of his ancestors in the context of the historical transformation which took place in France between 1919 and 1957.

The word *remise* means both a resetting of something into its place, and a storage shed or outbuilding on a farm, and so the title refers both to the psychological journey of the young hero, and to the setting of the crime. The programme included a poem by Planchon on the *remise* in which he spent part of his boyhood holidays on the farm. In the play, a police investigation into the killing of his grandfather leads a young man back to his father's birthplace, the village of Borée, and acquaints him, in spite of himself, with his origins. He discovers that Émile Chausson his grandfather, because he was obsessed with his land, worked his wife to death, drove his older son Célestin to leave home and his younger son Gabriel to suicide. Whilst the enquiry is taking place in the village, Célestin, who is the young man's father, is dying in a city hospital. Planchon admitted that the young man, Paul Chausson, represented himself:

I imagine that my brother (or I), knowing nothing of the story, comes into the Ardèche, learns everything and understands nothing. It is a kind of slow going back for this adolescent, in search of distant, long-dead beings. With, also, the fear of stirring up the past . . .[3]

Planchon rewrote the play in 1964, and again before publishing it in 1973. The time structure was the most experimental aspect of the work, and the part which Planchon changed most in successive revisions. Thre are four enquiry scenes, which take place in three days; the remembered action, however, spans the years from 1919 to 1954. Paul narrated the play. When he spoke of events discovered at second hand, the scenes were presented in a classical manner, with unity of time and place, and with presentation, climax, and outcome. When Paul told of events which he himself had lived through, on the other hand, there were jumps in time, flashbacks, sudden abridgements, abrupt transitions.

In the published version, Paul is not present at the enquiry scenes and there is no narrator. Planchon, however, retained the classical unity of time and place in the flashback scenes, and the more open structure of the enquiry scenes. Here, Chausson's elder son Célestin (Paul's father) is visible in his hospital setting during the enquiry scenes which take place in the village. His son Paul is usually by his side. We also see the various characters in the *remise*, the outhouse in which the enquiry is conducted, each giving a fragmentary account of the events leading up to the murder. The police commissioner visits Célestin in hospital; when Célestin asks questions of him, one of the characters answers from the *remise*. Thus the play in its published version has the kind of simultaneous multiple setting which Armand Gatti used in his play *La Vie imaginaire de l'éboueur Auguste Geai*. There the dustman Geai looks from a hospital bed upon several settings representing himself at various stages of his life. Jacques Rosner, Planchon's assistant, directed a production of *Auguste Geai* at Villeurbanne and in Paris in the same programme as *La Remise*. Gatti's experiment with time and place may well have influenced Planchon's successive productions of his own play.

In earlier productions too the sets were designed to convey the different levels of time and reality, as Planchon explained:

The events which Paul has lived through are in a real and precise framework (a real outhouse) whereas the classical scenes from the past are set in an 'exploded framework'.
Our classical set can indeed explode into its elements, these elements can in turn become an abstract outline. Transformable sets are generally used in the theatre to change the setting; this one on the contrary is used to describe the same setting in various ways.[4]

The 'exploded set' (*décor explosé*) opened up the setting and gave it the flexibility of the imagination. Gatti used the term *décor éclaté*, with a similar meaning, to describe the simultaneous presence onstage of various times and settings; the technique has been used by many directors since, notably Michel Parent and Ariane Mnouchkine.

In Planchon's productions of *La Remise* the classic set was almost naturalistic: a peasant's house with one wall removed in which one could see the crude table, the water boiling on the wood stove, the soup sending up a thick steam. For the enquiry scenes, the walls opened and were partially raised up, transforming the set into a stylised, non-realistic *remise*. Lighted panels gave the date of each scene. In the 1964 version, Allio added a revolving stage and no longer used lateral walls, although the sets were again raised into the flies for the enquiry scenes. Even when the action ranged to other settings, elements of the *remise* were always present; characters such as Chausson's younger son Gabriel who try to escape seem to carry its presence about with them. All the costumes were in shades of grey, and the sets were also stone-coloured or in dull beige tones.

In writing the play, Planchon tried to capture the flavour of the language which his grandfather spoke, because it was characteristic of the area in which he lived. It was a hard, rugged speech, the language of those who speak little but mean what they say. In order to recapture its quality, Planchon used sixteenth-century turns of phrase. Bernard Dort rightly compared Planchon's style in this play to Claudel's: one need only read the following speech by the embittered spinster Marie Giffard as she burns her never-used trousseau: 'It's a wretched piece of holland cloth, in the old style, which has never known either the dampness of the skin or the grass and the sun to dry it. The trousseau of a young girl from a great house with five cows, as spotless as on the first day.'[5] The 1962 text was rather elliptical in its attempt to recreate a terse peasant speech; the second was much clearer, and the published version has the conciseness and emphasis of the work of an experienced writer. (By 1973 Planchon had written five more plays not counting the musical comedies.) Here is Émile Chausson's poignant protest against the collapse of his world, as it appears in the 1973 text:

You have no land, you cannot understand. The government is replanting the woods, not chestnut-trees, but pine. Those filthy great trunks, of no use. In what had become a meadow or a field of rye, they're replanting pines. All the walls that were holding back the soil are crumbling more and more every winter, no one dreams of replacing the stones. And everyone bawling that the world is changing. Certainly it's changing: the rains make the soil slip downwards. Everything is decaying and everything is wearing

La Remise. The 'exploded' set

away. This soil, that our fathers and our fathers' fathers had carried back up in sacks, is sliding slowly towards its former place. As if all that sweat was to no purpose but to wear out their carcasses a little faster.[6]

When he first rewrote the play, Planchon filled out the minor characters. The police inspector, from the dull stereotype which he is in the 1962 version, became in the 1964 version a distinctive character with a wry sense of humour and a predilection for bacon sandwiches. Similarly, the old country doctor Isidore Gardien, from a mere witness, became in the second play an ex-socialist who has postponed leaving the Ardèche until he is too old to want to move after all. In the final version, the police inspector retains his wit, the doctor his regrets, but these are suggested and not dwelt upon; the figures are set back in relation to the major protagonists.

Planchon obviously took heed of the critics' opinions when he rewrote his play. In the 1962 script, for example, a journalist is present at the enquiry, looking for a sensational story. He speaks for the world outside, and ultimately represents its indifference, but the fluttering inquisitive figure, completely extraneous to the plot, annoyed many critics, and justifiably so. Planchon eliminated the character in the later versions.

Another justified criticism of the 1962 and 1964 plays was that, beside the towering figure of Émile Chausson, the young Paul seems faded and insignificant. Certainly as the flashbacks which we see are not a part of Paul's own memories, his role as a 'guide' is rather unnecessary. In the published play, Planchon eliminated the two speeches, at the beginning and the end of the play, in which Paul narrates the play. In the final version Paul is little more than a son worried and a little puzzled by his father's anguish over events long passed. Making Paul an outsider, Planchon focused on the remorse of Célestin, a remorse barely suggested in the first two versions of the play. Célestin's regret for the past is certainly more plausible than Paul's acquired grief. The underlying irony of the play is that Paul feels nothing for the land, save compassion for those who exhausted themselves upon it; by shifting the balance between Paul and Célestin, Planchon brought out this irony most clearly in the published text.

Planchon also altered the character of Marie Giffard totally in the last version of the play. She is a woman frustrated of her hopes of marrying Gaston, Émile Chausson's older brother, because in her youth she was seduced by Émile Chausson. In the published version she is not only a bitter old maid; she is also still Émile Chausson's mistress, bound to him by her desperate desire to have a child. Her final fury and her claim to be the murderess are far more plausible in the light of the cruel, hopeless, and cynical relations which Chausson has had with her, to the knowledge of the entire village. Mme Chausson was also changed; from a passive and docile beast of burden in the first two versions, she became, in the published play, a woman whose strength matches that of Émile Chausson, who can threaten to shoot him if he lays a hand on her son, and who scoffs bitterly at the despair of her husband's mistress Marie Giffard.

As Adamov had done in *Paolo Paoli*, Planchon intended here to show the larger events of international politics running parallel to local occurrences. Thus Borée's inhabitants are affected by two world wars as well as the war in Indo-China. The first two versions were criticised because the references to the Indo-Chinese war seemed to be artificial

and unconvincing additions. They do seem to be almost
afterthoughts. In an attempt to integrate them into the *fable*,
Planchon added to the published play the figure of a com-
manding officer under whom Gabriel Chausson served in
Indo-China; the man assumes, when he learns of Gabriel's
suicide, that the young man fell into despair after seeing
France surrender Indo-China. This opinion lends weight to a
speech by Gabriel, which appears in all three versions, and
which draws a parallel between the fighting in Indo-China
and the battle against progress in Borée:

Some things are a dead-loss before you start them. You clear a wood
for nothing. The soil is too sparse. You fight for nothing in the
paddy-fields. Have to clear out . . . I've learned to handle a
tommy-gun and a spade. That's something anyhow. (1973, pp.
142–3).

When Planchon spoke of *La Remise*, he said that its characters were important to him in themselves and not only as
victims of poverty and economic change. The peasants had a
sense of grandeur which fascinated him. Planchon himself
played Émile Chausson and, both as a playwright and as an
actor, he brought out brilliantly the nobility beneath the old
man's apparently stupid and futile resistance to change. The
ferociously uncompromising figure was so powerfully
drawn that some critics felt it overwhelmed the 'social'
theme. Certainly the portrait is central to the play: it is also,
however, central to the theme.
  Planchon created a character who was gassed during the
First World War, he had Gabriel fight in Indo-China and lose
a foot there in a land-mine explosion; he showed that during
the Second World War, the peasants, even the Chaussons,
prospered for a few years. The effects of the outer world on
Borée are all too evident. But it is the inexorable economic
change, the factory, the coming of electricity, the movement
of young people toward the cities, and finally the reafforest-
ation of the mountainsides which generations have painstakingly cleared away, which are the real marks of history on
this poor and isolated area. It is in Émile Chausson's proud
resistance to these signs of change that the social theme of
the play lies. He refuses to recognise economic change as the
principal force with which he must deal. When he wilfully
prevents 'the city' from installing electricity in Borée, when
he burns down the factory, he is not accepting them as the

opposition, but trying to eliminate their interference with his fight against the mountainside, which is his life's work. Émile Chausson is drawn as a being to be pitied but not forgiven; Planchon gives a perspective on him, on the cruelty and stupidity of his fight, but at the same time he makes the character infinitely moving. In his depiction of this old man's passion, Planchon showed a deep feeling for the Ardéchois, for their poverty, their remoteness, for their powerlessness over their own lives, for the fact that they have been left behind to watch their way of life disintegrating. The Ardéchois although they refer to France as another country are, inevitably and unfortunately for them, a part of it and of the world.

Claude Roy, in 1964, compared *La Remise* with Gatti's equally autobiographical play *La Vie imaginaire de l'éboueur Auguste Geai*:

> The two works have a forcefulness, a truth which comes from afar, and that knack of moving us because to begin with the author himself was moved, the straightforward tone of one who puts his hand on our arm and asks us: 'Can it be that you really consider it fair . . . Don't you think that one should do something . . . Don't you think?' It is not a tone which one hears so often in the theatre.[7]

It is the tone of all four of Planchon's peasant plays, a tone of compassion tempered by intelligence and enhanced by retrospective understanding.

Bleus, blancs, rouges ou Les Libertins (Blues, Whites, and Reds or The Libertines)
Planchon's play on the French Revolution, *Bleus, blancs, rouges ou Les Libertins* was first written and produced in 1967. It was rewritten and put on again in 1971. In October 1974 it was put on at the Birmingham Repertory Theatre by John Burgess and Michael Simpson, under the title *Blues, Whites and Reds*, in a translation by John Burgess. It was the first of Planchon's plays to be produced abroad by another company. Planchon spoke to the actors twice about the characters, but attended no rehearsals: the interpretation of the play was left to the two British directors.

In *Patte blanche* and in *Dans le vent* Planchon experimented with dramatic structure, placing the characters in a series of situations not connected by a linear plot. In *Bleus, blancs, rouges*, the events of the play are similarly unpredictable for the characters, but they are familiar to the audience as history. The plot is not linear, but made up of interconnecting stories which Planchon gleaned from biographies of the period.

Both versions of the play range in time from the year 1789 to the year 1800, and in place from France to the émigré routes, Florence, and Milan. The characters belong to various groups: first, that of the libertines led by Aubier d'Arbonne, a young aristocrat who refuses to consummate his marriage with a young *bourgeoise*; secondly, that of Aubier d'Arbonne's brother, a homosexual archbishop, and his associates; thirdly, that of the rejected wife Maurille, her mother Mme Renoir, and their sevants. Aubier d'Arbonne is imprisoned through the influence of Mme Renoir, who is incensed that he refuses to accept her daughter as a wife. During her husband's imprisonment, Maurille takes a lover, Édouard de Thierry, the bishop's erstwhile favourite. Aubier d'Arbonne is freed from his prison when revolutionaries take it over. When the Revolution begins to gain ground, Aubier d'Arbonne, Maurille, the archbishop, Édouard de Thierry, and Mlle Mignot, an old companion of Mme Renoir, emigrate together. Mme Renoir insists on staying behind. Aubier d'Arbonne's libertine friends, the archbishop's associates, and Mme Renoir's servants join different camps in the revolutionary struggles. Mme Renoir is guillotined, Hilaire her servant and Édouard de Thierry are both killed fighting for the royalist cause. The archbishop survives by leaning on his ecclesiastical counterparts in other countries. Aubier d'Arbonne, Maurille, and Mlle Mignot sink into greater and greater poverty and are finally compelled to depend on prostitution, theft, and arms trafficking in order to survive. The libertines, aristocrats, churchmen, and revolutionaries who survive become respectable citizens of Napoleon's empire.

In the 1967 script, the story of Aubier d'Arbonne and Maurille is central; the play dwells on their attitudes to love and on their relationship as much as on their reaction to the Revolution. The second version of the play, written after 1968, was noticeably politicised, and the subtitle *Les Libertins* abandoned. The emphasis of the later text is less on sentiment and libertine ideas and more on the ill-timed passivity of the characters in general and their inability to analyse historical events as they occur. The title *Bleus, blancs, rouges* refers to the different camps into which France was divided during the Revolution, that of the aristocrats, the whites, the bourgeoisie, the blues, and the common people, the reds. In the second version, Planchon made the rivalry between aristocrats and bourgeois much clearer, by making each character sharply and definitely aware of the group to which he or she belongs. Every quarrel and discussion in the play is more politicised, particularly those between Aubier d'Arbonne and his mother-in-law Mme Renoir, who represent the conflicting interests of two social classes.

Planchon set his play in the provinces partly in order that it should be more relevant to his audience. In the first version, one or two scenes take place in Paris, but in the second, all the action takes place either in the provinces of France or in Italy. Indeed it was after rewriting *Bleus, blancs, rouges* that Planchon became aware of the deep-seated provincialism of his work. Just as he had written about the Algerian war through the eyes of children in a provincial town, he was able to write about the Revolution only through the eyes of provincial characters. In this way he created a new perspective on the Revolution. Planchon's characters are intelligent beings who cannot estimate the events accurately, and who make a series of disastrous mistakes. By making his characters intelligent provincials, he made it possible for his audience to identify with them. Because the main events of the Revolution take place far away from where the characters live, it is not surprising that they misinterpret their relative and their ultimate importance. In fact the most important difference between Planchon's play and the Théâtre du Soleil's *1789* (also put on in 1971) was that, in Planchon's own words, '1789 shows the key moments of the Revolution, *Bleus, blancs, rouges* shows characters who live it from afar.'[8]

The major alteration which Planchon made in the 1971 play was to give the common people a voice. They are not represented in the play itself, but they appear between the scenes in *estampes populaires* (popular prints). Planchon felt that although it was the common people who had made the great events of the Revolution, such as the storming of the Bastille and the march to Versailles, nevertheless in reality power passed from the hands of the aristocrats straight into those of the merchants, the bourgeoisie. The dreams of those who 'made' the Revolution and were then excluded were represented in the short tableaux between the scenes. When a scene finished, a white curtain was lowered, with a banner attached reading '*La liberté ou la mort*' (Freedom or death). Through a back opening festooned with tricolours, cannon-balls and pikes, the ghosts of the people of Paris then marched onto the stage. They carried enormous puppets made of broom handles, strings, and old sheets, and they sang or recited speeches related to the events of the previous scene. Lochy's music for the songs recalled parts of *La Marseillaise* and of *carmagnoles* (roundelays popular at the time). Revolutionaries addressed the audience and tried to relate the Revolution to the public's own experience. When the company was on tour, the questions were written in the language of the audience on large banners held aloft by the people onstage. The common people were drawn off the stage on carts, posing, in the style of the 'revolutionary allegories' of public festivals, as 'Justice', 'Reason', etc. Planchon also had a *tricoteuse* (a woman knitter, like those who used to attend meetings and tribunals – and even, in Dickens' Mme Defarge's case, executions – knitting all the while) and a *sans-culotte* brandish standards to indicate the order and the subject of the scenes in the play. Through these tableaux, Planchon challenged the audience to evaluate the French Revolution and to consider what had become of its ideals. The role of these actors went much farther than that of the extras used in Planchon's productions of the classics: these moving tableaux became a parallel production, explicitly commenting on the themes of the main scenes of the play.

Planchon's play thus alternated between the point of view of the people, and that of the bourgeois and the aristocrats who profited from the Revolution or were destroyed by it. In the Théâtre du Soleil's *1789*, the audiences, standing in the 'pit' surrounded by the action, *became* the people, and could almost have been led to storm the Bastille all over again. In *Bleus, blancs, rouges*, the public could not identify whole-heartedly with the cause of the people for these were not the main characters; on the other hand, the principal characters' actions were shown up by the questions which 'the people' shouted at the audience during the tableaux scenes. Planchon thus demanded that the audience judge one viewpoint by juxtaposing it with another.

The play is obviously not didactic; Planchon himself said of it in 1967:

'Popular prints' from the Birmingham Repertory Company production of *Bleus, blancs, rouges*, translated by John Burgess, directed by Michael Simpson, set design by Pamela Howard, 1974

it is not a thesis play. No character is really the spokesman for the author. Placed in front of situations, the characters react. They are stuffed full of contradictions because history moves forward and the facts compel people to re-evaluate themselves. In this sense I am directly under the influence of Brecht. I do not like theatre in which a character takes the place of the playwright. I think, rather, that characters are cornered by situations. The play is to be deciphered by the public. It contains no lesson.[9]

Later Planchon was to consider even Brecht himself too didactic. In 1971, Planchon repeated that the play does not contain a message. He warned in the programme for the 1971 version that it would be over-simplifying *Bleus, blancs, rouges* to see in it only the theme that history destroys individuals. He summed up his basic preoccupation in the play in one question, which is included in the programme: 'How is it lived, that "historic" moment which will later convulse our lives, [but] which, right now, seems insignificant to us?'

In this play, critics could finally see clearly what Planchon has been saying even in the days of the Théâtre de la Comédie, with such plays as Adamov's *Paolo Paoli*: the individual is the creator and the product of history even when he wishes to ignore it. From the peasants of *La Remise* whose reason for living is slowly destroyed by the development of the French economy, to the bourgeois characters of *Dans le vent* who are determined by their comfortable social situation in the modern world, Planchon's characters are buffeted by history, against their will and sometimes without their knowledge. In *Bleus, blancs, rouges*, the effect of historical forces is more radical: the characters and their lives are transformed in the space of a few years. A critic wrote that 'Each in his own way, they try to ride out the storm. By dint of opportunism, heroism, crime, debauchery, or *assignats*. When the storm has passed, they are still there but they are no longer the same people. This revolution was also their own.'[10] Although the beings portrayed in this play are compelled to respond to a massive social upheaval, they do so as individuals. Though they do belong to different classes and, each in his own way, are representative of them, their relationships with one another are as complex and indefinable as in real life. Planchon creates here a perfect balance between individuality and historic determinism.

In *Bleus, blancs, rouges*, the characters who profess sincerely to have an ideology, be it religious or political, are no more likely to survive or to be crushed by events than the libertines who live in a moral limbo, divorced from the values of their class and unwilling to accept any others. Aubier d'Arbonne is proud of his rebellion against his arranged marriage, but his rebellion is meaningless without the social privileges which the Revolution has withdrawn from him. When they are penniless, his and his wife's libertinism is transformed into a sordid and compulsory means of survival, real prostitution. The characters who become revolutionaries are in the end killed, maimed, embittered, insane, or, most ironically of all, *embourgeoisés*. One character, as an officer in battle, has two of his erstwhile friends executed; after the Revolution, he cannot forgive himself for the killings. No ideology seems adequate in this play in which events have the upper hand.

Critics objected to Planchon that this was a play for intellectuals, and that, in the popular prints, he had overstated the similarities between the Revolution of 1789 and that of 1968. The tableaux, however, are what gives the play its real strength. The libertinism presented on the stage was one symptom of a decadent era; by contrasting to it the noisy and hopeful exuberance of the *estampes populaires*, Planchon created a remarkably dense picture of the Revolution. The characters of the play proper, libertines, servants, officers, priests, are like most of us in their desire to remain unscathed by history. When Planchon likened 1789 to 1968, he was not suggesting that the political issues were identical. He was provoking his public to see, in the characters' inability to cope with their own Revolution, a reflection of its own myopia in response to the contemporary situation.

The changes which Planchon made in the play emphasised not only its political aspects, but also the all-too-human tendency of the characters to remain passive. *Bleus, blanc, rouges* shows most clearly Planchon's approach to the dilemma of the individual within history. The play, more explicitly than any of his others, shows how people are involved in history, how they are changed by it, and how the decisions which they take in relation to it can affect their lives drastically. Because the play is set during the French Revolution, the events which its characters attempt to ignore are totally encompassing. Because the characters are intelligent provincials uncertain how to react, the play has a remarkable authenticity. It has a universal applicability which stems from its very provincialism. Planchon himself, in the 1971 programme, put the theme succinctly and well. *Bleus, blancs, rouges* illustrates perhaps more than any other play this basic paradox on which he has based his work as a director and as a playwright: 'History is ultimately the fabric of our days and what seems most external to our lives.'

L'Infâme (The Villain)

When he wrote *L'Infâme* in 1969, Planchon had already written seven plays including his musical comedies. It was the first of his own plays which he had published (in *Travail Théâtral* in 1970, and by Gallimard in 1975).

The play is based on a true story, that of the parish priest of the village of Uruffe, in Lorraine, L'Abbé Desnoyers. In 1956 Desnoyers killed his mistress, a local girl who was at the time nine months pregnant with his child; he cut out the foetus, christened it, killed it, and disfigured it for fear that it might be found to look like him. The incident shocked and astounded the entire country, and the subsequent trial provoked endless controversy. Plays, films, novels, and numerous studies have been made of the case of Desnoyers. Planchon chose to write a play based on the crime mainly because the incident had so deeply affected French people of all classes and all kinds; even in 1970 people remembered the case. Planchon thought that this widespread and lasting reaction was a mark of France's deeply-rooted Catholicism:

I believe that France is profoundly Catholic, I'm not speaking only of Catholics who go to mass, who practise, but of everyone. I have noticed many times that among atheists, there are great Christian themes which run through their reasoning, that men who claim to be quite unbelieving, who belong to parties of the left, continue to have their children baptised and send them to catechism classes.[11]

Planchon has admitted on many occasions that he is fascinated by madmen. He wrote this play after reading Georges Bataille's *Le Procès de Gilles de Rais (The Trial of Gilles de Rais)*, and so *L'Infâme* is really a forerunner to Planchon's *Gilles de Rais*; the two plays were published together in 1975. The actual Desnoyers, Planchon said in a press conference, behaved in a stupefying way after his crime:

Having arranged his alibi, he came back to the village, he had the alarm bell rung, directed the searchers, leading them in smaller and smaller circles around the body; when he had discovered it, he fell into prayer, crying, and told the peasants, who weren't asking for so much, that he knew the murderer, but could not denounce him, held back by the seal of confession. In the same way he gradually put the police on his track, whilst defending himself up to the final confession, with a profusion of details.[12]

Planchon's play is not an attempt to reconstruct the crime. It begins after the murder and ends with the arrest of the priest. Planchon turned his attention to the criminal's milieu and to the Church hierarchy in particular, showing how they react to an apparently irredeemable action committed by one of their number. Planchon described the various stages of the Church's reaction which were based on the actual events following the crime:

What interests me . . . is the reaction of the community to which this man belongs and it is in this case the Catholic Church. This community is at first completely divided. Its members adopt various and unexpected positions, following personal motives. There follows a veritable leap-frogging to the final position of rehabilitation of the lost member and to the expiation ceremonies which were organised at the time.[13]

Using the newspaper story only as a starting point, Planchon invented the characters freely. Desnoyer's name is changed to Duverger; the setting is changed from Uruffe (near Nancy) to Lauzun, a village in the Ardèche. The play is the portrait of a weak man carried along by circumstances, and of the village and the Church to which he belongs. As in his other productions and plays, Planchon was interested in exploring to what extent Duverger, his fellow priests, and his fellow villagers are determined by their principles, and to what extent by their emotions: '. . . what interested me was the blend of ideology and feelings, that is that under the pretence of feelings we speak of ideology, and that under the pretence of ideology we speak of feelings'.[14] This theme was one which he had already examined, most notably in his productions of *Tartuffe*.

Planchon made a few alterations in the first published text, and again in the later published text. They are minor changes which do not significantly affect the play as a whole. The most interesting aspect of the text is the contrast between the speech of the clergy and that of the villagers. The priests in the play have a common habit of speech, a tendency to use quotations in order to justify opinions. The quotations, in

inverted commas in the text, suggest the seminarian's training and sound like clichés; often they seem pathetic attempts
to integrate Duverger's barbaric act into a predefined dogma.
When, at the end of the play, the bishop finds that the peasants respond well to the idea of communal expiation ceremonies, he has his phrase ready: 'If they beat their breast, it is
because they recognise the sinner in themselves. What they
are perhaps giving us to understand, is the "mystery of the
culpability of all men".'[15]

The peasants' speech, unlike that of the priests, is vivid
and poetic. In *L'Infâme* as in *La Remise* Planchon makes his
feeling for the Ardèche evident in the powerfully terse expressions of its inhabitants. For some of the villagers the
countryside is alive with supernatural forces; most know,
however, that as a human community they are dying out. An
old schoolmistress lies dying, says the old *curé* '. . . silently
like a sweet melting in the sun' (sc. 9, p. 79). The shepherd
Célestin describes the area: 'This part of the country is no
longer what it was, in all the abandoned houses, with the roof
fallen in, there is nothing left of the lives people lived there.
An iron fork in the hearth which grows grey' (sc. 9, p. 77).
The peasant expressions can be startlingly beautiful; here
Duverger tells of one: 'I'm speaking of the purity of the snow
which covers everything here several months. Every year
some people fall into the snow-drifts. They aren't found until
the spring. We say then "The queen of the Winter has held
out her hand to them." The queen of the Winter, an invitation
which one doesn't refuse' (sc. 9, p. 73).

One character especially is the essence of the country, the
shepherd Célestin. Célestin accepts all creatures on the earth
with unshakable toleration for their vices, weaknesses, and
madnesses. He makes love to his ewes as naturally as to
women. In his pragmatic acceptance of his and other
people's driving forces, he is like Falstaff, like Schweyk, and
he looks forward to the character of Gédéon in *Le Cochon
noir*; like them he loves life at its most basic level more than
any morality or idea. All these roles at the Théâtre de la Cité
were played by Jean Bouise, and indeed those of Célestin and
of Gédéon may well have been written for Bouise, who is one
of Planchon's longest-serving and best actors. Célestin can
appreciate Duverger's behaviour with a rough humour and
an honesty at the antipodes from the attitude of the clergymen: 'A parish priest who steals the pants left to dry in the

L'Infâme, Théâtre Montparnasse. Roger Planchon as Duverger and Jean Bouise as Célestin

meadow does considerable harm to the Church. Everyone knows that you don't steal women's pants just to blow your nose. Duverger is not a bad sort but he has an itchy tail and his words go awry.' (sc. 1, p. 56). Although it is coarse and sardonic, although it is not the final word on the criminal, this is the most accurate and charitable account of Duverger in the entire play.

It is the old *curé* from the neighbouring village who sums up the dichotomy between the language of the Church and that of ordinary people in the Ardèche. He does not understand the expiation ceremonies or the Church's public rehabilitation of Duverger: 'I have lived too long amongst peasants. All these words of high spirituality, I can no longer articulate them, I distrust them. On the other hand, I speak willingly of ivy, nettles, fern, so poor, so miraculously elementary' (sc. 12, p. 81). The speech recalls Planchon's own remarks about elementary reality (see p. 25 above). The language of *L'Infâme* is particularly interesting because it reflects so clearly the social and intellectual differences between educated clergymen and the poor people who make up their provincial parishes.

In Duverger's speech the vivid style of the peasant and the correct parlance of the seminarian achieve an uneasy balance. Many of Planchon's characters are prisoners of a limited vocabulary; Duverger, on the other hand, is carried away by his own rhetoric. In his many speeches, the vigorous imagery of the villager usally outweighs the religious clichés of the seminary:

Fear is there, with its bones, in the bag of skin. The forces which were sweeping me along, Monsieur le Curé, were more powerful than the sugar-coated crap of holy books . . . As happens every now and then to farmhands, I fell into a cess-pit (sc. 4, p. 62).

Don't worry, mother, your son, like the great Saint George, is conquering the dragon . . . 'A great spiritual battle.' That's a seminary expression. (*To the old curé*) Rather comical, don't you think? (sc. 4, p. 63)

Eventually, ironically enough, it is through just such phrases that Duverger finds a way out: in the last scene, making himself histrionically repentant, he quotes from religious texts just as his fellow priests have done throughout the play, submitting in the end to the Church's decision to 'redeem' him.

Duverger is to a great extent the product of the type of village of which he is the parish priest. Within the village of Lauzun, the people are, like the characters of *La Remise*, the deprived and the forgotten, living in a past which should not have survived into this century. Like Borée in *La Remise*, like the village of *Le Cochon noir*, the community is closed in upon itself. They tolerate a licentious priest because hardly anyone believes that priests are celibate, and because they prefer to handle their own problems. They are totally imbued with an elementary Catholicism, which Planchon tried to portray in the stage language as well as the text.

Visually the production was very stark. Hubert Monloup designed the set. Interior scenes took place on a floor surface of five m by six (approximately sixteen by eighteen and a half ft) with very simple furniture, and with lights near the ground to suggest a low ceiling. The outdoor scenes took place in semi-darkness, an effect produced by quartz-lights, and on a sand-covered surface, with the boards from the interior 'floor' pushed to the side in a kind of palisade. Actors were seated on benches on either side of the playing area. When a scene finished, children's voices were heard reciting their catechism or their history lessons, singing childish songs, or asking one another riddles; they conveyed the whole ambience of a French Catholic childhood. The actors for the next scene came out onto the playing area when the sets were ready, passing through a complicated series of paths and little bridges. Before the action resumed three backcloths descended, hiding the stagehands and the actors not involved in the scene. These cloths were off-white, with three faded pink angels at the top suggesting both a childish religious faith and a decrepit reality. As in André Acquart's design for *Troilus and Cressida*, the sets could be changed easily: a few farm tables, for example, suggested, in different positions, a confessional, a bed, or an altar. The scene-shifting was stylised into a kind of liturgy in itself, accompanied by the children's voices.

The costumes were in a coarse pepper-and-salt material designed to be seen in a half-light. They suggested no specific period, but instead the imaginary world of Duverger's frightened self-questioning. Only the liturgical costumes were exact reproductions of reality: the Church finally regains its dignity and credibility through the liturgy.

The deliberately long scene changes were a distancing technique as well as a comment on Duverger's milieu. Staging and dramatic structure were inextricably linked in the play to give the portrait of Duverger the greatest density possible. One of the scenes (7, 1973 text; 6, 1975 text), like the published version of *La Remise*, has several simultaneous settings, in which the reactions of various characters to Duverger's crime are counterpointed, from that of the fiery Abbé Tardieu, defending his friend Duverger to a group of peasants, to that of the police inspector whose sympathies lie entirely with the victim. The scene is filled with brilliant juxtapositions, as when Tardieu's emotional appeal for

Duverger is followed immediately by Célestin's account of what he actually saw:

Tardieu: My heart trembles and I recognise in this the music of the Holy Ghost. Yes, the love which I have for him testifies to his innocence. I love this man, I respect him, I embrace his knees.
Célestin: He battered the head of the foetus with the heel of his shoe.[16]

The play provoked strong reactions. The mayor of Nancy banned performances which had been arranged in his city, purportedly out of consideration for the relatives of Desnoyers who lived in the area (although they had made no objection). Cultural, trades union, and political organisations responded to a call to protest at the banning made by the Théâtre d'Aujourd'hui (Theatre Today) Association in Nancy. Planchon later sued the city of Nancy and won his case in October 1973. A Lyons critic, Jean Beaumont, after reading only the programme, refused to see the play or even to attend a press conference about it, and roundly condemned a work which he had not read for its attack on the Church. Catholics and non-Catholics alike complained that the Church was presented as disunited.

Planchon certainly saw the Church as a social organisation, and it may be the humanity of his portraits which surprised critics accustomed to consider the clerical hierarchy either with special reverence or, impersonally, as an institution. He shows that within the structure of the Church, the secular social divisions still subsist, and that these have played their part in isolating Duverger. At the same time, however, he shows Duverger as a man driven to an insane act not only by the pressures of his situation, but by those of his faith. His fellow priests are driven not only by personal motives, but also by those of their beliefs. It is true that the Church's rehabilitation of Duverger is ironically treated. It is true also, however, that Planchon presents the characters who find this solution very sympathetically: a serious, cold Père Laurent, writing at night of his own doubts and feelings of ineffectiveness; a hot-headed Abbé Tardieu, blinded by his personal affection for Duverger; a weary, cancer-ridden old bishop, horrified by the crime, but determined to redeem the situation for the Church. Planchon's characters are intelligent and they act in good faith, but they have no predetermined principles with which to react to Duverger: they are left to sort out individually and collectively what is the most moral reaction, and what is the most practical, and to find a balance between the two. Above all, it is Planchon's portrait of the old curé in whom charity survives undiluted by considerations for the Church's worldly dignity, which shows that there is no desire to attack Catholicism or Christianity per se in this play.

Of Planchon's four peasant plays, L'Infâme is the one in which there are the fewest references to the outside world, and virtually no allusions to historical events in the nation or beyond it. Yet the reverberations of the crime in L'Infâme are nationwide, whereas the murders in La Remise and those in Le Cochon noir are known to few people, and those in Gilles de Rais occur before the mass media were even dreamed of. The journalists in L'Infâme, although they do not appear, are a constant presence in the background, and there is a feeling that the investigation is taking place in full view of the nation. The intervals during which children recite catechism and history lessons, riddles and songs, are far from being a mere structural device: they show the fundamental links between Duverger and his village, between that village and the rest of France, between the characters of the play and the people in Planchon's audiences. Based on an incident which shook the entire country and called into question some fundamental assumptions of Catholicism, the play could not be regarded as divorced from social realities.

Planchon's portrait of Duverger treats his shifting logic with a serious desire to illuminate all his fears and his bravadoes. Duverger faces not only his mother, the village, the police, and his superiors, but also himself, his guilt, his doubts, his terror. The quality of Planchon's compassion for the criminal priest misled critics into seeing, on the one hand, an attack on the Church, on the other, a play filled with faith; on the one hand, a madman, on the other, a cynic. Duverger alternately defies his milieu and complies with it. His attempt to live according to principles too severe for him ends in failure, and his shame leads him to a monstrous crime. Without minimising the crime, and although he does not share the faith which makes Duverger's guilt a torment, Planchon was able to present him as a man to be both judged and pitied, a criminal, but one struggling for self-respect.

The Lyons critic Jean-Jacques Lerrant thought that, although the subject of L'Infâme is shocking and sensational,

Planchon was right to use the story: 'It is the privilege and I will say even the duty of the poet to build . . . his work with the pitiable human material, the tainted blood and the mud of charnel-houses.'[17] Planchon succeeded in this play in transforming such material into a supremely understanding picture of a hunted criminal and lapsed priest.

Le Cochon noir (*The Black Pig*)

Le Cochon noir, the third of Planchon's peasant plays, was written in 1973 and published almost immediately. Planchon wrote the play in seven days, saying that it had been 'given' to him.

The play is set, once again, in a small village, in an unspecified area very like the Ardèche. It takes place during the *semaine sanglante* (bloody week) at the time of the Paris Commune of 1871 when the *communards* were finally unceremoniously executed. Like the first two peasant plays it depicts the villagers as apparently separated from historical events by their poverty and their isolation. 'The Ardèche', Planchon said in an interview with Colette Godard, 'has always been so poor that it didn't even experience feudalism. No lord, ever, came and imposed serfdom; though the inhabitants have known other oppressions, they did not know that one. They seem to me closer to Tuaregs than to the body of French peasants. One could even say that, of civilisation, the Ardèche knows only the sandwich wrappers.'[18]

Like the characters of *La Remise*, those of *Le Cochon noir* are affected by historical forces beyond their comprehension. Planchon told Colette Godard, in the same interview, that he considered the Commune of 1871 a historical turning-point: 'The Commune represents the beginning of the industrial world; an extraordinary ideological moment: for the first time, the proletariat takes the floor, it's the beginning of the death of the countryside.' The peasants of *La Remise* thus live through the final stages of a process of economic and ideological development which begins during the time of *Le Cochon noir*. There is an important historical link as well between *Le Cochon noir* and *L'Infâme*:

The affair of the curé of Uruffe was the starting point for *L'Infâme*. I'm convinced that this was the last time a Mass of Atonement was said in the whole of France. It wouldn't be possible nowadays. I have the same feeling about *The Black Pig*. After 1871 there couldn't be any more sorcerers, at least not like before. This par-

ticular juncture was at once their high point and the beginning of
the end. The triumph of the Church in *L'Infâme* is just the prelude
to the great thaw – they knew it had to come.[19]

The sorcerer of *Le Cochon noir* is also a descendant of François Prelati, the alchemist of *Gilles de Rais*.

This is the first of Planchon's peasant plays in which we
see the action taking place directly and in the present rather
than pieced together from an enquiry into the past. The
characters are defined not through the memories or the
impressions of others, or through their accounts of themselves, but through the action. We see the incidents in the
village, while the events of the *semaine sanglante* take place
in the background. In a way, Planchon's *Le Cochon noir* is to
Adamov's *Le Printemps 71* (a 1961 play on the Communards)
as his *Bleus, blancs, rouges* is to Ariane Mnouchkine's *1789*:
in neither instance does Planchon concentrate like his fellow
play-makers on the major events of the Revolution. Instead,
he shows the point of view of people not involved directly or
consciously in creating the events.

In rapid tableaux between the scenes of the play, Planchon
showed what was happening in Paris. In *Bleus, blancs,
rouges* the tableaux between the scenes developed into a
separate comment by the common people. In *Le Cochon noir*,
the historical sequences are far more subdued: they remind
us that a revolution is being quelled while the villagers go
about their affairs. John Burgess, who attended the rehearsals
of the play and saw it in performance, described one of these
silent scenes:

Two *communards*, stripped to the waist, drag a huge red cloth
down the sloping ramp. The red material spreads out until it covers
nearly a third of the stage. The *communards* kneel, holding the
corners over their shoulders, pulling the material taut. One by one
the villagers enter, holding pine branches in front of their faces.
They form up in a solid phalanx on the red material. Two shots are
heard. The *communards* fall forward on their faces.[20]

The Revolution and the recent Franco-Prussian war have had
their effects of the villagers directly. Just as in *La Remise* the
gassed and simple-minded Gaston Chausson appears as a
victim of the First World War, and then Gabriel, lamed, as a
veteran of the Indo-Chinese war, so in *Le Cochon noir* young
Toin, the bridegroom, comes to his wedding leaning on a
cane; he has been wounded and is on leave. There are far

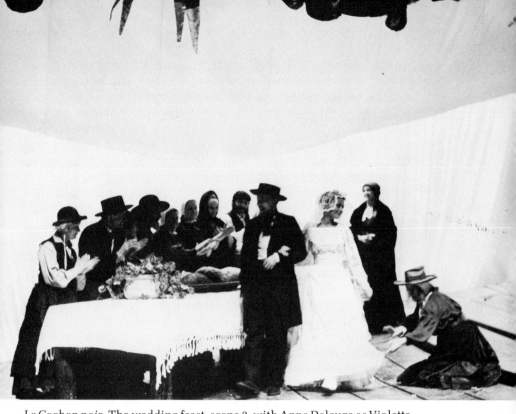

Le Cochon noir. The wedding feast, scene 3, with Anne Deleuze as Violette

more women than men at his wedding-feast. The villagers are strongly against the revolutionary *communards*, who are a threat to the social order which the peasants have always known. When the Solitaire (the Hermit), the local sorcerer, speaks solemnly of the honour of France, a widow who has lost two sons in the war protests drunkenly: 'To hell with the fatherland. Give me back the children I have lost. What the hell is the use of all your medals to me?'[21] Planchon himself said during rehearsals that this '. . . outburst . . . though soon stifled, is politically very important.'[22] It is the voice of those left behind for whom survival, for themselves and their loved ones, is more important than such abstractions as patriotism. It is the voice of those who would gladly let history pass them by and leave them in peace.

The central story in the play is that of Violette, who is raped by the village scoundrel Gédéon on the day her wedding is to take place. Afraid to say what has happened, she is thought to have been possessed by a devil. The Hermit, the sorcerer, who has been competing with the parish priest for power over the villagers' souls, subjects Violette to an 'exorcism' in order to impress everyone with his supernatural talents. Afterwards, the girl runs off to kill herself.

Once again Planchon's feeling for the Ardèche and its people suffuses the entire play. One of the characters, the brutal Rank (le Grand Charretier – the Great Carter) was based on a real person well-known in the Ardèche when Planchon spent holidays there as a child. Backward, superstitious and ignorant, the Ardèchois of 1871 are not so different from the medieval characters of Gilles de Rais and, significantly, they are not so different either from those of La Remise or L'Infâme. Planchon's style had matured by the time he wrote Le Cochon noir. The region, its mentality, its prejudices, are presented with the greatest possible economy of means.

The play was inspired in part by Ibsen's Peer Gynt and in part by Geneviève de Bollème's La Bibliothèque bleue, a compendium of the popular literature of France from the sixteenth to the nineteenth centuries.[23] Planchon openly borrows incidents and images from Ibsen, entire sentences from Bollème. The speech of the peasants is certainly authentic, even in its coarseness: its directness and energy reflect the hardness of the peasants' lives and of their outlook.

Planchon's former assistant director, Jacques Rosner, who was now a director in his own right, put on a reading of Le Cochon noir at Avignon in August 1973. Rosner said that, having moved away from Villeurbanne, he had become sensitive to a quality which Planchon often neglects when he directs his own work, 'What it contains of shadow, of mystery, its mythical aspect . . .'[24] Rosner's reading emphasised the personal relationships between characters, and the presence of the village as almost a character in itself. In my opinion, Le Cochon noir is both in substance and in style the most poetic of all Planchon's plays to date.

Luciano Damiani's design for Planchon's production of the play in Caen in December 1973 suggested a bleak countryside, with a floor made of black wood, and a sky of colourless moving draperies. The stage sloped slightly to suggest the hill where Violette is raped. The draperies were stretched into different shapes, lowered to produce a claustrophobic feeling or raised to create an atmosphere of lightness and relief. André Diot the lighting technician borrowed an idea which Chéreau had used in his production of La Dispute earlier that year: '. . . 32 small quartz lamps in the flies, angled up onto reflectors, which give a general diffused light seeping down from above – just like daylight in fact . . . ordinary tungsten lights can then be used to mould-in areas as required'.[25] Four musicians using fiddles, hand-bells and hand-rattles played authentic French folk music, which Planchon described as '. . . slow, sad, desperate, and very serene'.[26] The tone was set by this sad, thin sound, just as in *L'Infâme* the atmosphere was created by the sing-song voices of the children.

In *La Remise* we see in passing that pagan celebrations have survived, integrated into religious festivities. Planchon believes that Catholicism used the old superstitions of the countryside in order to implant itself in people's minds. Once religion was established, paganism adopted the vocabulary of Catholicism in order to survive. In *Le Cochon noir*, paganism is incarnated in the figure of the Hermit, who speaks the same language as the parish priest with whom he is in conflict. Planchon pointed out in a discussion of the play in Rheims, which I attended, that 'The parish priest and the Hermit invoke the same saints.'[27] He also pointed out there that he writes about religion because, 'Even in violently revolutionary works I see a Catholic framework.'

The parish priest in this play is almost a medieval carica-ture of a *curé*, a lecherous old man who, even on his death-bed, cannot resist embracing all the women who visit him. He has denounced the Hermit as a charlatan in public, and thus made an enemy of him. The parish priest has little mastery of language; because he is ill, like the bishop in *L'Infâme*, his phrases and images tend to refer to his own body, his pain, and his fear of death. Planchon said that the audience should see in this character '. . . a man literally dying of fear'.[28]

The Hermit, on the other hand, has the great oratorical advantage of good health. He is a 'holy man', one of the last descendants of a primitive paganistic tradition. The villagers are not completely taken in by him, but they fear him enough to go along with his bogus ritual. He preaches Christian virtues, and his self-abnegating way of life makes him a fairly convincing saint, particularly in comparison with the sen-sual parish priest. He combines religion and paganism skil-fully, having Mme Victorine swear, for example, both on a boar's foot, an amulet, and on a cross, a Christian symbol. To

Le Cochon noir. Roger Blin as the Hermit

a great extent his ascendancy over the villagers comes from the sheer vitality and poetry of his 'prophetic' language:

This morning, I saw a rent in the clouds. A terrible redness. As though the entire firmament was breaking its back. The joy of souls. Io. Death has wielded its scythe. Io. Io. Io. (*The Hermit dances.*) sc. 2, pp. 23–24

The world has a centre you know! If I lie, let them put a glowing ember on my tongue. Look about you, look: the mountain is quivering. Look at its buttocks, its flanks, its breasts. sc. 8, p. 56

Like his speech, the ceremony of exorcism which the Hermit organises is filled with colour and solemnity. His purpose in the exorcism is to discredit the dead parish priest by convincing everyone that the parish priest's soul has taken

satanic possession over Violette's. The physical circumstances surrounding the exorcism are horrific: Violette is
whipped every seven hours for a week before the ceremony;
on the day, she is made to lie on the parish priest's cadaver,
still in its blood-stained sheets. To frighten away devils, the
villagers smear themselves with dog's blood and soot and
beat their sabots together rhythmically. Roger Blin, who
played the Hermit in Planchon's production, conducted the
exorcism like a long-forgotten ceremony, with frequent hesitations. When at one point he asked the villagers to pray with
him they stood about uncertain what to do. Thus the acting
made it clear that this ritual is a relic from the past, and that
no one is quite taken in by it although it exerts a fascination
on everyone. Violette resists the Hermit stoutly at first, then
humours her tormentor by pretending that the evil spirit is
saying 'je sors' (I am coming out) from her lips, and finally,
under the Hermit's persistent pressure her mind breaks and
she submits to the ritual.

Planchon said early on in the rehearsals that after the
exorcism there should still be tension between the Hermit
and Violette because she has not accepted the exorcism. He
explained her suicide as an attempt to break out of the isolation imposed on her by the community since the day of the
rape, an isolation culminating in the exorcism during which
she is, in reality, put on trial. Planchon added that she 'thinks
of death as her bridegroom and going to meet him she will no
longer be alone.'[29] In a discussion of the play at Caen, Planchon said that the scene was actually the opposite of an
exorcism: Violette is the victim of a *possession complète*
(a total possession).[30] It is the Hermit's spiritual rape of
Violette, and her only escape is death.

Quite young and quite alone against the villagers, Violette
nevertheless puts up a good defence before breaking down.
All the women characters in this play are magnificently
strong. One of them, *La Veuve* (the Widow) is lustily reminiscent of Chaucer's Wife of Bath. She first appears at the
parish priest's bedside, ready to pit all the supernatural
forces which she can command against the death of her
husband. Her words are a fierce incantation:

I've been to all the churches in the valley. In all of them, I've had
candles burned. He's been cold for two days already. But if everywhere we pray very hard, if we say masses, if we burn candles, God
will take him out of the kingdom of the dead . . .

> Must I throw myself head first against the stone of the high altar for God to hear me? Light the candles, I tell you. Give me credit, I'll pay later, I'll sell my hair in the city. sc. 2, pp. 20–1

When her husband does not after all come back to life, she begins to pursue Gédéon, and the vitality of her desire is as overpowering as that of her grief. Like the old troll-woman in *Peer Gynt*, she threatens to seize her share of her man's caresses from a younger rival. She finally wins over the old man, partly by threatening to denounce him to the police. After Gédéon's daughter Eulalie has been stoned to death in revenge for his own crimes, the Widow's healthy positivity is also a welcome comfort.

One of Planchon's constant preoccupations, evident in his treatment of such plays as *Tartuffe* and *Troilus and Cressida*, as well as *l'Infâme* and *Le Cochon noir*, is the relation between people's ideology and their behaviour. When he wrote *Le Cochon noir* Planchon had come to believe that people's 'mortality' or ideology were abstractions with no real effect on their behaviour:

> Moralities are useless. They touch only the superficial part of life. We use them to explain, to justify. We use them all the time, and everywhere, including the realm of politics. But they change nothing as far as actions go. Reality is outside these abstract codes.[31]

In this play two people live quite outside the conventions of the village: Gédéon and his daughter Eulalie. They are lovers, but their incestuous relations were not intended to be shocking; incest was fairly common in peasant families in the past, as a way of keeping the inheritance whole. Morality is invoked by Gédéon and Eulalie without real reference to their behaviour. Eulalie uses conventional precepts to try to shame her father for failing as a provider; Gédéon quotes religious commandments of filial obedience in order to seduce Eulalie. Like Peer Gynt, Gédéon has dreams of splendour, and also strange visions. As Peer Gynt's troll-son is brought to him, so Gédéon's 'child' is presented to him in a dream by Violette: an ugly pig, which he sees as black. The famous wild buck of Peer Gynt's fantasy becomes, in Gédéon's frightened vision, the Emperor Napoleon. Eulalie at one point appears to him as Napoleon, and treats him as a tempting female, to his great terror. Colette Godard was certainly right when she wrote that 'Roger Planchon is not a misogynous writer.'[32]

Gédéon is the ancestor of Célestin in *L'Infâme*, albeit a less healthy, more destructive ancestor. It is through Gédéon that human tenderness intrudes into the play. Despite his swaggering, his rapes, his killing, he is able to conceive of affection as well as desire. Even his rough advances to Eulalie are mixed with tenderness:

> You have your mother's stomach. Beautiful thighs, nice and soft. Your body has a thousand good qualities. Myself, I have always taken you with much pleasure. I am indebted to you for an infinity of joys. All those who take you after me will agree with me. sc. 1, p. 16

When Gédéon and the Widow look forward to their life together, they speak of affection, too (in a passage borrowed almost word for word from *La Bibliothèque bleue*):

> *The Widow*: Each has his humour. His faults. It happens sometimes that a husband and wife will fall out with each other. But we will not take things too far.
> *Gédéon*: No. After a quarrel which has gone too far tenderness is no longer the same. sc. 6, pp. 50–1

To such a character as Gédéon, as to Célestin in *L'Infâme*, moral categories are irrelevant; people are driven by needs, desires, affections, and these are what matter and what must survive.

All the characters in the play have an ambivalent attitude to moral codes. They are very human. Mme Victorine, Violette's mother, wants above all that her daughter should marry well; she pushes the villagers into accepting the exorcism, bribes and threatens them, and even allows her daughter to be whipped so that the marriage can take place. She considers the Hermit a fool and a fraud, but she needs his help to restore Violette's marriage chances and so she pretends to believe in him. Privately she hesitates and suffers. Planchon reveals a great compassion for his characters as he shows them caught in this kind of indecision. Violette, if she admits she had been raped, condemns herself to a life of spinsterhood and shame; by remaining silent instead, she unwittingly becomes the Hermit's tool in discrediting the dead parish priest. Like other characters she faces a conflict which cannot be resolved by her own moral code. Planchon's characters, Émile Chausson, L'Abbé Duverger, try and fail to relate their actions to their moral beliefs, and they fail because those beliefs are inadequate in the face of real events and genuine passion.

During the discussion with the audience in Caen,[33] one of the spectators complained that all the characters in *Le Cochon noir* seemed abnormal. Planchon disagreed and said that he thought most of us were like them. At the same time he admitted that he has a certain tenderness for insane people, and that he often found it hard to distinguish between the normal and the abnormal. (It is without doubt this fascination which led him to write about Gilles de Rais and about Desnoyers.) Spectators were sceptical, as well, about the degree of ignorance and the backwardness of the peasants as presented by Planchon; they were, after all, supposed to be living in the late nineteenth century. Planchon again explained that the Ardèche was an isolated region which had retained many customs long after they had disappeared in other areas. One might add that, at the time when *Le Cochon noir* was being presented, the film *The Exorcist* was attracting crowds of 'normal', 'modern' cinema-goers. The supernatural exerts a certain fascination on everyone. It is not so unlikely that its influence would be stronger in an isolated rural village in a time before industrialisation had reached as far as provincial France.

The last words in *Le Cochon noir* belong to Gédéon and the Widow. Despite the deaths of Eulalie and of Violette, which Planchon described well as a 'massacre of the innocents'[34] life will go on almost unperturbed in the village. In Paris, too, the troubles are over. The Revolution has been put down quickly, efficiently, and bloodily. It is the Widow in her elementary, hard positivity, who triumphs. The village swallows up its events and goes on, unaware that historical forces already alive will eventually destroy it.

Gilles de Rais

Gilles de Rais bears a striking resemblance to *L'Infâme* with which it is published. It was first put on at Villeurbanne in January 1976. Planchon calls the play a '... history play as seen by the imagination'.[35] Gilles de Rais, one of Joan of Arc's comrades-in-arms and a *maréchal de France* (Field-Marshal), was condemned to be burned at the stake in 1440 in Nantes for the sexual abuse, torture, and murder of hundreds of children over a period of years, and for dabbling in alchemy and devil-worship. The case is quite well documented, and an account of it exists in Georges Bataille's *Le Procès de Gilles de Rais* as well as in Geneviève Bollème's

La Bibliothèque bleue. Although it is not strictly speaking a play about peasants, it depicts the ideological landscape in which the mentality of the other three plays has its roots.

Gilles de Rais's crimes are even more horrible than the double murder committed by Desnoyers. Planchon portrays Gilles, as he did Desnoyers, at the time when he is being gradually cornered by his opponents. In the case of Gilles, however, we also see the trial. Once again, Planchon was interested in the reactions of others to the criminal, but this play focuses more on the man himself. It is an attempt to understand the mind of one who could commit such horrific acts:

> if I can't understand a character in real life, I try in the theatre to walk in their footsteps, to see how far I can follow them . . . It's one of the strengths of a theatrical story – not just to purge evil thoughts – but that it allows us to meditate on crime and see how far we can go along with it.[36]

Gilles de Rais lived in a medieval society whose mentality was pre-scientific. There is in the play a prevailing sense of the spiritual, which is not always distinguishable from superstition, and which precludes rational investigation into civil offences. It is the world from which that of *Le Cochon noir* emerged, one filled with religious language and paganistic belief intermingled. Many passages recall the incantations of the Hermit, particularly the speeches of Gilles's alchemist, François Prelati: 'You term "dreams" that which you do not know. Look! The sun is rising and the things I say are as certain as the sun. I am speaking of light.'[37] François Prelati plays a similar role in relation to Gilles as the Hermit did in relation to the village. Prelati is taken very seriously, as Gilles also loves him. Gilles's other attendants, jealous of his affection for Prelati, are predisposed to regard the alchemist as the fraud which he no doubt is.

Planchon saw Gilles de Rais as one of a dying breed – the knight – but as one who at the same time experimented with new values: 'We're living in the ruins of the cathedrals and in the ruins of the Greeks. It's interesting to recognise in Gilles the first man who saw the cathedral as a ruin.'[38] Because he lives long before the philosophy of 'everything is permitted' was dreamed of, Gilles defies his society by searching for a transcendent evil. The evil which he seeks out, however, is one defined within the prevailing ideology of that same society: God is good, Satan is evil. He derives insane pleasure from slitting children's throats ('I am the child whose throat I slit and I scream with them. It is my fear that I slaughter', sc. 5, p. 43). He derives a certain philosophical pleasure from his rejection of 'good' for 'evil'. Each of his followers in his eyes is allied in some way with the devil. Yet they are petty, squabbling people, his alchemist is a fraud, and he himself is mad. Even Gilles's attempt to conjure up the devil strikes an amusingly cowardly note – he leaves Prelati a letter for Satan: 'Come at my behest and I will give you everything you want, except my soul and the abbreviation of my life' (sc. 1, p. 13).

Gilles's affections are strong: at one point he kisses the feet of each person in his retinue, and the scene is filled with tenderness. His affections however are besmirched in the pettiness, cowardice, and bickering of his entourage. In scene 5, Gilles and his friends dress up as women and taunt the enemy whom they think is near. The incident recalls that in the Villeurbanne *Édouard II* in which Gaveston and other favourites parade in women's clothes. Planchon said during rehearsals that 'The scene tells the story of a defeat. Everyone is afraid except La Meffraye [Gilles's procuress] and perhaps Roger [Gilles's companion].'[39] The mad dressing-up scene is the men's manner of defying their own fear as much as the enemy. Yet it comes to nothing, for the enemy is not there. The scene was played with an emphasis on the silences, the heavy emptiness between speeches. In a sense it typifies Gilles de Rais's rebellion against the values of his day – energetic, but finally pointless.

La Meffraye is a much-coarsened descendant of Marie Giffard in *La Remise* and the Widow and Mme Victorine in *Le Cochon noir*. She is filled with vigour and humour from the start, lying ruthlessly to Gilles's potential victims, unmoved by François Prelati's rhetoric or by Gilles's fear of it, and claiming stoutly to be on familiar terms with both God and the devil. Even at bay she remains fearless, encouraging Gilles to drink rather than tremble, taunting the enemy in outrageous terms, telling the Soldat Errant (the Wandering Soldier, another woman character) to defy everyone, chaffing Gilles's followers so that they will stop quarrelling and present a united front. She behaves as though neither God nor Satan exists or at least as though they are not worth too much notice; in a way, her applied sceptisicm goes much

Gilles de Rais, Villeurbanne, 1976, scene 5. Gilles and his companions depart, leaving the peasant boy asleep

deeper than Gilles's frightened theoretical forays into demonism.

Gilles's attempts at devil-worship are no more than a pretext for the Duc de Bretagne to have him arrested. For the duke, Gilles's arrest and execution are profitable: the two men have had a long dispute over land-ownership, and Gilles's castle is a tempting morsel as well. He hesitates because Gilles is a Field-Marshal, and because the King might support him against the duchy; he acts only when he has assurances to the contrary from the King. Gilles's crimes are no more in the duke's eyes than violent acts in a violent age. He is more intrigued than repelled by the rumour that Gilles speaks with the devil. When his mistress is dying he even asks Prelati for a miracle – although a few moments later, fearing divine retribution, he quickly orders a few masses to be said and charitable donations to be made to placate God. This is a world finely balanced between personalised good and personalised evil, in which, if God does not 'work', one is very tempted to try the devil. People bargain with either in order to achieve their ends. Nevertheless, the forces for action in the play are secular ones: Gilles's punishment comes not from an offended God but from human beings with a mercenary interest in his downfall.

The second half of the play consists of Gilles's trial and his execution. The trial is presented as a kind of morality play[40] complete with medieval staging, put on before an audience

Gilles de Rais, Villeurbanne, 1976, scene 7. Gilles prepares to kill the boy, his action paralleled by six children who plunge knives into loaves of bread and collapse as though dying

consisting of Gilles de Rais's historical judges (the Duke of Brittany, the Bishop of Nantes, Jean Blouyn the inquisitor) and some heavenly visitors, the Virgin Mary, God, the child Jesus, and a few angels. These scenes can be looked at as Gilles's own perception of his trial, in which he believes that he is acting out essential human themes (murder, despair, suicide) before an audience which includes not only his civil and religious adversaries, but the whole universe, that is to say the inhabitants of a medieval Catholic heaven. The heavenly visitors are vaguely comical and very human (Mary comments on the actors' diction, on provincial actors . . .) because they are products of Gilles's imagination.

Gilles begins with a straightforward self-defence, recounting his role in the war, his honours from King Charles VII, etc. The role of heroic warrior, however, does not suit him any longer, and his judges demand that he play Cain. Dream, drama, and reality alternate and are sometimes superimposed as Gilles goes through with the performance of the Mystery play. When Gilles as Cain asks God who accuses him of murder, Jean Blouyn steps in with the names of the historical Gilles de Rais's actual accusers. Gilles is then compelled to play Judas, with Prelati as Despair tempting him to suicide. As his performance nears its end, preparations are made for his execution, he climbs up to the stake where he is to be burned and, to the surprise and displeasure of his celestial audience, he laughs.

The set, designed by Patrick Dutertre and Paul Hanaux, is described in the designer's notebook:

The walls of the stage are hung with dusty white canvas. At the back a painted sky. On the floor a landscape in relief, with red-brown soil looking as if the rains have eroded all vegetation from it – a cross between the burnt-looking soil of an Italian primitive painting and volcanic lava. In the folds of the hills there nestle three small model castles.

Spanning this landscape and running out towards the audience is a ramp made up of three huge baulks of timber painted a pale grey colour and bound at the corners with iron brackets. This ramp is capable of splitting into two unequal halves to reveal a pit underneath . . .[41]

Until the trial/Mystery-play scene, the action took place on this 2.32-metres-square (25-foot-square) ramp, and this concentration into a small space created a feeling of mounting tension and claustrophobia. For scene 9, the trial, it opened up (like the sets of *La Remise*). The sky was rent to reveal gold-tipped mountains and a bright backcloth with a reproduction from *Les Très riches Heures du Duc de Berry* (an exquisitely illustrated medieval book of prayers and meditations). This *éclatement*, bursting open, of the set had a strong emotional impact: the play was suddenly delving, not into remembered time as in *La Remise*, but into a dream time, a strange mixture of levels of reality. Just as children played the chorus in *L'Infâme*, here, grouped at the front of the ramp, they formed an audience for Gilles's performances in the Mystery plays, representatives, perhaps, of his victims.

The last scene takes place on several time levels. Gilles and his companions are already spirits looking at the world they have left; they are alive and awaiting their execution; they are being burned at the stake. The dialogue alternates between Gilles's conversations with his two friends, and the preparations of his executioners. The lines of the 'dead' are spoken in a slow and relaxed manner; those of the Captain at a normal pace. Jean Blouyn, Gilles's chief enemy, is nervous, exhausted, and worried: he speaks hurriedly. The Duke of Brittany, on the other hand, urbanely discusses his brother's greed and comments in a detached way on the interesting details of a burning at the stake. On the pyre, Gilles has a final vision of one of his victims, covered in blood, carrying lilies and coming toward him smiling forgiveness. A procession then fills the stage, to triumphal music.

Because of Gilles's rank, there were beautiful costly obsequies after his death, complete with a triumphal funeral procession. The irony of a lavish funeral after a criminal's death must be looked at in the context of a rigidly hierarchical society. In Planchon's plays there is always a commonsense view included, a down-to-earth perspective. Here it is expressed by the Captain, Gilles's guard. He is doing his duty by arresting Gilles, but is too respectful of the man's rank to tie his hands, for instance. He speaks, in Planchon's words, 'like a dazzled concierge'[42] of his own memories (partly invented) of the man's former wealth and of his parentage. Like the old *curé* of *L'Infâme* he is full of kindly, totally inadequate advice; he is blind to the metaphysical aspect of Gilles's revolt, and sees in him only a ruined knight. It is important that he is an old man, for the values which he expresses are already growing less firmly established in his society.

The portrayal of Gilles bears many similarities with that of *L'Infâme*. Both men are intoxicated by their own words, caught between spiritual aspirations and the needs of the flesh, histrionic, self-deluding, and nevertheless to be pitied as much as they are blamed. We see Gilles kill one of his victims onstage, but there is little sense of pity for the child; in fact one critic wrote after seeing the play that '. . . were it not for one scene in which Gilles de Rais murders a child beneath our eyes, we could believe that the accusations made against him by some old fogeys – the bishop, the duke – are false and invented in order to lay hold of his riches'.[43] As in *L'Infâme*, there is in *Gilles de Rais* a sympathetic portrayal of a guilty, hunted madman. This is both the strength and the weakness of the play. Planchon fails to make us share his

Gilles de Rais, Villeurbanne, 1976. The Mystery play, scene 9. Gilles (Roger Planchon) as Cain and Jean Blouyn (Michel Beaune) as Abel

own fascination with the figure. What emerges in the end is a sense of the smallness of Gilles himself; there is a great irony in the gulf between his aspirations to be a wrongdoer in the face of the universe, and his reality as a child-killer executed more for the sake of financial expediency and weariness with scandal than for fraternising with the Evil One. This is a remarkable attempt to penetrate the mentality of a madman, but not, in theatrical terms, a successful one. The conclusion of the play is confusing, its symbolism overdone.

PART III

Roger Planchon: director and playwright

9

Popular theatre: problems and possibilities

IN the course of his career Planchon has shown both a concern to reach wider audiences and a need to experiment
artistically with new ideas and forms. The question has
always been whether or not these two aims can be recon-
ciled.

The dilemma of 'popular' theatre directors has been that,
even when they themselves (like Planchon) have humble
origins, the culture and education which they have acquired
by participating in a theatrical endeavour separates them
from their potential public. Directors could, on the one hand,
choose to stage the traditional plays developed in response
to the needs of the middle class, a category in which
everyone would include the boulevard play (equivalent to a
West End comedy), and some would include the classics of
European drama. This type of play was definitely unrelated
to the needs and the interests of a working-class public. They
could, on the other hand, put on 'revolutionary' plays which
challenge the contemporary social structure. Most of them,
believing like Planchon that theatre should not be *sécurisant*
(reassuring) but, rather, *inquiétant* (disquieting), chose the
latter type of play. Brecht, O'Casey, Gatti, the playwrights
wryly enumerated in Planchon's *La Mise en pièces du 'Cid'*,
all recurred again and again in the repertoire of the popular
theatres of the 1960s. Were they what was needed? The
problem was not only that of giving working-class people
information about and access to the theatre: it was one of
repertoire.

The question of subsidies further complicated the matter.
Popular theatres were generally left-wing to a greater or
lesser extent. It is not surprising that their political sympathies often irritated conservative local authorities or the
Gaullist Ministry of Culture. When Maurice Druon took
office as Minister of Culture in 1973, he infuriated the theatre
groups by stating that 'People who come to the door of this

213

ministry with a begging-bowl in one hand and a Molotov cocktail in the other will have to choose.'[1] A demonstration of several thousand people in Paris protested against this decision to 'bury freedom of speech'. Yet Druon's attitude was typical, and had in fact already been expressed; Claude-Gérard Marcus, then Paris representative of the Union des Démocrates pour la République (the main Gaullist party), had said that:

Certainly artistic creation must be free, but there's a difference between freedom and state subsidy. Many think . . . that public funds are not *necessarily* intended to help prepare the disintegration of the state and that, although the revolutionary theatre has a right to exist, it does not stand to reason that it must do so at the taxpayers' expense.[2]

The government was understandably reluctant to subsidise those who seemed bent on destroying the kind of society which it represented. The theatres, on the other hand, believed that theatre is a basic right, to be publicly sponsored; they also resented the kind of 'financial censorship' which would reduce them to putting forward, if only by default, the values and interests of those in power.

To argue that 'good' theatre should be able to pay for itself is to see theatre as a commodity for the few and not a service for all. Limiting the repertoire to what will pay means ignoring those for whom it is still a mysterious irrelevance quite eclipsed by television and the cinema. If one is to seek out an audience, and to give them the very highest artistic standards of which one is capable, one must have the means to do so. Of course agit-prop theatre which, rather than questioning the basis of society, tries to provoke its active destruction, must expect to remain on the fringe: you can't have your sponsor and beat him, too. The problem is that of deciding at what point dissidence becomes incitement to violence. Theatre groups are understandably reluctant to leave this decision in the hands of the state, which has a tendency to lump all its opponents together as a dangerous influence.

When Planchon mocked self-censorship with his *auto-censure* in *La Mise en pièces du 'Cid'* he was touching on a sensitive issue. Was it really possible for the directors of subsidised theatres, the *troupes permanentes*, the *centres dramatiques*, the *maisons de la culture*, to retain their artistic independence when they were subsidised by authorities whose views they often opposed? There is more than a little irony in the situation itself. One can't help recalling George Grosz's imaginary tale about Erwin Piscator (the German director whose revolutionary plays were attended by wealthy spectators) in which a rich man pays eagerly to hear himself abused.[3] The paradox by which revolutionary art becomes récupéré (retrieved) as a fashionable, and even, as in America, a marketable, commodity, is a painful one for left-wing directors. They can protest publicly if government agencies withhold subsidies in order to hinder their work. There is little they can do if they feel they are being subsidised because their work is harmless: the frustration leads either to attempts to be less acceptable, to shock, to 'make revolution', or else to an acceptance that, in the present social framework, it is not possible to bring a really disquieting theatre to working-class people.

There are still those who believe that the non-public can be reached by avoiding a paternalistic approach at all costs. They put on shows which are great spectaculars meant to appeal to people on a variety of levels (productions such as the Théâtre du Soleil's 1789 or the plays of Jérôme Savary's Grand Magic Circus); or they create small productions addressed to a number of people who can be talked to, or who can, in some cases, participate (as in André Benedetto's work with La Nouvelle Compagnie d'Avignon). This second type of production seems to be more fruitful. Not only do the small groups go out to their audiences and give shows where they find them, creating not only street theatre, but also council-flat and factory theatre; they also take infinite pains to know their spectators. There is a gulf separating people for whom long hours are spent each day on menial, repetitive, and often physically exhausting work, and those involved in a profession which, however precarious and demanding its conditions, has the undeniable human advantage of being creative. If it can be bridged at all, it is by small community-based groups not averse to going from door to door to invite people to come and have a chat, and capable of giving to the ideas and interests emerging from these discussions a form which is relevant and potent. During a railwaymen's strike in Avignon in 1971, Benedetto and his actors played out various roles connected with the strike, for the benefit of the strikers. As blacklegs in Avignon are called renards (foxes), one actor, wearing a yellow mackintosh and a fox mask, played a silent character who danced with the boss, swept the floor in front of him, etc. The railwaymen were deeply impressed by this image in particular. 'We had represented', said Benedetto, 'a concept, a reality, which is terrible for them; and the fox took on a very great force as a caricature. It was a tangible image of what was going on in their minds, a projection of the popular imagination.'[4]

Thus a production can be meaningful to a working-class audience if the company has prepared it by getting to know its public, their concerns, their manners of expression, and if they are able to dramatise convincingly what they have learned. Enrique Vargas, organiser of the Gut Theater in New York, said the same thing of street theatre in poor neighbourhoods there: 'You've got to know what touches the people. What they laugh at, what they read; what comic strips are preferred; what approaches the local preachers use to reach them.'[5] Vargas spent days 'casing' a street before putting on a production in it, observing its rhythms and activities at all hours of the day. This is the sort of in-depth work necessary to reach the culturally disinherited.

There is little room for the individual author in such theatre. Politically-committed writers and even committed theatres can easily make the mistake of preaching rather too solemnly. 'It is . . . the laughter of life that we need', said Jack Ralite, then mayor of Aubervilliers, 'Planchon, with his *Trois Mousquetaires*, had succeeded in producing it . . . What is necessary is not passing from seriousness to laughter, but a dialectical mixture as in our daily life – of laughter and seriousness.'[6] It is absurd to believe that less educated people will be attracted *only* by what is funny, light, escapist entertainment. It is patronising to stage political dissertations in order to 'educate' or to 'liberate'. Theatre must embody the real preoccupations of the audience which it wants, in a form which seems directly relevant to them (as Benedetto's fox did to the Avignon strikers), and which never excludes humour.

It is interesting that a few years ago, Planchon was already slightly embarrassed by the memory of his *Trois Mousquetaires*, a production which had been a success with all kinds of audiences. By becoming a dramatist himself and by taking a position at the head of a national theatre, Planchon has taken a very different course from that of many of his colleagues. Planchon and Chéreau seem to have decided that the ambition of creating a theatre which would attract the working classes in representative numbers is unrealistic in our present society. Chéreau's first production at the TNP, Villeurbanne, of Marlowe's *The Massacre at Paris*, was a theatrical experiment of considerable impact, but it was extremely difficult to follow: characters wore dark clothing and moved about on a sombre stage; it was often impossible to determine who was speaking, and therefore difficult to concentrate on the text. When I saw it, it was booed (8 June 1972). Perhaps, as for Planchon's *Troilus and Cressida*, one would need to see the show twice in order to appreciate it. Leaders of theatre-goers' associations complained about the production: 'On the aesthetic level, *The Massacre* was extraordinary: but the text was totally incomprehensible, inaudible. All the people who saw this show now have a prejudice against the TNP. Some will refuse to come back.'[7] The critic Bertrand Poirot-Delpech wrote that this was an example of non-popular art; Chéreau, however, replied quite vehemently that he, Planchon, and other leaders of the popular movement have been trying, since 1968, to define a radically new role for the theatre in a society whose mentality has changed.[8] Certainly it would be stultifying both for the director and for the audience to put on only facile productions; certainly the artist has every right to experiment. Nevertheless, it cannot be denied that such experiments as Chéreau's *The Massacre at Paris* are likely to drive away new spectators, and possibly even old ones, for good.

In 1974, the Arts Council in Britain subsidised a publicity campaign, to be conducted at factory gates and on council estates by arts associations in Birmingham, Sheffield and Bristol, in order to '. . . attract the cloth-cap worker to the theatre'. A public-relations officer at Bristol remarked that 'If at the end of the experiment, the people still don't go to artistic events, it will not be because they don't know about them . . . It will be because they don't bloody want to.'[9] Planchon, after an effort which has been intelligent, sensitive, and far-reaching, has concluded that 'they don't bloody want to', but he remains sympathetic to people who are cut off by lack of education, lack of time and energy after a working day, and by the irrelevance of even the best-intentioned theatre to their own reality. Planchon saw his role, in 1974, as that of at least trying to make people aware that they are missing out on something valuable:

I have said it often, workers go into the theatres only to build them. I am all the more troubled by this because, in a very autobiographical way, I know that there is a cultural gap and that it is large, real, brutal. I don't believe that theatre can have an effect upon a state of things which only a change in civilisation could modify. I hope to see the dawn of that change, but, in the meantime, what a theatre such as the one I direct can do is to recall constantly that a violent cultural gap exists. Our role is to keep the wound open.[10]

Although the *troupes permanentes*, *centres dramatiques*, and *maisons de la culture* had succeeded in attracting only a small percentage of working-class people, they could say, as Vilar did, that they had brought to the theatre many people who had not previously gone, and built up a following amongst them. In the provinces and on the periphery of Paris, the presence of a resident troupe in a community gave a continuity to the programme from year to year. The company developed a repertoire which became more sophisticated as the audience became more demanding. Planchon has noticed important changes in his public, who are educated not only by the cinema, but also by televised plays and serials and, too, by his own work and that of his colleagues.

The new TNP has carried out its intention of touching as wide a public, geographically, as possible. Since 1972, they have toured the cities of France regularly (with Paris considered as just one of many) and, as described in chapter 1, their appearance in each city is prepared in advance by the resident theatre companies. In each town the in-depth work of informing various associations and organisations, of discussing a production with the public, explaining it, and gauging the reactions to it, is done by the host theatre troupe. Planchon and his actors are as approachable as possible and engage in discussions after their productions. It is work which Planchon still considers essential: '. . . in our action in the provinces, we must try to make certain that the trades unions and teachers' unions, that the youth movements give us our support. This support is important because theatre is always at risk of becoming peripheral.'[11]

The TNP festivals have remained their principal work. There are problems, of course: touring is expensive, especially when one considers Planchon's predilection for enormous machine-like sets. To alleviate the possible financial strain which a TNP visit might put on a local theatre centre, the TNP pay for a good proportion of the costs of their productions on tour. They almost always fill the theatre and ticket sales therefore almost cover salaries. They never visit the same city two years in succession, and so a local theatre would have a chance to make up its losses if there were any. In any case, the TNP is invited to each town it visits.

The aim is not only that defined by Planchon, of bringing out the latent need for culture which exists everywhere. They also hope that they can influence relations between local theatre groups and municipal authorities, if only by showing how large a potential audience there is, or by letting some of their own prestige rub off on a local drama group.

As he has continued this work of making known the existence of a cultural gap, of keeping the wound open, Planchon's own artistic approach has been evolving. The world of dreams, the methods of surrealism, the interest in individual psychology and madness which Planchon relegated to the background in his earlier work has been given increasing scope in his later productions and plays. He remains an artist passionately interested in history and in politics, but he is interested in their mechanisms, in how they work, how 'progress' is affected by and affects individuals, each with his or her own dreams, aspirations, limitations. As his texts have become more poetic and more austere, so has the content of his plays become richer. The recurring themes in Planchon's work, the relation of ideology to behaviour, the relation of the individual to his or her social and economic circumstances at a specific point in history, the discrepancy between traditional interpretations of history and the way in which it is lived by ordinary people, all these concerns reveal a belief in the dialectical interaction of the human being and his society. Planchon's work is deeply rooted in a specific time and place because he takes his inspiration from the milieu which he and his public know. In this way his work is distinct from that of the absurdist movement of the 1950s and 1960s. Like Gatti, he belongs to the movement which is descended from Brecht. The absurdist universe is based on the premise of utter human impotence, whereas that of the heirs of Brecht is founded on the premise that human beings are both created by and creators of their environment, their experiences, their circumstances, and their era.

All Planchon's plays are a picture, drawn consciously, of a given society at a particular historical moment. Be it through its business dealings, its forms of entertainment, its love relationships, its myths, through its great or humble people or its madmen, each society is depicted both critically and with compassion. Planchon's plays show an ever deeper and more mature social and human analysis. In the early plays, great social or intellectual revolutions are taken into account in the localised and specific situations of the plot; in the later plays they are expressed through them. Planchon has moved gradually away from Brecht, whose theories may have been right for his time and place, but not for Planchon's public, in France, today. Planchon's work has been shaped by years of contact with his audience, an audience which now includes the theatre-going intelligentsia and any self-respecting critic, but whose core has always been basically provincial, and basically fresh to the theatre. As this audience has changed, so have Planchon's productions altered. Of contemporary directors, he is perhaps the most able to draw out the relevance for us, here and now, of other people's plays. As a playwright, he has added to this talent extraordinary poetic and analytical gifts. His productions are an increasingly profound reflection on our dilemma as individuals interacting with our society.

Chronology

Plays marked with an asterisk were premieres in France
1950 June *Bottines et collets montés* at Mâçon
  Oct. *Bottines et collets montés* in Lyons (Salle paroissiale du quai St-Antoine)
1951 June *Twelfth Night*, Lyons festival
  Summer *Bottines et collets montés* and *Twelfth Night*, La Lorelei, East Germany
  Winter *The Merry Wives of Windsor*, Lyons region
1952 Mar. René Char's *Claire** and Calderon de la Barca's *La Vie est un songe*
  June *Twelfth Night*, Lyons festival
  31 Dec. Opening of Théâtre de la Comédie with *Rocambole* (Lucien Dabril, after Ponson du Terrail)
1953 Mar. Michel de Ghelderode's *La Balade du grand macabre**
  Apr. Arthur Adamov's *Le Sens de la marche** and *Le Professeur Taranne**
  May. *Burlesque-Digest* (parody of Jean Tardieu plays)
  Oct. Ferenc Molnar's *Liliom*
  Dec. *Cartouche* (created by Planchon) for three months
1954 May Heinrich von Keist's *La Cruche cassée*
  June Marlowe's *Edward II** (trans. Adamov) and Brecht's *La Bonne Ame de Sé-Tchouan** at Lyons festival
  Oct. *La Bonne Ame de Sé-Tchouan*
  Dec. *Casque d'or* (after Jean-Marie Cérure)
1955 Jan.–Mar. *Casque d'or*
  Apr. Jean Clervers and G. Hannoteau's *La Belle Rombière*
  June–July Caldreon de la Barca's *L'Alcade de Zalaméa*, adapted by Planchon, in old Lyons (Musée de Gadagne) for two weeks
  Sept. Eugène Ionesco's *Comment s'en débarrasser*
  Nov. John Millington Synge's *The Shadow of the Glen* and Kleist's *La Cruche cassée*
  Dec. Jacques Prévert's *La Famille tuvau de poêle*, and Roger Vitrac's *Victor ou les enfants au pouvoir* and Brecht's *La Bonne Ame de Sé-Tchouan*
1956 Mar. Brecht's *Grand-peur et misères du Troisième Reich**
  15 Apr.–15 May *La Bonne Ame de Sé-Tchouan*, *Grand-peur*

et misères du Troisième Reich (Brecht), *Les Soldats* (Lenz), *Le Professeur Taranne* (Adamov), *La Cruche cassée* (Kleist) at Théâtre d'Aujourd'hui, Paris

May–June Ionesco's *La Leçon* and *Victimes du devoir*, Théâtre de la Comédie and *Twelfth Night*, Musée de Gadagne

24 Oct. Michel Vinaver's *Aujourd'hui ou Les Coréens**

1957 Jan. Planchon presents himself as a candidate for the directorship of the Théâtre Municipal de Villeurbanne

25 Mar. Planchon is accepted as director

24 May Adamov's *Paolo Paoli**, Théâtre de la Comédie

June *Paolo Paoli*, Théâtre du Vieux-Colombier

31 Oct. Opening of Théâtre de la Cité de Villeurbanne with *Henry IV*

1958 12 May *Les Trois Mousquetaires**, TCV

June *Les Fourberies de Scapin* (directed by J.-M. Boeglin)

23 Sept. *Les Trois Mousquetaires*, Liège

Oct. *George Dandin*

7 Nov. *Henry IV*, TCV

Dec. *La Bonne Ame de Sé-Tchouan*

1959 Jan. First publication of *Cité-Panorama*

13 Feb.–15 Mar. Marivaux's *La Seconde Surprise de l'amour* and Musset's *On ne saurait penser à tout*

12–31 May *Henry IV*, Montparnasse, Paris

2–14 June *Falstaff*, Montparnasse, Paris

16–28 June *La Seconde Surprise de l'amour*, Montparnasse, Paris

Nov. *Les Trois Mousquetaires*, Ambigu and Palais de Chaillot

18 Dec. *Les Trois Mousquetaires*, TCV

1960 15–17, 29–31 Jan. *Henry IV*, TCV

12 Feb. *Les Ames mortes**, TCV

17 Mar.–10 Apr. *Les Trois Mousquetaires* and *George Dandin*, Rhône–Alpes region and Italy

20 Apr.–30 May *Les Ames mortes*, Odéon, Paris

11–12 June *Les Trois Mousquetaires*, Zurich

17–19 June *Les Trois Mousquetaires*, Geneva

June *Les Trois Mousquetaires*, Mulhouse

27–28 June *Les Trois Mousquetaires*, Anvers

5–10 July *Les Trois Mousquetaires*, Marseilles

28 July *Henry IV*, Orange

31 July *Edward II*, Orange

14–24 Aug. *Edward II* and *Les Trois Mousquetaires*, Baalbeck

Aug. *Les Trois Mousquetaires*, Edinburgh

Sept. *Les Trois Mousquetaires*, London (Aldwych)

Oct. *Les Trois Mousquetaires*, Frankfurt and Charleroi

18–27 Nov. *George Dandin*, TCV
2–18 Dec. *Les Trois Mousquetaires*, TCV
23 Dec.–8 Jan. 1961 *La Seconde Surprise de l'amour*, TCV
1961 20 Jan.–12 Feb. *Edward II*, TCV
4–10 Oct. TCV, *Schweyk dans la deuxième guerre mondiale**.
11–29 Oct. *Schweyk dans la deuxième guerre mondiale*, Paris
11 Oct. *Schweyk*, Théâtre des Champs-Eylsées, Paris
23 Oct.–2 Dec. *Edward II*, Paris
30 Oct.–6 Dec. *Les Trois Mousquetaires*, Paris
9 Nov.–7 Dec. *George Dandin*, Paris
1962 12 Jan.–4 Feb. *Schweyk*, TCV
16 Feb.–11 Mar. Armand Gatti's *La Vie imaginaire de l'éboueur Auguste Geai** (directed by Jacques Rosner)
23 Mar.–15 Apr. *La Remise**, TCV
23 Nov.–16 Dec. *Tartuffe*, TCV
1963 4–27 Jan. *La Villégiature* (Michel Arnaud after Goldoni) (directed by Jacques Rosner), TCV
22 Feb.–17 Mar. *O M'man Chicago**, TCV
18–21 Apr. *George Dandin*, TCV
        On tour with *Les Trois Mousquetaires, George Dandin*, as follows:
26–29 Apr. Warsaw
2–5 May Cracow
8–10 May Timisoara
12–19 May Bucharest
22–26 May Sofia
31 May–3 June Budapest
19–26 June Festival of Holland, *George Dandin* in the Hague, Groningen, Utrecht, Amsterdam, Deventer, Tilburg
2–12 Sept. *Les Trois Mousquetaires, George Dandin, Tartuffe*, Moscow
16–26 Sept. *Les Trois Mousquetaires, George Dandin, Tartuffe*, Leningrad
19–27 Oct. *Les Trois Mousquetaires*, TCV
22 Nov.–1 Dec. *La Remise*, TCV
1964 10 Jan.–2 Feb. *Troilus and Cressida*, TCV
21 Feb.–16 Mar. *Troilus and Cressida*, Odéon, Paris
12 Mar.–13 Apr. 3–8 June *Tartuffe*, Odéon, Paris
6–26 Apr. *La Remise*, Odéon, Paris
4 May–1 June *Auguste Geai*, Paris
14–26 Oct. *George Dandin*, Oran, Sidi-Bel-Abbès, Algiers, Constantine, Annaba
4–15 Nov. *George Dandin*, TCV
27 Nov.–20 Dec. *Schweyk*, TCV
1965 20–31 Jan. 24–28 Feb. *Patte blanche**, TCV

28 Jan.–14 Feb. Maupassant recitals by Gérard Guillaumat
6–30 May Marivaux's *La Fausse Suivante* (directed by Yves Kerboul), TCV
27 Oct.–21 Nov. *Henry IV*, TCV
26 Nov.–22 Dec. *Falstaff*, TCV
1966 21 Jan.–13 Feb. Sean O'Casey's *Purple Dust* (directed by Jacques Rosner), TCV
3–27 Mar. *Bérénice*, TCV
22–23 Apr. *Les Trois Mousquetaires*, Hamburg
25–27 Apr. *Les Trois Mousquetaires*, *Le Tartuffe*, Copenhagen
28–29 Apr. *Les Trois Mousquetaires*, Malmö, Sweden
2–4 May *Le Tartuffe*, *Les Trois Mousquetaires*, Stockholm
5 May *Les Trois Mousquetaires*, Upsala
9–16 May *Tartuffe*, *Les Trois Mousquetaires*, Bratislava
1–3 June *Tartuffe*, St-Étienne
8–9 June *Tartuffe*, Zurich
11–12 June *Tartuffe*, Thonon
16–17 June *Tartuffe*, the Hague
18 June *Tartuffe*, Amsterdam
20 June *Tartuffe*, Esch sur Alzette
22–25 June *Tartuffe*, Caen
24 July–4 Aug. *Richard III* and *George Dandin*, Avignon
19–20 Sept. *Le Tartuffe*, Venice
10–11 Oct. *George Dandin*, Amiens
13–15 Oct. *George Dandin*, Caen
18 Oct.–13 Nov. *George Dandin*, Toulouse
25 Nov.–11 Dec. *George Dandin*, St-Étienne
13–15 Dec. *George Dandin*, Clermont-Ferrand
17–18 Dec. *George Dandin*, Thonon
1967 4–22 Jan. John Arden's *Armstrong's Last Goodbye* (directed by Jacques Rosner)
25–31 Jan. Dickens recital by Gérard Guillaumat
21 Feb.–19 Mar. *Richard III*, TCV
5–23 Apr. *Bleus, blancs, rouges* ou *Les Libertins**, TCV
11 July–6 Aug. *Bleus, blancs, rouges* ou *Les Libertins* and *Tartuffe*, Avignon
On tour with *Le Tartuffe*, as follows:
10–11 Oct. Chambéry
13–20 Oct. Milan
23 Oct. Mulhouse
24–28 Oct. Strasbourg
31 Oct.–3 Dec. TCV
6–9 Dec. Marseilles
14–16 Dec. Montpellier
3 Nov.–10 Dec. Maupassant recital in Beaune, Toulouse, Caen, Clermont-Ferrand, TCV (Gérard Guillaumat)

1968 16 Feb.–16 Mar. *Dans le vent**, TCV
      19 Apr.–11 May *Les Trois Mousquetaires*, TCV
      25 June–14 July *Les Trois Mousquetaires*, *Le Tartuffe*,
      George Dandin, New York
      22 Nov.–15 Dec. Roger Vitrac's *Le Coup de Trafalgar*
      (directed by Jacques Rosner), TCV
1969 17 Jan.–8 Feb. *La Mise en pièces du 'Cid'**, TCV
      11–29 Mar. *L'Infâme**, TCV
      14–16, 24–26 Apr. *Bérénice*, London (Aldwych)
      17–23 Apr. *George Dandin*, London
      4–5 May *Bérénice*, Rome
      10 Nov. *La Mise en pièces du 'Cid'*, Montparnasse
1970   Paris, Montparnasse season continues with:
      15 Feb.–Mar. *L'Infâme*, then Vitrac's *Le Coup de Trafalgar*
      (directed by Rosner)
      3 Apr.–May *Bérénice*
               Villeurbanne, Maison des Sports and Centre
               Culturel (during renovations at the TCV):
      10 Feb. *Nicomède*, (directed by Rosner)
      7 Apr. *Homme pour Homme* (directed by Rosner)
      12 May Chekhov recital by Guillaumat
      Sept. On tour with *Bérénice*, *L'Infâme*, *O M'man Chicago*
      5 Oct. *Bérénice*, Caen
      26 Oct.–10 Nov. *L'Infâme*, Rouen
      16–21 Nov. *Bérénice*, Strasbourg
      Nov. *Bérénice*, Rennes
      23–28 Nov. *L'Infâme*, Strasbourg
      Nov. Mayor of Nancy forbids two scheduled presentations
      of *L'Infâme* at Nancy, purportedly to avoid offending rela-
      tives of Desnoyers in the area. Planchon refuses to put on
      scheduled performances of *Bérénice*. Numerous groups
      protest at the mayor's censorship.
      30 Nov.–1 Dec. *L'Infâme*, Grenoble
1971 May First public announcement that Patrice Chéreau is to
      co-direct the Théâtre de la Cité de Villeurbanne
      8–9 May Partially rewritten *Bleus, blancs, rouges* at Nîmes
      12 May TCV leaves on extended tour with *Tartuffe*, *Bleus,
      blancs, rouges*, and Guillaumat's Maupassant recital in
      Bulgaria, Yugoslavia, Austria, Rumania. Further renova-
      tions get under way at the Villeurbanne theatre.
      Oct.–Dec. *Bleus, blancs, rouges* on tour in Nice, Venice,
      Toulouse, Marseilles, Perpignan, Montpellier, Rheims,
      Grenoble, Thonon, Chalon, Rennes, Rouen, Tours, Bor-
      deaux, Caen.
1972 Jacques Duhamel, Minister of Cultural Affairs, announces
      that Planchon is to direct the new Théâtre National
      Populaire based at Villeurbanne.

19 May–10 June TNP (en préfiguration) opens with Chéreau's production of Marlowe's *The Massacre at Paris*, in J. Vauthier's adaptation.

Oct. The theatre wins its lawsuit against the municipality of Nancy for cancelling two performances of *L'Infâme* in Nov. 1970.

La Langue au Chat:

10–16 Oct. Marseilles*

20–28 Oct. Rheims

3–25 Nov. TNP, Villeurbanne

29 Nov.–2 Dec. Nice

1973 1 Jan. The Théâtre de la Cité de Villeurbanne officially becomes the new Théâtre National Populaire.

12–27 Jan. Tankred Dorset's *Toller* (directed by Chéreau), TNP

2–24 Mar. Michel Vinaver's *Par-dessus bord**, TNP

June-July Planchon tours Chili, Uruguay, and Brazil with new production of *Tartuffe*

24 Oct.–Nov. Marivaux's *La Dispute* (directed by Chéreau), Paris (Gaîté-Lyrique)

11 Dec. *Le Cochon noir**, Caen

1974 Jan.–Mar. On tour in Arles, Caen, Chambéry, Clermont-Ferrand, Grenoble, Nice, Tours, with *Tartuffe* and *La Dispute*

22 Apr.–May *Toller*, Paris (Odéon)

7 May *Le Cochon noir*, Paris (Porte St-Martin)

1 June *Par-dessus bord* opens, Paris (Odéon)

8 June–20 July *Tartuffe*, Paris (Porte St-Martin)

Oct. *Blues, Whites, and Reds*, trans. by John Burgess, directed by Michael Simpson, at Birmingham Repertory Theatre

1975 28 Jan. *A.A. Théâtres d'Arthur Adamov**, TNP

8 Apr. Bond's *Lear* (Chéreau) TCV

9–12 Apr. *Folies bourgeoises**, St-Étienne

16–20 Apr. *A.A. Théâtres d'Arthur Adamov*, St-Étienne

23–27 Apr. Edward Bond's *Lear* (Chéreau), St-Étienne

5–7 May *Folies bourgeoises*, Tours

13–15 May *Folies bourgeoises*, Lille

14–15 May *Lear*, Caen

20–22 May *A.A. Théâtres d'Arthur Adamov*, Lille

21–23 May *Lear*, Tours

28–30 May *Lear*, Lille and *A.A. Théâtres d'Arthur Adamov*, Tours

5–7 and 10–14 June *Lear*, TNP

4 Oct. *Lear*, Brussels

21–29 Oct. *Tartuffe*, Créteil

4–8 Nov. *Tartuffe*, TNP

17 Oct.–16 Nov. *Lear*, Paris (Odéon)
21–29 Nov. *Lear*, Créteil
1976 6–24 Jan. *Gilles de Rais**, TNP
2–20 Mar. *Folies bourgeoises*, TNP
9–13 Apr. *Tartuffe*, Strasbourg
22–24 Apr. *Tartuffe*, Amiens
24–29 Apr. *La Dispute* (Chéreau), TNP
27–29 Apr. *Folies bourgeoises*, Amiens
4–6 May *Tartuffe*, Lille
5–7 May *La Dispute*, Amiens
11–13 May *Tartuffe*, Chalon/Saône
12–14 May *La Dispute*, Lille
18–21 May *Tartuffe*, Toulouse
22–26 May *La Dispute*, Strasbourg
24–29 May *Folies bourgeoises*, Toulouse
31 May–2 June *La Dispute*, Chalon/Saône
18 Sept. *La Dispute*, Belgrade
12–16 Oct. *Tartuffe*, TNP
9–13 Nov. *La Dispute*, TNP
17–20 Nov. *Tartuffe*, National Theatre, London (Lyttelton)
23–27 Nov. *La Dispute*, National Theatre
23 Nov.–18 Dec. *A.A. Théâtres d'Arthur Adamov*, Chaillot
1977 4–26 Jan. *Gilles de Rais*, Chaillot
22 Feb.–2 Mar. Jean-Paul Wenzel's *Loin d'Hagondage**
(directed by Chéreau), Paris (Porte St-Martin)
12 Apr.–14 May *Loin d'Hagondage*, TNP
6 May *Folies bourgeoises*, Porte St-Martin
1978 26 Apr.–17 June *Antony and Cleopatra*, *Love's Labours
Lost*, and *Pericles*, on alternate evenings
1979 May–June Pinter's *No Man's Land*, Paris. Also Racine's
Athalie, Molière's *Dom Juan*
1980 28 Apr.–7 June *Athalie Don Juan*, TNP

Notes

1 THE BIRTH AND LIFE OF THE THÉÂTRE DE LA CITÉ DE VILLEURBANNE

1 Quoted by Jean-Jacques Lerrant, Le Progrès (Lyons), 4 Apr. 1954.
2 Interview on 1 Jan. 1969, recorded by Denis Gontard in La Décentralisation théâtrale en France 1894–1952 (Paris: Société d'Édition d'Enseignement Supérieur, 1973), pp. 327–8. A tape recording of the interview is available at the Institut d'Études Théâtrales, rue de Santeuil, Paris v^e.
3 Éditorial, Cité-Panorama, no. 9, os (Feb. 1960).
4 'Roger Planchon nous parle de Villeurbanne', Théâtre Populaire, no. 28 (Jan. 1958), p. 12.
5 Lettres Françaises, 11 Feb. 1959.
6 Recorded in Travail et Culture (Lyons), 20 Oct. 1960.
7 In a discussion recorded in Lettres Françaises, 9–15 July 1959.
8 Recorded in Le Monde, 15 Apr. 1964.
9 'Notre réponse', Cité-Panorama, no. 4, NS (Jan.–Feb. 1965), p. 10.
10 'Creating a theatre of real life', detailed interview with Michael Kustow, Theatre Quarterly, vol. II, no. 5 (Jan.–Mar. 1972), p. 46.
11 For an account of these theatres, see Philippe Madral, Le Théâtre hors les murs (Paris: Éditions du Seuil, 1969).
12 Reproduced in Madral, Le Théâtre hors les murs, pp. 245–50.
13 'Un théâtre populaire baroque?' in Le Théâtre 1968. I – Cahiers dirigés par Arrabal (Paris: Christian Bourgois, 1968), p. 122.
14 Interview by G. de Véricourt, L'Express, 3 Nov. 1969.
15 'Une mort exemplaire', Partisans No. 47, Théâtres et politiques (bis) (Apr.–May 1969), p. 68.
16 Recorded in 'Quand l'imagination se surprend à prendre le pouvoir', draft of an article by Lucien Attoun, archives of the TNP, Villeurbanne, 1972.
17 Recorded by Yves Léridon, Le Figaro, 3 Mar. 1972.

2 PLANCHON'S APPROACH TO THE THEATRE

1 'Note sur le théâtre épique à propos de La Bonne Ame', Le Travail au Théâtre de la Cité, no. 1 (Paris: l'Arche, 1959), pp. 2–3.
2 'Roger Planchon nous parle de Villeurbanne', Théâtre Populaire, no. 28 (Jan. 1958), p. 15.
3 Planchon, quoted in Le Soir, 6 Apr. 1965.
4 'Où en sommes-nous avec Brecht? Entretien avec Roger Planchon et

René Allio' in Arthur Adamov, *Ici et maintenant* (Paris: Gallimard, 1964), p. 214.

5 Interviewed by Michel Richard, *Nouveau Clarté*, 1969.

6 Jean-Louis Martin-Barbaz, at a conference reported in *Méridional* (Marseilles), 1 Aug. 1966.

7 'Le travail du décorateur', *Théâtre Populaire*, no. 28 (Jan. 1958), p. 24.

8 Allio, recorded in *Lettres Françaises*, 24–30 Oct. 1963.

9 'Le travail du décorateur', *Théâtre Populaire*, no. 28, p. 24.

10 Claude Lochy, 'La musique de scène', *Le Travail au Théâtre de la Cité*, p. 10.

11 'Le décor', *Le Travail au Théâtre de la Cité*, pp. 7–8.

12 'Le peintre au service du théâtre', *Jardin des Arts* (Feb. 1963).

13 'Dessiner un serpent avec des pattes', *Le Travail au Théâtre de la Cité*, pp. 1–2.

14 'Creating a theatre of real life', detailed interview with Michael Kustow, *Theatre Quarterly*, vol. II, no. 5 (Jan.–Mar. 1972), pp. 52–3.

15 Recorded in *Libération*, 12 Mar. 1962.

16 Planchon in a discussion recorded by Claude Olivier, *Lettres Françaises*, 9–15 July 1959.

17 Recorded in *Journal de Genève*, 18 Dec. 1966.

18 9 Jan. 1969, recorded by Jacques Blanc in an unpublished thesis on the staging of *Bérénice* and *Dans le vent* for the University of Lyons, 1969, p. 63. Archives of the TNP, Villeurbanne.

19 'Creating a theatre of real life', *Theatre Quarterly*, vol. II, no. 5, p. 52.

20 Recorded by G. de Vericourt, *L'Express*, 3 Nov. 1969.

21 Recorded by Michele Manceaux, *L'Express*, 20 Feb. 1964.

22 'Creating a theatre of real life', *Theatre Quarterly*, vol. II, no. 5, p. 51.

23 Ibid., p. 48.

24 Recorded in *Le Progrès* (Lyons), 8 Mar. 1965.

25 Recorded in *Dernière Heure Lyonnaise*, 17 Dec. 1964.

26 Recorded in *Nouvelles Littéraires*, 12 Feb. 1970.

27 'Creating a theatre of real life', *Theatre Quarterly*, vol. II, no. 5, p. 54.

28 Recorded in *Presse de Tunisie*, 22 Aug. 1970.

29 Recorded in *Le Soir* (Marseilles), 12 May 1969.

30 Recorded by Michele Grandjean, *Le Provençal* (Marseilles), 2 Oct. 1972.

31 'Creating a theatre of real life', *Theatre Quarterly*, vol. II, no. 5, p. 53.

32 Georg Lukács, *The Meaning of Contemporary Realism* (London: Merlin Press, 1962), p. 123.

33 Recorded in *Presse de Tunisie*, 22 Aug. 1970.

34 Claude Roy, 'Théâtre Bonheur Malheur', *La Nouvelle Revue Française*, 1 July 1964.

3 CONTEMPORARY DRAMA: THE SOCIAL CONTEXT

1 Recorded in *La Tribune de Genève*, 20 June 1958.

2 *Arts*, 7–13 Jan. 1959.

3 Ibid.

4 Recorded in *Lettres Françaises*, 12–18 Oct. 1961.

5 In *The Manchester Guardian*, 21 Nov. 1961.

6 In *Lettres Françaises*, 18–24 Oct. 1961.

7 Bernard Dort, 'Schweyk dans la deuxième guerre mondiale de Bertolt Brecht, musique d'Hans Eisler', Itinéraire de Roger Planchon 1953–1964 (Paris: l'Arche for Théâtre Populaire, 1970), pp. 79–80. Planchon replied in an article, 'Orthodoxies', Théâtre Populaire, no. 46 (2ᵉ trimestre 1962), pp. 122–5.

8 Le Monde, 18 Oct. 1961.

9 Bulletin du Théâtre de la Comédie, no. 5 (Oct. 1956).

10 Recorded in 'Marx, les fruits et la spéculation. A propos de Par-dessus bord', La Nouvelle Critique, no. 85, NS (June–July 1975), p. 35.

11 In 'La genèse de Par-dessus bord', leaflet, archives of the TNP, Villeurbanne.

12 Recorded in 'Marx, les fruits et la spéculation', La Nouvelle Critique, no. 85, p. 35.

13 'La genèse de Par desus bord', archives of the TNP, Villeurbanne.

14 Lettres Françaises, 25 Mar. 1970.

15 Alain Prévost, Lettres Françaises, 20 May 1958.

16 Arts, 27 Apr. 1960.

17 Nikolai Gogol, Dead Souls, trans. David Magarshak (Harmondsworth, Middlesex: Penguin Books Ltd, 1961) pt. I, p. 58.

18 Recorded by Jacqueline Autrusseau, 'Comment on répète au Théâtre de la Cité', Théâtre Populaire, no. 36 (4ᵉ trimestre 1959), pp. 15–22.

19 Ossia Trilling, The Observer, 24 Apr. 1960.

20 Adamov, Ici et maintenant, Collection Pratique du théâtre dirigée par André Veinstein (Paris: Editions Gallimard, 1964), p. 116; p. 111.

21 Arts, 27 Apr. 1960.

22 L'Homme et l'enfant (Paris: Gallimard, 1968), p. 13.

23 Ibid. p. 127

24 Le Progrès (Lyons), 3 Feb. 1975.

4 ENGLISH CLASSICS: THEMES FOR THE TWENTIETH CENTURY

1 'Roger Planchon nous parle de Villeurbanne', Théâtre Populaire, no. 28 (Jan. 1958), p. 16.

2 André Gisselbrecht, 'Henry IV de William Shakespeare', Itinéraire de Roger Planchon 1953–1964 (Paris: L'Arche for Théâtre Populaire, 1970), pp. 48–9.

3 Lettres Françaises, 11–17 June 1959.

4 Recorded by Mireille Boris, Humanité, 18 Feb. 1964.

5 Ibid.

6 Text of Troïlus et Cressida, archives of the TNP, Villeurbanne, pt II, p. 10.

7 In a debate entitled 'Shakespeare aujourd'hui', recorded in Cité-Panorama, no. 2, NS (Apr. 1964), p. 7.

8 Lettres Nouvelles (June 1964), p. 179.

9 Gilles Sandier in Arts, 4–10 Mar. 1964.

10 Special Correspondent, The Times, 30 July 1964.

11 Recorded by Mireille Boris, Humanité, 18 Feb. 1964.

12 In 'Troïlus et Cressida de William Shakespeare', Itinéraire de Roger Planchon 1953–1964, p. 106

13 Recorded by Claude Sarraute, Le Monde, 21 Feb. 1964.

14 Gilles Sandier in Arts, 4–10 Mar. 1964; B. Poirot-Delpech, Le Monde, 21 Feb.–4 Mar. 1964.

15 In 'A propos de Troïlus et Cressida', Itinéraire de Roger Planchon 1953–1964, p. 120.
16 Quoted in 'Shakespeare aujourd'hui', Cité-Panorama, no. 2, NS, p. 7.
17 Recorded in L'Accent (programme for the Avignon festival), July 1966.
18 Jan Kott, Shakespeare notre contemporain, trans. Anna Posner (Paris: René Julliard, 1962), pp. 51–2.
19 Arts, 10–14 Aug. 1966.
20 Ibid.
21 Lettres Françaises, 16 Mar. 1967.
22 Recorded in L'Accent, July 1966.
23 In Humanité, 30 July 1966.
24 The 'Cartel des Quatre' was formed in 1939 by Gaston Baty, Charles Dullin, Louis Jouvet, and Georges Pitoeff, partly in order to take a stand against the tyranny of drama critics of the day. Their style and repertoire are now sometimes cited as examples of 'old-fashioned' theatre, that is, politically uncommitted, concerned with individual psychology, and based on traditional dialogue, etc.
25 Pierre Seller, 'Édouard II d'après Christopher Marlowe (1960–1961)', Itinéraire de Roger Planchon 1953–1964, p. 86.
26 Ibid.
27 Special Correspondent, The Times, 8 Aug. 1960.
28 Arts, 1–7 Nov. 1961.
29 Lettres Françaises, 2–8 Nov. 1961.

5 FRENCH CLASSICS: HUMAN BEINGS AND SOCIAL BEINGS

1 Quoted in Nouvelles Littéraires, 12 Feb. 1970.
2 Jean-Jacques Lerrant, in L'Accent (programme for the Avignon festival), July 1966.
3 Lettres Françaises, 23–29 Nov. 1961.
4 'Notes pour Dandin', Théâtre Populaire, no. 34 (2ᵉ trimestre 1959), p. 47.
5 L'Accent, July 1966.
6 Henry Hewes, Saturday Review, 13 July 1966.
7 'Notes pour Dandin', p. 48.
8 L'Accent, July 1966.
9 Lettres Françaises, 24 Mar. 1966.
10 The Fronde, the civil war, lasted from 1648 to 1653, and Le Tartuffe was written in 1669.
11 Recorded in Paysans, Apr.–May 1964.
12 Planchon, in Lettres Françaises, 24 Mar. 1966.
13 Émile Copfermann, Roger Planchon (Lausanne: Editions l'Age d'Homme, 1969), p. 134.
14 Nouvelles Littéraires, 25 June 1959.
15 'Pour Marivaux. Les miroirs', Le Travail au Théâtre de la Cité, p. 19.
16 Ibid.
17 'Pour Marivaux. Note au comédien qui joue Lubin', Le Travail au Théâtre de la Cité, p. 27.
18 Claude Lochy, 'Pour Marivaux. La musique', Le Travail au Théâtre de la Cité, p. 27.
19 Planchon, 'Pour Marivaux. Dans un monde humain', Le Travail au Théâtre de la Cité, p. 22.

20 Planchon, interviewed by Martine Monod, *Lettres Françaises*, 14–20 May 1959.
21 Planchon, 'Creating a theatre of real life', detailed interview with Michael Kustow, *Theatre Quarterly*, vol. ii, no. 5 (Jan.–Mar. 1972), p. 51.
22 'La Seconde Surprise de l'amour de Marivaux', *Itinéraire de Roger Planchon 1953–1964* (Paris: l'Arche for *Théâtre Populaire*, 1970), p. 68.
23 *Lettres Françaises*, 25 June–1 July 1959.
24 *Cité-Panorama*, no. 2, os (Feb. 1959), p. 2.
25 Guillot in *Lettres Françaises*, 26 Feb.–4 Mar. 1959.
26 Planchon in programme note on *Bérénice*, archives of the TNP, Villeurbanne. Brecht, 'Cultural Policy and the Academy of Arts' in *Brecht on Theatre. The Development of an Aesthetic*, ed./trans. John Willett (London: Methuen and Co. Ltd, 1964), p. 269.
27 Programme note on *Bérénice*, archives of the TNP, Villeurbanne.
28 Roland Barthes, *Sur Racine* (Paris: Editions du Seuil, 1963), p. 98.
29 *Lettres Françaises*, 24 Mar. 1966.
30 Planchon, programme note on *Bérénice*, archives of the TNP, Villeurbanne. Louis XIII died in 1643, leaving the throne to Louis XIV who was then five years' old. France was governed by Mazarin under the regency of Anne of Austria, and it was toward the end of this regency that the love-affair between Louis XIV and Marie Mancini took place. On the death of Mazarin in 1661 Louis XIV began his personal reign. *Bérénice* was written in 1670.
31 Barthes, *Sur Racine*, p. 43.
32 Planchon in a letter to Richard Demarcy, in response to an assessment of the play, *Travail Théâtral*, no. 2 (Jan.–Mar. 1971), p. 161.
33 Recorded by Jacques Blanc in an unpublished thesis on the staging of *Bérénice* and *Dans le vent* for the University of Lyons, 1969, pp. 38, 39. Archives of the TNP, Villeurbanne.
34 Irving Wardle, *The Times*, 15 Apr. 1970.
35 *La Pensée*, Oct. 1970.

6 FIVE MUSICAL COMEDIES: THE MORE THE MERRIER

1 Recorded in *Lettres Françaises*, 2 May 1958.
2 De Winter: 'Messieurs les Français, vous ne serez jamais que des . . .
   Tous les Anglais: Pa-pistes.
   Jussac: Messieurs les Anglais, vous n'êtes que des . . .
   Tous les Français: Hu-guenots.
   Les Anglais: Féti-chistes.
   Les Français: Héré-tiques.'
   From the Nov. 1960 text of *Les Trois Mousquetaires*, archives of the TNP, Villeurbanne, sc. 18, p. 52. Further quotations are from the same text.
3 *New York Times*, 7 July 1968.
4 'Vous avez fini ce tintamarre? On va pouvoir dormir? Moi la journée, je travaille!' *Les Trois Mousquetaires*, sc. 9, p. 40.
5 'Seuls? Non, nous n'étions pas seuls, il y avait un cardinaliste dans chaque bosquet. Moi, je n'oublie pas ce qui a suivi, l'éclat que fit le Roi,

poussé sans doute par Monsieur le Cardinal, Madame de Chevreuse ma seule amie, condamnée à la retraite. Moi-même privée de déssert pendant quatre mois.' Ibid., sc. 11, p. 47.

6 'Bon d'accord! Gustave-Francoué ou je ne sais quoué. Viens-t-en donc arquebouter l'échelle . . . Bonhomme si tu te plais pas en bas y'a de l'ouvrage sur la hauteur.' Ibid., sc. 11, p. 47.

7 'Je représente Madame Bonacieux. Je suis une jeune personne de 25 à 26 ans. J'ai le teint marbré de rose et d'opale, le nez légèrement retroussé, je n'ai pas de moustache . . ' Ibid., sc. 6, p. 28.

8 Interviewed by Xavier Salomon, Le Progrès (Lyons), 27 Sept. 1968.

9 New York Times, 7 July 1968.

10 Libération, 9 Nov. 1959.

11 Le Monde, 8 Nov. 1959.

12 Oeuvres et Opinions (Moscow), Jan. 1964.

13 At the University of Lyons, recorded in Le Progrès (Lyons), 14 Mar. 1963.

14 'Ils vous servent sur plateau en hors-d'oeuvre, un massacre, et à côté de celui-là, la guerre de sécession était une partie de campagne', et, 'Al, ton petit gars me rouille les éperons avec ses propos éthiques.' From the text of O M'man Chicago, archives of the TNP, Villeurbanne, sc. 10, p. 59 and sc. 1, p. 1.

15 'Y'a pas de danger, Inspecteur. Moi, mon métier c'est d'acheter les types qui vous paient.' Ibid., sc. 10, p. 64.

16 Lettres Françaises, 21–27 Mar. 1963.

17 Interviewed by Nicole Zand, Le Monde, 20 Nov. 1969.

18 '. . . est-il possible de continuer à faire du théâtre si le sang coule sur les barricades, faut-il continuer à jouer Corneille?' From the text of La Mise en pièces du 'Cid', archives of the TNP, Villeurbanne, pt. 1. p. 60. The text is not divided into acts or scenes. Further quotations will be from the same text.

19 Le Monde, 27 July 1968.

20 'J'ai été révolutionnaire. Oui, dans La Mort de Danton, chez Vilar, en 56. J'ai joué Brecht, O'Casey et Gatti.' La Mise en pièces du 'Cid', pt. 2, p. 71.

21 Plays in which actual historical documents form a part or a whole of the text, such as Vilar's Le Dossier Oppenheimer (1964), Peter Weiss's Die Ermittlung, put on at Aubervilliers in 1966, André Benedetto's Le Napalm, a 1966 Avignon production on Vietnam, to name only a few.

22 'Pas de toilettes lorsqu'on passe son bac . . . Que disent-ils au fond de la salle? Ils contestent. Ils contestent le baccalauréat? (Fafurle décroche un téléphone.) Monsieur le Ministre, l'examen ne peut pas se poursuivre, ils contestent le baccalauréat.' La Mise en pièces du 'Cid', pt. II, p. 23.

23 Corneille: 'Ceux qui se font presser à la représentation de mes ouvrages m'obligent infiniment; ceux qui ne les approuvent pas peuvent se dispenser d'y venir gagner la migraine, ils épargneront de l'argent et me feront plaisir.'
Bourdolle et les esthètes: 'Nous voulons un théâtre dégoûtant, sali, qui pue, qui répugne, qui ne craigne ni la boue ni le crottin, un théâtre qui n'ait pas peur d'avoir les mains sales.'

Corneille: 'Chacun a sa méthode; je ne blâme point celle des autres et me tiens à la mienne . . .'
Ibid., pt II, p. 81. Corneille's lines are from the letter of dedication for *La Suivante*, first published in 1637. In *Théâtre complet de Corneille*, vol. 1 (Paris: Editions Garnier Frères, n.d.), p. 313.

24 *Germaine*: 'Regarde-les, Léon, ils vont la construire eux-mêmes, ils sont ingénieux ces gens de théâtre. Regarde-les se dépatouiller! Ils coupent une scène par-ci par-là, ils fendent en deux une réplique, ils rafistolent un acte ou deux et hop, l'auto-censure est montée.'
Fafurle: 'Elle est jojotte votre guimbarde! Ça a plutôt l'air d'une brouette que d'un engin de compétition mais je reconnais que les coussins sont tout confort. Le débrayage est automatique, quelle merveilleuse marche arrière. L'échappement est plus ou moins libre, mais on ne peut pas tout avoir!'
Ibid., pt II, p. 61.

25 *France Soir*, 17 Nov. 1969.

26 In Jorge Lavelli's production of Oscar Panizzi's *Le Concile d'amour* in Nov. 1968 at the Théâtre de Paris, a large star-studded phallus was exhibited and then cut up. Phalluses also featured in Gabriel Garran's Aubervilliers production of Adamov's *Off Limits* in March 1969, and in Peter Brook's production of Seneca's *Oedipus* at the Old Vic in March 1968; the list is endless.

27 *Quinzaine Littéraire*, 1–15 Dec. 1969.

28 *Europe*, Mar. 1970.

29 'Mais qui sont ces gens? des acteurs, des spectateurs, du non-public?'
La Mise en pièces du 'Cid', pt I, p. 17.

30 '– Monsieur Ionesco est mort, victime du devoir.
– Monsieur Adamov est mort en criant: vivent les talons aiguilles et la sociale . . .
– Le mystérieux Monsieur Beckett meurt depuis toujours, il n'en finit pas d'agoniser.
– . . .
– . . . Le bon Monsieur Beck a mangé de la viande rouge, Monsieur. Il est mort en pacifiste de mort violente.
– Monsieur Grotowski s'est crucifié, eh oui, Monsieur, en jurant qu'il était athée.
– L'exquis Monsieur Strehler est mort sur scène comme une diva dans les draps blancs de Damiani.
– Monsieur Brook a eu un accident de voiture, sa Shakespeare s'est retournée dans un faubourg de Londres.
– Planchon est mort gâteux, Monsieur, on l'a enterré en Ardèche.
– Le bouillant Chéreau, héroiquement est monté au sommet d'une barricade mais il est déja blessé à mort.'
Ibid., pt II, pp. 85–6.

31 Recorded by E. Santy, *Le Soir*, 9 Oct. 1972.

32 *Bretzel*: 'Les vents putrides qui se déplacent d'est en ouest ne parviendront pas à soulever – on s'en doute – le couvercle de plomb que nous avons sur nos têtes. Ainsi vivrons-nous aujourd'hui comme hier sous les fluorescents' (sc. 2, p. 2).
Le Chat: '. . . la zone de dépression s'étend vers l'ouest et dans tous les

coeurs. Les brouillards crasseux se lèveront à minuit. Mais alors, une pluie de suie tombera sur toute la région' (sc. 7, p. 4).

Louis: 'Les usines déversent des flots de jus vert sur nos sympathiques cités. Ce matin toutes les surfaces de béton armé sont couvertes de mousse chimique' (sc. 8, p. 1).

From the text of *La Langue au Chat*, archives of the TNP, Villeurbanne. Further quotations will be from the same text.

33 'Certains d'entre vous se suicident toujours aussi bêtement, les imbéciles sont les imbéciles.' Ibid., sc. 12, p. 2.

34 'Ces hommes avaient une façon d'expliquer le monde dans leurs discours, dans leurs éditoriaux et voilà que le monde est parti au galop . . .

Le monde parti au galop a laissé des questions sans réponse et les questions sans réponse ont sécrété des microbes insidieux qui ont pourri leurs idéologies. Le sang idéologique qui irriguait leur cerveau s'est décomposé, a pourri. Maintenant leurs artères craquent.' Ibid., sc. 6, p. 5.

35 Rehearsal of 29 Sept. 1972 at Villeurbanne.

36 'Puis on bouffe. Petite sieste. Exercice pieux. Rebouffe. T.V. Prière et dodo. Notre vie sacerdotale s'est audacieusement simplifiée.

Tous mariés. Grignotés par la psychanalyse ou la politique. Les derniers obscurantistes espagnols sont devenus militants. La Révélation a été remplacée par la Révolution.' *La Langue au Chat*, sc. 11, p. 4.

37 'Un petit sucre de LSD et Jésus fait boum dans vos tempes.' Ibid., sc. 13, p. 5.

38 'Ce soir, j'aimerais me frotter à vous pour une petite bouffée de tendresse . . . La tendresse aujourd'hui coûte un prix fou, n'est-ce pas M. Louis?' Ibid., sc. 10, pp. 4–5.

39 'Prenez mon chewing gum. Un petit bout chacun. Il a été un peu machouillé mais il a gardé toute sa saveur.' Ibid., sc. 8, p. 7.

40 Recorded by M. Grandjean, *Provençal-Dimanche* (Marseilles), 15 Oct. 1972.

41 '. . . il est maintenant vingt heures. Toutes les familles sont réunies autour de la bonne soupe synthétique. Le néon flambe au dessus de vos têtes. C'est chouette. Bouffez rapidement votre sou-soupe. Et glissez-vous dans le chat aseptisé de vos compagnes.' *La Langue au Chat*, sc. 9, p. 3.

42 '. . . cher producteur: sur les pots de confiture funéraires mettez des étiquettes en couleur. Ça apporte un peu de gaieté.' Ibid., sc. 12, p. 2.

43 'Si, tout le monde se paie votre tête et depuis toujours. Aujourd'hui, un homme totalement délirant vous parle. Un cinglé adresse un sourire de complicité à tous les timbrés de la terre. Aux saints, aux mystiques, aux demeurés qui aboient la nuit dans les couloirs du métro. A tous les aliénés qui se jettent tête en avant contre le mur de leur cellule. Cette civilisation va sombrer mais je m'en fous, je suis un chat.' Ibid., sc. 2, p. 5.

44 'Studio de télévision préhistorique avec, se prenant pour un chat . . .' Ibid., sc. 14, p. 4.

45 At the Théâtre Populaire de Reims, 26 Oct. 1972.

46 Recorded by Colette Godard, *Le Monde*, 3 Apr. 1975.

47 Ibid.

48 From the text of *Folies bourgeoises*, archives of the TNP, Villeurbanne, act I, sc. 5, p. 10. Further quotations will be from the same text.

49 'Ah! l'époque des bals syphilitiques et des soupers en musique à la Rotonde. L'époque de l'amiral Godefroy Meronay de Saint-Gril. Époque somptuesuse où la belle Madame Meronay de Saint-Gril attestait son ardeur espagnole en prenant deux amants à la fois.' Ibid., act I, sc. 8, p. 17.

50 Brieux, *Le Bourgeois aux champs* in *La Petite Illustration*, no. 62 (9 May 1914), act I, sc. 2, p. 4. Georges Rivollet, *Jérusalem* in *La Petite Illustration*, no. 50 (14 Feb. 1914), act III, sc. 7, p. 17. *Folies bourgeoises*, act III, sc. 6, p. 9.

51 Pierre Veber and Marcel Gerbidon, *Un Fils d'Amérique* in *La Petite Illustration*, no. 51 (21 Feb. 1914), act I, sc. 8, p. 14. *Folies bourgeoises*, act III, sc. 6, p. 9.

52 *L'abbé*: 'pouvantable.
Gustave: Scandale. Courir. Ratrapper.
Le ministre: Où. Où.
Toutes entrant avec des béquilles: Rose disparue?
Tous: Disparue.
Toutes: Dis?
Tous: Arue.
Gustave: Arue. Arue. Arue.
Folies bourgeoises, act IV, sc. 4, p. 10.

7 TWO MODERN COMEDIES

1 Recorded by Gérard Guillot, *Lettres Françaises*, 21–7 Jan. 1965.

2 Recorded by Otto Hahn, '*Patte blanche* de Roger Planchon, vu des répétitions', *Cité-Panorama*, no. 4, NS (Jan.–Feb. 1965), p. 5.

3 'Le sexe, c'est pour les vieux pervers de vingt ans.' From the text of *Patte blanche*, archives of the TNP, Villeurbanne, pt I, p. 7. The text is not divided into acts or scenes. Further quotations will be from the same text.

4 'Capone, l'as-tu vu, le journal parle de la mort de "Salut-mon-Z'ami". Seulement il faut être très malin pour la trouver; il n'y a que trois lignes et il s'appelle Mohammed-quelque-chose-impossible-à-prononcer.' Ibid., pt. II, p. 133.

5 Planchon expressed this view of *Patte blanche* in a discussion after a reading of *Le Cochon noir* at the Théâtre Populaire de Reims, 26 Oct. 1972.

6 Recorded in *Vie Lyonnaise*, 2 Feb. 1968. *Hitler?, connais pas* (*Hitler? Never heard of him*) was the title of a 1963 film by Bertrand Blier, a documentary in which several young people were interviewed and revealed themselves, for the most part, as apolitical and pleasure-seeking.

7 Recorded in *La Tribune de Genève*, 10 Feb. 1968.

8 A thorough and detailed account of the rehearsals exists in Jacques Blanc's unpublished thesis on Planchon's productions of *Bérénice* and *Dans le vent* for the University of Lyons, 1969. Archives of the TNP, Villeurbanne.

9 Fourth rehearsal, 11 Jan. 1968, recorded by Jacques Blanc, thesis on *Bérénice* and *Dans le vent*, p. 80.

10 Recorded by John Burgess, 'Roger Planchon's *The Black Pig* at Villeurbanne', *Theatre Quarterly*, Vol. IV, no. 14 (May–July 1974), p. 70.

11 '... un prince est entré dans ma vie. Tu es mon prince, mon chevalier ...' From the text of *Dans le vent*, archives of the TNP, Villeurbanne, sc. 3, p. 17. Further quotations will be from the same text.

12 'ce ne sont pas les jeunes qui sont dangereux, ce sont tous ceux qui espèrent me laver le cerveau, qui veulent extirper ma singularité. J'ai la liste de tous ceux qui appartiennent à ce complot, une gigantesque machination internationale qui est décidée à liquider les derniers Grecs afin qu'il ne reste plus face au récepteur de télévision que des petits bourgeois dépolitisés et aseptisés.' *Dans le vent*, sc. 6, p. 57.

13 'J'ai un clou planté au sommet de l'occiput.' Ibid., sc. 6, p. 59.

14 Thesis on *Bérénice* and *Dans le vent*, pp. 164–5.

15 *Le Progrès* (Lyons), 15 Feb. 1968.

16 In a discussion with drama students after a reading of *Le Cochon noir*, at the Théâtre Populaire de Reims, 26 Oct. 1972.

8 THE PROVINCIAL PLAYS

1 Recorded by Colette Godard, *Le Monde*, 2 May 1974, p. 19.

2 Recorded by Claude Sarraute, *Le Monde*, 2 Apr. 1964.

3 Recorded by Claude Cézan, *Nouvelles Littéraires*, 28 Mar. 1964.

4 Recorded by Mireille Boris, *Humanité*, 4 Apr. 1964.

5 'C'est une saleté de toile écrue, à la façon ancienne, qui n'a jamais connu ni la sueur de la peau, ni l'herbe et le soleil pour la sécher. Le trousseau d'une jeune fille de grande maison à cinq vaches, aussi net qu'au premier jour.' From the 1964 text of *La Remise*, archives of the TNP, Villeurbanne, sc. 13, p. 89.

   Bernard Dort thought that this style should be compared to Claudel rather than to Zola, as many critics had suggested: 'La Remise de Roger Planchon', *Itinéraire de Roger Planchon 1953–1964* (Paris: L'Arche for *Théâtre Populaire*, 1970), p. 92.

6 *La Remise*, Collection Le Manteau d'Arlequin (Paris: Editions Gallimard for the NRF, 1973), p. 122. Further quotations from the 1973 text will give the page number only.

7 *Nouvelle Revue Française*, 1 July 1964.

8 Recorded by Colette Godard, *Le Monde*, 2 Dec. 1971, p. 15.

9 Recorded by Robert Butheau, *Le Monde*, 7 Apr. 1967.

10 A. Sayac, *Nice Matin*, 8 Oct. 1971.

11 Recorded by J.-J. Olivier, *Combat*, 17 Feb. 1970.

12 Recorded in *Dernière Heure Lyonnaise*, 7 Mar. 1969.

13 Recorded by Henri Terrière, *Ouest-France* (Rennes), 18 Nov. 1970.

14 Recorded by J.-J. Olivier, *Combat*, 17 Feb. 1970.

15 *L'Infâme* in *Travail Théâtral*, no. 1 (Oct.–Dec. 1970), sc. 12, p. 80. Unless otherwise indicated, further quotations from the play will be from the same text, and will give the scene and page numbers only.

16 *L'Infâme*, Collection Le Manteau d'Arlequin (Paris: Gallimard, 1975), sc. 6, p. 139.

17 *Ouest-France* (Rennes), 18 Nov. 1970.

18 *Le Monde*, 15 Dec. 1973.

19 Recorded by John Burgess, 'Roger Planchon's *The Black Pig* at Villeurbanne', *Theatre Quarterly*, vol. IV, no. 14 (May–July 1974), p. 52.

20 'Paris', *Plays and Players* (July 1974), p. 52.
21 *Le Cochon noir*, Collection Le Manteau d'Arlequin (Paris: Gallimard, 1973), sc. 3, p. 31. Further quotations from the play will give the scene and page numbers only.
22 Recorded by Burgess, 'Planchon's *The Black Pig*', *Theatre Quarterly*, p. 61.
23 *La Bibliothèque bleue: la littérature populaire en France du XVIe au XIXe siècle présentée par Geneviève Bollème*, Collection Archives (Paris: Julliard, 1971).
24 Rosner, recorded by Colette Godard, *Le Monde*, 10 Aug. 1973.
25 Burgess, 'Planchon's *The Black Pig*', *Theatre Quarterly*, p. 86.
26 Ibid., p. 58.
27 With drama students at the Théâtre Populaire de Reims, after a reading of *Le Cochon noir*, 26 Oct. 1972.
28 During rehearsals, recorded by Burgess, 'Planchon's *The Black Pig*', *Theatre Quarterly*, p. 66.
29 Ibid., p. 71.
30 With the audience at the Comédie de Caen in December 1973, information kindly communicated by Dr Dorothy Knowles.
31 Planchon recorded by Colette Godard, *Le Monde*, 15 Dec. 1973.
32 Ibid.
33 Information supplied by Dr Dorothy Knowles.
34 Recorded by Burgess, 'Planchon's *The Black Pig*', *Theatre Quarterly*, p. 80.
35 Recorded by John Burgess, 'Roger Planchon's *Gilles de Rais* at Villeurbanne', *Theatre Quarterly*, vol. VI, no. 22 (Summer 1976), p. 3.
36 Ibid., p. 23.
37 *Gilles de Rais*, Collections Le Manteau d'Arlequin (Paris: Gallimard, 1975), sc. 1, p. 15. Further quotations from the play will be from the same text.
38 Planchon, recorded by Burgess, 'Planchon's *Gilles de Rais*', *Theatre Quarterly*, p. 23.
39 Ibid., p. 11.
40 The historical Gilles de Rais loved spectacle. In 1429, Orléans, besieged by the English, had been saved by Jeanne d'Arc; this was the start of her military career. In 1435 Gilles de Rais spent a large part of his fortune in reconstructing the entire siege and battle, playing his own historical role once again. He also helped to plan his own funeral ceremonies. Making the trial into a play is thus appropriate.
41 Transcribed by Burgess, 'Planchon's *Gilles de Rais*', *Theatre Quarterly*, p. 18.
42 Ibid., p. 14.
43 Guy Dumur in *Le Nouvel Observateur*, 19 Jan. 1976.

9 POPULAR THEATRE: PROBLEMS AND POSSIBILITIES

1 Recorded by Louis Dandrel, *Le Monde*, 15 May 1973.
2 Recorded in *Le Monde*, 21 Oct. 1971, p. 17.
3 'Hach, Erwin, insult me, will you? Say something really filthy.'
'You unscrupulous capitalist.'

'Hach, again. Hach, isn't that charming? Erwin, here's a blank cheque. Any amount, any amount . . .'
Quoted by John Willett in *Erwin Piscator – Political Theatre 1920–1966* (London: Arts Council of Great Britain, n.d.), p. 12.

4 Recorded by Françoise Kourilsky, 'Avec André Benedetto et les Comédiens de la Nouvelle Compagnie d'Avignon', *Travail Théâtral*, no. 5 (Oct.–Dec. 1971), pp. 14, 15.

5 Recorded by John Lahr in *Acting Out America: Essays on Modern Theater* (Harmondsworth, Middlesex: Pelican Books, 1972), p. 45.

6 Recorded by Philippe Madral in *Le Théâtre hors les murs* (Paris: Éditions du Seuil, 1969), p. 188. Aubervilliers is a Parisian dormitory city in which Gabriel Garran's Théâtre de la Commune d'Aubervilliers has been active since 1965.

7 Unidentified young woman at a meeting at the TNP, Villeurbanne, recorded in *Le Progrès* (Lyons), 27 Sept. 1972.

8 B. Poirot-Delpech criticised the production in *Le Monde*, 27 May 1972, p. 31; Chéreau replied in *Le Monde*, 20 July 1972, p. 11.

9 Recorded in *The Guardian*, 27 May 1974.

10 Recorded by Yvonne Baby, *Le Monde*, 2 May 1974, p. 20.

11 Ibid., p. 19.

Select bibliography

PRIMARY SOURCES

Planchon's unpublished plays, translations and adaptations

Bleus, blancs, rouges (1970)
Bleus, blancs, rouges ou Les Libertins (1967) (1971)
La Contestation et la mise en pièces de la plus illustre des tragédies françaises 'Le Cid' de Pierre Corneille suivies d'une 'cruelle' mise à mort de l'auteur dramatique et d'une distribution gracieuse de diverses conserves culturelles (1969)
Dans le vent (1968)
Édouard II (after Marlowe and Brecht, 1961)
Henri IV (Shakespeare, adaptation, 1957)
L'Infâme (1969)
La Langue au Chat (1972)
O M'man Chicago (1963)
Patte blanche (1965)
La Remise (1962, 1964)
Richard III (Shakespeare, adaptation, 1966)
Troïlus et Cressida (Shakespeare, adaptation, 1964)
Les Trois Mousquetaires (1960)

Planchon's published plays

Le Cochon noir. La Remise. Le Manteau d'Arlequin, Paris: Gallimard for the NRF, 1973.
Gilles de Rais. L'Infâme. Le Manteau d'Arlequin. Paris: Éditions Gallimard for the NRF, 1975.
L'Infâme in *Travail Théâtral*, no. 1 (Oct.–Dec. 1970), pp. 55–83.

Planchon's articles and interviews

Planchon, R. 'Notes pour *Dandin*'. *Théâtre Populaire*, II 34 (2ᵉ trimestre 1959).
    'Orthodoxies'. *Théâtre Populaire*, 46 (2ᵉ trimestre 1962).
    'Un spectacle pour gens distingués'. *Lettres Françaises* (12 Nov. 1969).
    'Adamov'. *Lettres Françaises* (25 Mar. 1970).

'Taking on the TNP: theatre as social and artistic adventure'
(montage of various articles ed. and trans. by John Burgess).
Theatre Quarterly, 25 (Spring 1977), 25–33.

Baby, Y. 'Le Territoire de Roger Planchon'. *Le Monde* (2 May 1974),
19–20.
Kustow, M. 'Roger Planchon: actor, director, playwright (interview, assessment and checklist)'. *Theatre Quarterly*, 5
(Jan.–Mar. 1972), 42–57.
Olivier, C. 'Autour du micro des *Lettres Françaises*: Planchon et
l'équipe du Théâtre de la Cité de Villeurbanne'. *Lettres Françaises*, 9–15 July 1959).
'Roger Planchon nous parle de Villeurbanne'. *Théâtre Populaire*,
28 (Jan. 1958).

SECONDARY SOURCES

Adamov, Arthur. *L'Homme et l'enfant*. Paris: Gallimard, 1968.
Ici et maintenant. Paris: Gallimard, 1964.
Arrabal, Fernando. *Le Théâtre 1968. I – Cahiers dirigés par Arrabal*.
Paris: Christian Bourgois, 1968.
Autrusseau, Jacqueline. 'Histoire et histoires'. *Travail Théâtral*,
no. 6 (Jan.–Mar. 1972), 164–6.
Baecque, A. de. *Les Maisons de la culture*. 2nd edn. Paris: Seghers,
1967.
Barthes, R. *Sur Racine*. 2nd edn. Paris: Seuil, 1963.
Bataillon, M. 'A propos des *Folies bourgeoises*', *ATAC Informa-
tions*, 68 (May 1975).
'Les finances de la dramaturgie', *Travail Théâtral*, no. 7
(Apr.–June 1972), 49–56.
Blanc, J. Unpublished dissertation on the productions *Bérénice*
and *Dans le vent* at Villeurbanne for the University of Lyons,
1969. Archives of the TNP, Villeurbanne.
Bollème, G. *La Bibliothèque bleue: la littérature populaire en
France du XVIe au XIXe siècle*. Collection Archives. Paris:
Julliard, 1971.
Brecht on Theatre. The Development of an Aesthetic. Ed. and trans.
by John Willett. London: Methuen, 1964.
Brook, P. *The Empty Space*. 2nd edn. Harmondsworth, Middlesex:
Penguin, 1972.
Burgess, J. 'Paris', *Plays and Players* (July 1974), 50–2.
'Roger Planchon's *The Black Pig* at Villeurbanne', *Theatre
Quarterly*, 14 (May–July 1974), 56–86
'Roger Planchon's *Gilles de Rais* at Villeurbanne', *Theatre Quar-
terly*, 22 (Summer 1976), 3–24.
Cité-Panorama nos. 1–29 OS (Jan. 1959–May 1961), nos. 1–19 NS
(Feb. 1964–May 1970).

Copeau, J. *Le Théâtre populaire*. First published in *Théâtre Populaire*, 36 (4ᵉ trimestre 1959), 79–115.

Copfermann, É. *Le Théâtre populaire, pourquoi?* Paris: Maspero, 1965.

Roger Planchon. Lausanne: La Cité, 1969.

Théâtres de Roger Planchon. Lausanne: La Cité, 1977.

'Roger Planchon et la compagnie du Théâtre de la Cité de Villeurbanne', *Bref*, Special edition (May–June 1966).

'La mousse, l'écume. Entretien avec Patrice Chéreau', *Travail Théâtral*, no. 11 (Apr.–June 1973), 3–28.

'L'écriture enchevêtrée et l'indifférencié du langage. Entretien avec Michel Vinaver', *Travail Théâtral*, no. 12 (July–Sept. 1973), 70–9.

Dort, B. *Théâtre public*. Paris: Seuil, 1967.

Théâtre réel. Essais de critique 1967–1970. Paris: Seuil, 1971.

'Un théâtre sans public, un public sans théâtre', *Théâtre Populaire*, no. 5 (Jan.–Feb. 1954).

'Entre la magie et l'histoire ("le Cochon noir")'. *Travail Théâtral*, no. 17 (Oct.–Dec. 1974), 49–51.

Dullin, C. *Ce sont les dieux qu'il nous faut*. Ed. by C. Charras. Paris: Gallimard, 1969.

Dumur, G. 'Les Ames mortes au Théâtre de France'. *Théâtre Populaire*, no. 38 (2ᵉ trimestre 1960).

Duvignaud, J. 'Roger Planchon et le Théâtre de la Comédie à Lyon'. *Théâtre Populaire*, no. 5 (Jan.–Feb. 1954).

Ertel, E. 'Notes sur deux spectacles (*le Cochon noir*, mise en scène Jacques Rosner, Théâtre Ouvert, XXVIIe Festival d'Avignon)'. *Travail Théâtral*, no. 13 (Oct.–Dec. 1973), 84–8.

Gaudy, R. *Arthur Adamov*. Collection Théâtre Ouvert. Paris: Stock, 1971.

Gontard, D. *La Décentralisation théâtrale en France 1895–1952*. Paris: Société d'Edition d'Enseignement Supérieur, 1973.

Gozlan, G. and J.-L Pays. *Gatti aujourd'hui*. Paris: Seuil, 1970.

Gourdon, A.-M. ' "Le Théâtre Populaire": point de vue du public du TNP'. *Travail Théâtral*, no. 8 (July–Sept. 1972), 9–19.

Itinéraire de Roger Planchon 1953–1964. Paris: l'Arche for *Théâtre Populaire*, 1970.

Jacquot, J. *Shakespeare en France: mises en scène d'hier et d'aujourd'hui*. Collection Théâtres, Fêtes, Spectacles. Paris: Le Temps, 1964.

and D. Bablet. *Les Voies de la création théâtrale*. Paris: Editions du Centre National de la Recherche Scientifique, 1970.

Kilfoil, M. E. '*Roger Planchon – animateur de théâtre*'. Unpublished B.A. thesis, University of Liverpool, 1962.

Knowles, D. 'Problèmes du théâtre populaire en France'. *Problèmes des genres littéraires* (Lodz, Poland), no. 6 (1963), 27–43.

Kott, J. *Shakespeare notre contemporain*. Trans. By A. Posner. Paris: René Julliard, 1962.

Kourilsky, F. *et al.* 'Deux Schweyk'. *Théâtre Populaire*, no. 46 (2ᵉ trimestre 1962).

Laurent, J. *La République et les Beaux-Arts*. Paris: René Julliard, 1955.

Madral, P. *Le Théâtre hors les murs*. Paris: Seuil, 1969.

Monod, R. 'Entre la fable et le collage'. *Travail Théâtral*, no. 10 (Jan.–Mar. 1973), 95–8.

Nouvelle Critique, no 54, NS (June–July 1972); no. 65, NS (June–July 1973); no. 69, NS (Dec. 1973–Jan. 1974); no. 85, NS (June–July 1975).

Organon, no. 3 (July–Oct. 1970).

Promesses, no. 78 (June 1973).

Rolland, Romain. *Le Théâtre du peuple. Essai d'esthétique d'un théâtre nouveau*. Paris: Paul Ollendorff, 1899.

Roy, C. *Jean Vilar*. Paris: Seghers, 1968.

Temkine, R. *L'Entreprise théâtre*. Paris: Cujas, 1967.

Théâtre de la Cité de Villeurbanne. *Le Travail au Théâtre de la Cité*. Paris: l'Arche for *Théâtre Populaire*, 1970.

Tréteaux 67, no. 4 (Aug.–Sept. 1967).

Yale French Studies, no. 46 (1971).

Glossary

A-effect	Alienation effect, Brecht's *Verfremdungseffekt*, a device, usually a stylisation of sets or of acting, intended to make the theatricality of a production obvious to the spectator, so that he or she remains critically detached.
Agit-prop theatre	'Agitation', the use of slogans, parables, and half-truths to exploit the grievances of the uneducated, and 'propaganda', the reasoned use of historical and scientific arguments to indoctrinate the educated, were both strategies considered by Lenin as essential to political victory. 'Agit-prop' theatre is generally street theatre put on by groups with an anti-establishment message.
Blocking	Director's plan of where actors are positioned at any given point, how they move, etc.
Création collective	A production created as a group effort by the entire company.
Décor explosé, éclaté	An 'exploded' set, representing several settings at once, or one which can open up to do so.
Enchaînement	The connecting of two scenes, the linking of one scene with the next.
Événements	The events of May 1968, the revolutionary strikes, demonstrations, and sit-ins by students and workers in France.

244

Fable	The basic sequence of events and actions making up the plot – what *happens*, not what is discussed.
Mise en place	Blocking.
Mise en scène	The staging and direction of a production, literally a 'putting on the stage'.

Index

note: RP = Roger Planchon

246

Index